Related Titles of Interest

The T.A.T., C.A.T., and S.A.T. in Clinical Use, Fifth Edition
Leopold Bellak
ISBN: 0-205-13933-7

The MMPI-2/MMPI: An Interpretive Manual
Roger L. Greene
ISBN: 0-205-12525-5

The MMPI: Use with Specific Populations
Roger L. Greene
ISBN: 0-205-10104-6

Helping People Change: A Textbook of Methods, Fourth Edition
Frederick H. Kanfer and Arnold P. Goldstein (Editors)
ISBN: 0-205-14382-2 Paper   0-205-14383-0 Cloth

Clinical Use of Story Telling: Emphasizing the T.A.T. with Children and Adolescents
Hedwig Teglasi
ISBN: 0-205-13938-8

Tactical Psychotherapy of the Personality Disorders

An MCMI-III–Based Approach

Edited by
Paul D. Retzlaff
University of Northern Colorado

Allyn and Bacon
Boston • London • Toronto • Sydney • Tokyo • Singapore

Copyright © 1995 by Allyn & Bacon
A Simon & Schuster Company
Needham Heights, Massachusetts 02194

All rights reserved. No part of the material protected by this copyright notice may be reproduced or utilized in any form or by any means, electronic or mechanical, including photocopying, recording, or by any information storage and retrieval system, without written permission from the copyright owner.

Library of Congress Cataloging-in-Publication Data

Tactical psychotherapy of the personality disorders : an MCMI-III
  –based approach / [edited by] Paul D. Retzlaff.
     p.   cm.
   Includes bibliographical references and index
   ISBN 0-205-15932-X
   1. Personality disorders—Treatment. 2.Psychotherapy.
  I. Retzlaff, Paul D.
     [DNLM: 1. Personality Disorders—diagnosis. 2. Personality
  Disorders—therapy.   3. Personality Inventory.   4. Psychotherapy.
  WM 141 T119 1995]
  RC554.T33 1995
  616.85é8—dc20
  DNLM/DLC
  for Library of Congress   94-445
                                                                          CIP

Printed in the United States of America
10 9 8 7 6 5 4 3 2 1 99 98 97 96 95

Contents

Foreword   ix

Preface   xiii

Acknowledgments   xv

About the Authors   xvii

1 **Clinical Application of the MCMI-III**   1
   by Paul Retzlaff
   MCMI-III Scales   1
   MCMI-III Item Content   3
   Development of the MCMIs   8
   Reliability   11
   Base Rate Scores and Scale Interpretation   11
   Internal Corrections   15
   Validity   16
   An Interpretation Approach to the MCMI-III   19
   Summary   21

2 **Domain-Oriented Personality Theory**   24
   by George S. Everly, Jr.
   Personality and Personality Disorders   25
   Millon's Model of Personality Disorders   26
   The Prototypal Model   27

Clinical Prototypal Domains of Personality   28
Treatment and Domain-Related Theory   32
Summary   38

3 **Use of the MCMI-III in Behavior Therapy**   **40**
by Dennis Donat
Behavior Therapy   40
Behavioral Expressions of Personality   46
Case Study   58
Summary   62

4 **Interpersonal Psychotherapy and MCMI-III–Based Assessment**   **66**
by Robert J. Craig
Interpersonal Psychotherapy   67
Relationship-Based Assessment and Millon's Theory   75
Case Study   84
Summary   88

5 **Cognitive Therapy and the MCMI-III**   **90**
by Thomas E. Will
Theoretical Assumptions and Clinical Techniques   91
Cognitive Therapy and the Personality Disorders   95
Case Study   104
Summary   106

6 **Object Relations Theory and the MCMI-III**   **111**
by Eric J. Van Denburg
Object Relations Theory   112
Object Relations and Millon's Personality Domains   118
The Personality Styles   122
Case Study   128
Summary   132

7 **The MCM-III and Treatment of the Self**   **137**
by Joseph T. McCann
Theory and Therapy of the Self   138
Treating the Personality Disorders   145
Case Study   152
Summary   156

**8 An Intersubjective Approach to Assessing and Treating Ego
Defenses Using the MCMI-III**   158
by Steven R. Kubacki and Paula R. Smith
An Intersubjective Model of Assessment and Therapy   *159*
An Intersubjective Approach to Personality Disorders   *166*
Case Study   *178*
Summary   *183*

**9 Psychoanalytic Psychotherapy of the Personality Disorders
toward Morphologic Change**   186
by Darwin Dorr
Psychoanalytic Psychotherapy   *187*
Morphologic Organization of the Personality Disorders   *193*
Case Study   *205*
Summary   *209*

10 Experiential Mood Therapy with the MCMI-III   210
by Lee Hyer, Jeff Brandsma, and Lucinda Shealy
Experiential Therapies   *211*
Affect of the Personality Disorders   *220*
Case Study   *228*
Summary   *232*

Author Index   *235*

Subject Index   *241*

Foreword

BY THEODORE MILLON

What a brilliant conception, that of connecting the diagnostic assessment process to the goals and techniques of therapy! We have all heard the comment, "What good does diagnosis do—once we decide on the disorder, we go ahead and use the same techniques to which we are accustomed." An historic and still frequently voiced complaint about diagnosis, be it based on the official classification system or not, is its lack of utility for therapeutic purposes. As noted in the preceding comment, most therapists, whatever their orientation or mode of treatment, pay little attention to the possibility that diagnosis can inform the philosophy and technique they employ. How different are we from chiropractors, a profession some tend to disparage owing to their supposed use of essentially the same method, "spinal manipulation," for colds, cancers, and cardiac arhythmias alike? Are we much better when we insist on using "family systems" approaches for almost all of our patients, or psychodynamic therapies, or cognitive-behavioral techniques for the great majority of all our patients?

In the past decade or two we have seen the emergence of so-called "integrative" and "eclectic" approaches, a willingness and open-mindedness to explore different modalities. Important and progressive though this movement has been, questions remain as to what techniques we should employ and integrate; on what logical basis we should choose which methods, in what order, and in which combinations. As my colleagues and I have noted elsewhere (Millon, Everly, & Davis, 1993), integrative therapies require a foundation in a coordinated theory; that is, they must be more than a schema of eclectic techniques, a hodgepodge of diverse alternatives assembled anew with each case.

Although the assembling of diagnostic criteria in the *DSM* manuals is a decent step in that they provide a potential rationale for selecting appropriate therapeutic techniques, they fall far short of their promise. They must be comprehensive and comparable, that is, systematically constructed so as to be genuinely useful for diverse modalities of treatment planning. I am convinced that the foundations of a personality science will advance when we construct a set of clinical domain criteria that are genuinely designed for therapy.

It is in this latter realm of domain and treatment correspondence that Professor Retzlaff and his co-authors have provided a new approach of considerable promise in the field of personologic psychotherapy. Here they have drawn on earlier work of mine that specified eight major clinical domains, each of which possesses a distinctive criterion for every diagnostically relevant characteristic, and aligns them with every personality disorder. For example, if the domain "interpersonal conduct" was deemed of value in assessing personality, then a singular diagnostic criterion was specified to represent the characteristic or distinctive manner in which each personality conducted its interpersonal life. By composing a taxonomic schema that included all the relevant clinical domains (e.g., behavior, mood, cognition) and specifying a defining feature in each domain for each of the 14 *DSM-III* and *DSM-IV* personalities, the proposed model would be fully comprehensive in its clinical scope and possess parallel and directly comparable domain criteria for therapeutic intervention.

In this volume the eight clinical domains have been separated and given individual chapters. The domains are divided conceptually into what have been termed *functional* and *structural* attributes, the former defined as "expressive modes of regulatory actions," the latter as "deeply embedded dispositions of a quasi-permanent nature." Among the functional processes are expressive behaviors, cognitive styles, interpersonal conduct, and regulatory mechanisms. The structural components include object representations, self-image, morphologic organization, and mood/temperament. Among other useful purposes, a profile composed of these clinical domains can be an especially helpful tool for identifying which sphere of thought, behavior, or feeling should serve as the initial focus of therapy.

Although Lazarus (1981) approaches the domain-oriented assessment task from an appreciably different perspective, an atheoretical eclectic therapy, as opposed to an integrative personality theory, our approach and Lazarus's "BASIC ID" method intersect in many ways, and their implications point to similar concerns regarding therapy interventions. In our work we have replaced the DSM's somewhat noncomparable and noncomprehensive diagnostic criteria with a full set of clinical domains. No longer are criteria specified at different levels of generality within and across the personality disorders. Rather than being a hodgepodge, each is derived from a broad-based theoretical model and is composed of attributes of approximately equal levels of generality across the various realms in which personality pathology is expressed.

As instructed by Professor Retzlaff, each contributor has focused on one of the major domains as his or her sphere of expertise, addressing three broad mandates: first, to provide a thoughtful analysis of the history and logic of the main subject of their chapter (e.g., to present the rationale for an object relations approach); second, to examine the characteristics of each of the 14 personality disorders and to indicate how these personalities can best be approached by utilizing the domain approach espoused; and, third, to provide a case history vignette to demonstrate the utility of the designated domain as a form of therapy.

Professor Retzlaff has seen an intriguing way to organize this impressive work on personality treatment. The field has grown in the past two decades to immense proportions. Retzlaff is to be commended for having organized and highlighted its major issues and therapeutic possibilities in a most intelligent and logical fashion. I am especially impressed by the balance among diverse viewpoints that the editor and his authors have given and the skill with which they have executed the task of representing these alternative models. This is an illuminating format through which to conceive therapeutic work. This landmark work, a first of its kind, utilizes an integrative therapeutic model, creating thereby a balanced and pioneering book. Enormously valuable for mature clinicians of various theoretical persuasions, the book should prove eminently useful to students as well, owing to its clear and straightforward presentation of the major therapeutic modalities.

References

Lazarus, A. (1981). *The practice of multimodal therapy.* New York: McGraw Hill.
Millon, T., Everly, G., & Davis, R. (1993). How can knowledge of psychopathology facilitate psychotherapy integration? *Journal of Psychotherapy Integration, 3(4),* 331–352.

Preface

All too often psychological testing and psychotherapy are viewed as separate aspects of clinical work. There are excellent books on testing and there are excellent books on psychotherapy. Rarely, however, are the two areas joined.

It is the purpose of this book to bring together the Millon Clinical Multiaxial Inventory-III and psychotherapy. To that end, selected MCMI-III researchers who are practicing psychotherapists have each contributed their view of the use of the MCMI-III within each of their particular theoretical frameworks.

The first two chapters cover the foundations. Chapter 1 provides a background in the use of the MCMI-III. It covers the test from a psychometric perspective, pointing out the strengths and weaknesses of the test and its scales. Chapter 2 provides a theoretical background across all of the theoretical domains. The chapter ties together the seemingly discrepant approaches and schools of thought regarding the personality disorders. Using Millon's theory of psychopathology, target diagnostic symptoms for the personality disorders are delineated across the domains. These two chapters should give the reader a sufficient understanding of the test and theory to make good use of the therapy chapters.

The domains of therapy covered in this work include behavioral, interpersonal, cognitive, object relations, self-image, defense mechanism, psychic organization, and mood/temperament. The chapters are all structured to give the reader a fundamental understanding of the particular therapeutic theory and techniques, an appreciation of the personality disorders from that perspective, the application of the therapy to each of the personality disorders, and, finally, a case example tying all of the chapter together.

Acknowledgments

Many people contribute to the success of a project like this—they are all fully appreciated, although I am not able to list all of them here.

National Computer Systems and specifically Terri Foley, Kristi Everson, Kathy Gialluca, and John Finken must be thanked for their support of the researchers and writers in the field. Their gracious allowance of early MCMI-III material allowed this project to be completed as the test was being released.

Early versions of individual chapters and the entire book were reviewed by Steve Strack (Los Angeles VA Outpatient Clinic) Rodney Vanderploeg (Tampa VA Medical Center), Mark-David Janus (Ohio State University Hospitals), Mark Marusih (National Computer Systems), and Donald Williams (Mayo Clinic). Their comments were uniformly excellent and were incorporated into the work.

Above all others, Ted Millon must be thanked for the underlying theory, the MCMI-III, and the delineation of the domains of therapy. Most of the tables and "grist" of this work have been liberally borrowed from his many fine works.

About the Authors

Paul Retzlaff, Ph.D., is an Associate Professor at the University of Northern Colorado and a Consulting Psychologist at the VA Medical Center in Cheyenne, Wyoming. He has published extensively on the MCMI-I, MCMI-II, and the MCMI-III. His psychometric research interests include hit rate/operating characteristics, factor structures of items and scales, biased test taking, and high point codes. Patient-oriented research has included military mental health retention, alcoholic subtyping, disability prediction, and general inpatient and outpatient outcome.

Jeff Brandsma, Ph.D., is a Professor of Psychiatry at the Medical College of Georgia. His research and writings involve psychotherapy including the therapeutic relationship, group therapy, and religious issues.

Robert J. Craig, Ph.D., ABPP, is the Clinical Director of the Drug and Alcohol Treatment Unit at West Side VA Medical Center and a Professor of Psychology at the Illinois School of Professional Psychology in Chicago. He has published books on the MCMI including an edited research volume and an interpretive guide.

Dennis Donat, Ph.D., is the Chief of Psychology at Western State Hospital in Staunton, Virginia, and Assistant Professor in the Department of Psychiatric Medicine at the University of Virginia Medical School. His clinical interests are in the behavioral treatment of substance dependence. He has published on therapy outcome using the MCMI.

Darwin Dorr, Ph.D., is currently the Director of Clinical Training at Wichita State University in Wichita, Kansas. Prior appointments include Duke University Medical Center and Highland Hospital in North Carolina. In addition to psychoanalytic psychotherapy, his interests include the Rorschach and the MACI.

George S. Everly, Jr., Ph.D., is Chief Psychologist and Director of Behavioral Medicine at Union Memorial Hospital, Baltimore, Maryland, and Chairman of the Board of the International Critical Incident Stress Foundation. Past appointments have included Visiting Lecturer in Medicine at Harvard Medical School and a Harvard Scholar visiting in the Department of Psychology, Harvard University. He has written extensively on personality disorders and the MCMI.

Lee Hyer, Ph.D., is a Psychologist at the VA Medical Center, Augusta, Georgia, and has an appointment with the Medical College of Georgia. He has published extensively on the MCMI and has a particular interest in PTSD.

Steven R. Kubacki, Ph.D., is on the faculty at the University of Wyoming, where he teaches personality assessment, modern psychodynamic theory, and psychodynamic play therapy. His private practice specializes in both childhood and severe characterological disorders.

Joseph T. McCann, Psy.D., J. D., is currently in private practice in Binghamton, New York. Recent appointments have included Erie County Medical Center and School of Medicine at the State University of New York at Buffalo. Clinical and research interests include adult and adolescent assessment and forensic evaluation.

Lucinda Shealy, M.S., is currently a Psychologist at the Patrick B. Harris Psychiatric Hospital in Anderson, South Carolina. She completed her clinical psychology internship at the Medical College of Georgia/Augusta VA Medical Center Consortium. Her interests include the interpersonal and affective aspects of trauma survivors.

Paula R. Smith, M.S., is a Doctoral student in clinical psychology at the University of Wyoming. Her interests are cross-cultural psychology, adult personality development, and insight-oriented psychotherapy.

Eric J. Van Denburg, Ph.D., is a Staff Psychologist and Director of Clinical Training at the Lakeside VA Medical Center and on the faculty at Northwestern University Medical School, Chicago. He is a co-author of the *Interpretive Guide to the MCMI.*

Thomas E. Will, Psy.D., M.P.H., is the Chief of Neuropsychology at Group Health in Minneapolis, Minnesota, and a faculty member of the Fielding Institute in Santa Barbara, California, and the Minnesota School of Professional Psychology in Minneapolis.

1

Clinical Application of the MCMI-III

PAUL RETZLAFF

This chapter introduces the reader to the Millon Clinical Multiaxial Inventory (MCMI-III) (Millon, 1994). First, the 28 scales and their groupings are reviewed. Next, the development process utilized in the construction of the MCMI through its three revisions is presented, and the psychometric characteristics of the MCMI are examined. Finally, the chapter presents the concept of base rate scoring utilized in the MCMI and offers a hierarchical interpretation approach to the MCMI-III. This chapter serves as a foundation for the remainder of the text. When the reader is able to understand and interpret MCMI-III profiles, the nature of particular personality disorders can be described and conceptualized. It is only in that context that specific psychotherapeutic approaches for different personality disorders can be explicated.

MCMI-III Scales

The MCMI-III is composed of 175 items that are scored on 28 scales. The first four scales assess validity and response style. The first scale is labeled Validity and primarily assesses whether or not a patient read the items. The second scale, Disclosure, assesses the tendency to overreport or underreport psychopathology. The third validity scale is Desirability. It is similar to social desirability scales commonly found in other psychological tests. The final validity scale is Debasement, which assesses self-perception primarily in terms of self-esteem.

Millon (1994) breaks personality disorders into two types: basic and severe. Basic personality disorders include schizoid, avoidant, depressive, dependent, histrionic, narcissistic, antisocial, sadistic, compulsive, negativistic, and self-defeating. Individuals with basic personality disorders may experience mild to moderate levels of impairment in their ability to function socially or occupationally. With a basic personality disorder, patients may be able to continue to work and maintain an intimate interpersonal relationship. In addition to the basic personality disorders, Millon identifies three severe personality disorders: schiztotypal, borderline, and paranoid. These personality disorders are usually severely disabling; it would be difficult for such patients to function effectively socially, occupationally, or academically.

The first 11 scales of the MCMI-III evaluate Millon's (1994) Basic Personality Disorders. These scales are a superset of the *DSM-IV* (American Psychiatric Association, 1994) personality disorders. The *DSM-IV* dropped the sadistic and self-defeating disorder diagnoses found in the *DSM-IIIR* (American Psychiatric Association, 1987), while adding a depressive personality disorder diagnosis. While the MCMI-I and MCMI-II were faithful to the prior editions of the *DSM* (American Psychiatric Association, 1980, 1987), the MCMI-III has kept all the personality disorders rather than stay in lock step with the *DSM-IV*. Thus the MCMI-III includes 11 personality disorder scales, not just the 9 personality disorders found in the *DSM-IV*. The MCMI-III, therefore, includes the Sadistic and Self-Defeating personality disorders from the appendix of *DSM-IIIR* as well as the new Depressive personality disorder found in the *DSM-IV*. Finally, Negativistic personality disorder, as it has been termed from the very first MCMI, continues as such in the MCMI-III. The *DSM-IV* has added the Negativistic label to the Passive-Aggressive diagnosis.

The MCMI-III Severe Personality Disorders scales represent those three personality disorders, schizotypal, borderline, and paranoid, that are severely impairing. Here begins some of the hierarchical nature of the MCMI-III; these scales are viewed as largely superseding the Basic Personality Disorder scales and, from an interpretation perspective, form their own block.

As it does with the personality disorders, the MCMI-III breaks clinical syndromes into two types: basic and severe. Basic Clinical Syndromes scales include Anxiety, Somatoform, Bipolar, Dysthymia, Alcohol Dependence, Drug Dependence, and Post Traumatic Stress Disorder (PTSD). Again, individuals with elevations on the Basic Clinical Syndrome scales can probably function with only mild to moderate impairment.

The Severe Clinical Syndromes scales include Thought Disorder, Major Depression, and Delusional Disorder. These three scales represent more severely debilitating and more complex clinical syndromes and subsume elements of the Basic Clinical Syndrome scales. Breaking these three Severe

TABLE 1-1 MCMI-III Scales

Validity Scales
Validity
Disclosure
Desirability
Debasement

Basic Personality Disorders
Schizoid
Avoidant
Depressive
Dependent
Histrionic
Narcissistic
Antisocial
Sadistic
Compulsive
Negativistic
Self-Defeating

Severe Personality Disorders
Schizotypal
Borderline
Paranoid

Basic Clinical Syndromes
Anxiety
Somatoform
Bipolar
Dysthymia

Alcohol Dependence
Drug Dependence
PTSD

Severe Clinical Syndromes
Thought Disorder
Major Depression
Delusional Disorder

Clinical Syndromes out from the others aids interpretation. Within the clinical scales the mild to severely impairing differentiation is less clear than within the personality disorder scales, as evidenced by Bipolar and PTSD being grouped with the "Basic" Clinical Syndromes.

MCMI-III Item Content

The content of the scales of the MCMI-III is an admixture of Millon's (1969, 1981, 1986a, 1986b, 1990) theory (see Chapter 2) and *DSM-IV* criteria honed during the construction of the test. Since the most fundamental aspect of a psychological test is the items, an initial approach to orienting the reader to the scales of the MCMI-III will be to present a sample item from each scale. That single item will be the first "prototypical" (Millon, 1986a) item found in the test for each of the scales. As will be seen later, the MCMI-III scoring procedure gives added weight to the items that performed the best across the various construction hurdles. As such, they are viewed as being prototypical of the domains and are the best exemplar items. Looking at a single item for each scale often does poor justice to the larger set of items. It would, however, be impractical to discuss all items on all scales. Chapter 2 of this book will further develop the content of the personality disorder scales from a theoretical perspective, and chapters 3 through 10 will look at each of the disorders from a specific domain perspective.

Response Bias Scales

The response bias or style scales respresent those scales that point to possible test-taking response problems (Retzlaff, Sheehan, & Fiel, 1991). The first scale, Validity, is composed of only three items, each of which has extremely unusual content. An example is "I was on the front cover of several magazines last year." This item should not be endorsed by anyone in a clinical population. If patients answer true to any of these three items, it either implies that they could not or did not read and appropriately respond to the items. The scale, therefore, flags profiles where the patient has a reading or gross motivational problem.

The Disclosure scale is based upon a formula that is a function of the personality disorder scale scores. The assumption is that patients who present clinically should fall within a particular window of personality disturbance. If they report too much personality disturbance such that they obtain elevated scores on seven or eight personality disorder scales, they are probably overreporting psychopathology. Conversely, if they report no personality disturbances, they are probably underreporting psychopathology. This is a relatively unique approach to the assessment of response bias.

The Desirability scale includes items such as "I think I am a very sociable and outgoing person." This captures more of a histrionic than desirability theme. It seems, therefore, to lack face validity.

The Debasement scale suffers from similar content validity problems. Here the item "People make fun of me behind my back, talking about the way I act and look" seems to tap more avoidant or schizotypal characteristics than it does debasement. Later in this chapter, problems with the Desirability and Debasement scales will be discussed as being secondary to methodological weaknesses during scale development.

Basic Personality Disorders

The first prototypical item from the Schizoid scale is "I've always had less interest in sex than most people do." This item comes from not only Millon's theory (1994) but also the *DSM-IV* criteria "little, if any, interest in having sexual experiences." It certainly captures the aloof and nonsocial nature of the schizoid.

The Avoidant personality disorder scale item "In social groups I am almost always very self-conscious and tense," includes some of the schizoid features seen in the prior item, but adds the affective and anxiety component found in the avoidant. Indeed, the *DSM-IV* criteria of "is preoccupied with being criticized or rejected in social situations" certainly seems to be represented by this item.

The Depressive personality disorder item "I have been downhearted and sad much of my life since I was quite young" encompasses the "dejection, gloominess, cheerlessness, joylessness, and unhappiness" of the DSM-IV criteria. The characterlogical nature of the depressive content is reflected in the phrase "much of my life." It further represents Millon's idea of melancholic mood (see Chapter 10).

The Dependent personality disorder item "I am a very agreeable and submissive person" goes to the core of the dependent personality in terms of a number of the *DSM-IV* criteria. It includes the "[need for] others to assume responsibility" and the "difficulty expressing disagreement with others" criteria.

The Histrionic personality scale includes as its first prototypical item "I think I am a very sociable and outgoing person." Here is perhaps a difference from the *DSM-IV*, which tends to focus upon the excessive emotionality, the attention seeking, and the rapidly shifting emotionality of patients. DSM-IV's social aspects include being theatrical and exaggerating social interaction. This item is more of the traditional affiliation or sociability dimension that we find in psychology.

Under Narcissism is "I know I'm a superior person, so I don't care what other people think." This taps the *DSM-IV* criteria of "a grandiose sense of self importance." Also, the not caring what other people think goes to some of the lack of empathy that is found in the narcissist. Millon sees this as an admirable self-image (see Chapter 7).

The Antisocial personality disorder scale includes "As a teenager I got into lots of trouble because of bad school behavior." This largely attempts to go back and find evidence of the conduct disorder that is one of the criteria necessary for an antisocial personality disorder *DSM-IV* diagnosis. This impulsive conduct is a focus of Millon's expressive acts domain (see Chapter 3). Indeed, other items within this item set attempt to capture the adult aspects of the antisocial personality.

The Sadistic scale includes "I often criticize people strongly if they annoy me." It's hard to know whether or not this item truly maps onto a sadistic personality disorder because the DSM-IV has dropped this disorder. It probably does share some of the domain with the "cruel, demeaning, and aggressive behavior" construct of the DSM-IIIR appendix criteria. This item reflects the abrasive interpersonal interactions of the sadistic (see Chapter 4).

Compulsive personality disorder includes the item "I keep very close track of my money, so I am prepared if a need comes up." This taps into the *DSM-IV* criteria of "miserly spending style . . . hoarded for future catastrophes." In the MCMI-II the Compulsive personality disorder scale had more to do with social respectability. The MCMI-III item pool is probably in closer concord with the DSM approach to the construct.

The Negativistic personality disorder scale includes the item "If my family puts pressure on me, I'm likely to feel angry and resist what they want." This maps onto the criteria of "sullen and argumentative" and "resists fulfilling routine social and occupational tasks." At a more general level it also taps into the angry quality of the negativistic personality. The item has Millon's affective component that has largely driven the trend to a new negativistic personality disorder from the passive-aggressive personality disorder.

The Self-Defeating personality disorder item "I often think that I don't deserve the good things that happen to me" seems to capture the criteria, which in the initial "options" draft of *DSM-IV* (American Psychiatric Association, 1991) included "perceives himself or herself as undeserving of being treated well." Again, self-defeating was dropped for the DSM-IV and is also a victim of a lack of concordance in professional opinion. The undeserving self-image is central to Millon's theory of this disorder (see Chapter 7).

Severe Personality Disorders

The Schizotypal personality disorder item is "People make fun of me behind my back, talking about the way I act and look." Referring back to the Debasement scale, this item is not a good debasement item but is probably an excellent schizotypal item. In *DSM-IV* it gets to the "odd, eccentric, or peculiar" aspects of the behavior and also has elements of the excessive social anxiety that the schizotypal individual can have.

The Borderline personality disorder scale item "Lately, I have begun to feel like smashing things" probably doesn't get to the instability of identity, cognition, or affect, but it does go to the instability of behavior. Indeed, the *DSM-IV* criteria, "difficulty controlling anger," probably is manifest by this item. Millon refers to this as being "expressively spasmodic" (see Chapter 3).

The Paranoid personality disorder scale includes the item "People have never given me enough recognition for the things I've done." This item has

Millon's cognitive suspiciousness element (see Chapter 5). It also parallels the *DSM-IV* criterion of "others are exploiting, harming, or deceiving."

Basic Clinical Syndromes

The Anxiety scale item is "Lately, I've been sweating a great deal and feel very tense." This does a very good job of picking up the autonomic aspects of a generalized anxiety disorder. It could also pick up elements of a phobia or agoraphobia and the situational aspects of a panic disorder. Obviously, the clinical scales on the MCMI-III are compilations of five or six different *DSM-IV* clinical syndromes.

The Somatoform item "I have a hard time keeping my balance when walking" is probably a poor item. Patients in nursing home or orthopedic units will answer this item true. Here the problem is that some domains and constructs within psychology simply do not lend themselves to the development of items and the construction of scales. In essence, a somatoform disorder is an unconscious process driven by the defense mechanisms (see Chapter 8) and the morphological organization of the psyche (see Chapter 9). Yet the conscious mind of the patient is asked to endorse these items. An item would have to be something like "When I'm upset with my spouse, I tend to get headaches driven by unconscious primary gain." Patients aren't going to endorse an item like that. The MCMI-III has done as good a job as possible building this scale, but somatoform disorder is an unconscious domain and as such does not lend itself to objective testing.

The Bipolar item "I enjoy doing so many different things that I can't make up my mind what to do first" certainly does tap some of the specific energy of the bipolar, but also energy in general. Hence the scale is best viewed as an energy scale much as scale 9 of the MMPI-II is interpreted.

Dysthymia's "I began to feel like a failure some years ago" is a good depression item in that it has the personal failure quality to it. It also attempts to get patients to estimate how long they have been depressed. The "some years ago" mimics the *DSM-IV* criteria that dysthymia lasts more than two years. This is to differentiate it from a major depression. A problem with this is that patients, in their own phenomenology, are unable to make chronological differentiations of their depression. We're going to find a lack of specificity among dysthymia, major depression, and the new depressive personality disorder both in the MCMI-III and the *DSM-IV*. That aside, the Dysthymia scale of the MCMI-III is an excellent scale of depression in general.

The Alcohol abuse item is "I have a drinking problem that I have tried unsuccessfully to end." This again comes right from the *DSM-IV* substance dependence criteria and relates to the failure to stop a substance use. As with most of the other alcohol dependence items, this is an item that is behavioral and obvious. If patients want to deny that they are drinking, they can do it on interview by saying "No, I don't drink." They can also do it on a test by saying, "No, I don't drink." Alcohol and drug dependence are so behavioral in nature that patients, if they want to lie to you, certainly can. It's a good scale, not in identifying whether or not someone is an alcoholic, but for quantifying the severity of the alcohol dependence.

The same goes for the Drug Dependence item "My drug habits have often gotten me into a good deal of trouble in the past." Someone who wants to deny this can do so on an interview or on the MCMI-III. Again, though, while the scale should not be used for identification, it can be used for quantification.

The PTSD scale has "The memory of a very upsetting experience in my past keeps coming back to haunt my thoughts." This not only encompasses combat types of traumas, but other physical and sexual types of traumas in patients' pasts. Here again, though, is the double-edged sword of face validity. If a clinician is in an adjudication system, such as a VA Medical Center, patients who want to "prove" that they have PTSD, perhaps for financial gain, are probably going to be able to spot these items and endorse them as true.

Severe Clinical Syndromes

For Thought Disorder the item is "Ideas keep turning over and over in my head, and they won't go away." Ideas that turn over and over in your head do not necessarily represent a thought disorder. It could be the worry component of a generalized anxiety disorder or some element of a paranoid personality disorder.

Major Depression has "Lately, my strength seems to be draining out of me, even in the morning." Here the fatigue elements and perhaps some of the terminal insomnia elements of the major depression symptom are evident. Again, patients may not be able to differentiate this from a Dysthymia item or from a Depressive personality disorder item.

Finally, Delusional disorder includes as its first key item "Many people have been spying into my private life for years." Here the phenomenology of someone with a delusional disorder is extremely narrow and focused. Indeed, delusional disorders are extremely difficult to find on interview because they are so focal. Delusional disorder patients may not endorse this item as true for some small technical reason. They might say, "Well, many people are not attempting to spy into my life, just those two people at my office."

Development of the MCMIs

The various versions of the MCMI have integrated all three of the traditional approaches to test construction: clinical content, statistical homogeneity, and empirical validation. This sequential, multimethod integration is referred to as a *domain construction approach* (Nunnally, 1978; Suen, 1990). Clinical theory, understanding, and need have driven what scales are to be developed. Items are developed and retained within scales based on their homogeneity and high reliability. Finally, the validity analyses are conducted to demonstrate that the test will cross-validate and generalize.

MCMI-I Development

The foundation of the current MCMI was actually laid with the development of the MCMI-I (Millon, 1977). All MCMI revisions have followed from the prior version, and all used approximately the same combination of test construction techniques.

Construction began with content techniques through the development of an initial, large, face-valid item pool. Judges wrote items that they viewed as essential to the theoretical domains of each scale. Items were then eliminated based upon readability levels. If an item was too scholarly, complex, or awkward, it was eliminated. Items were then shown to patient groups who were asked, "Do these items make sense to you as a patient?" If an item didn't make any sense to patients, it was eliminated.

The next step was critical. The initial item pool was reduced by clinician sorting. Naive clinicians were asked to sort each item into its appropriate domain(s). If an item was "I like robbing convenience stores," and five out of the eight clinicians put it into the antisocial domain, then it stayed. They also had a chance to put it in other domains keyed either true or false. By being sorted by a group of clinicians, the items enjoy a broad-based consensus support (Retzlaff & Gibertini, 1987; Gibertini & Retzlaff, 1988).

Considerations of the internal statistical structure were the next phase. At this point the provisional form of 1,100 items was split into two equivalent forms, each with 566 items. After having patient groups endorse these forms, items with the highest item total correlations were retained. An item total correlation is the correlation of the endorsement of each item (zero for false, one for true) with the total score of the 40 or 50 initial items in that domain. Those items that are most core or key to that domain are retained; this is homogeneity. Homogeneity or internal consistency is operationalized by the Cronbach Alpha reliability statistic.

The next step was that the 440 remaining items were reduced to 289, based upon multiscale correlation patterns. Antisocial items should be positively keyed on Antisocial, perhaps Sadistic, and maybe Negativistic. They may also be negatively keyed on Dependent or Self-Defeating. These patterns were all consistent with the underlying theory.

Next, the empirical approach was utilized. Here 167 clinicians gave the test to and completed diagnostic rating forms on actual patients. On the basis of this validity analysis the items were reduced to 154.

For a number of reasons, the Hypochondriasis, Obsession-Compulsion, and Sociopathy scales were eliminated from the original MCMI. In the place of those three scales were added Hypomania, Alcohol Dependence, and Drug Dependence. New item sets were developed and went through the same construction procedures. The final MCMI-I included 175 items that were keyed 733 times.

MCMI-II Development

After a number of years it was deemed appropriate, with the publication of the *DSM-IIIR*, to revise the MCMI. In order to do this, a provisional MCMI-II of 368 items was developed by adding sufficient initial items to develop Sadistic and Self-Defeating scales. All the construction steps were repeated as with the MCMI-I for these two scales. Additionally, other scales were strengthened by the addition and deletion of items.

Forty-five of the 175 original MCMI-I items were changed. The 175 new MCMI-II (Millon, 1987) items ended up with 953 keyings. Also, at this time a multipoint keying system was added where an item was given a weight of 1, 2, or 3 based upon how the developers of the test believed it survived the various hurdles. If an item was sorted well, had a very high item total correlation, and had a high validity correlation, it was given 3 points. Lesser-quality items were given 2 or 1. This multipoint scoring has come under attack as unnecessary (Retzlaff, Sheehan, & Lorr, 1990).

After the majority of the development process, the Desirability and Debasement scales were empirically derived. A number of graduate students were asked to go through the 175 items and endorse those items that they viewed as being socially desirable or debasing. If the majority of these graduate students agreed on an item, it was added to that scale. This construction method is why these scales are not as strong as they could be. Had items for social desirability and debasement been generated in an initial item pool and gone through all the rigorous and sophisticated steps as did the rest of the scales, they would be better scales.

MCMI-III Development

With the advent of the *DSM-IV* in 1994, the MCMI-II was revised. The provisional MCMI-III that was developed had 325 items. It added sufficient items to encompass a Depressive personality disorder and a PTSD scale. Additionally, and somewhat atypical of most tests, a number of critical items were added that would suggest Eating Disorders and Child Abuse. These are not truly scales and are only output by the computer scoring as critical items.

Ninety of the 175 MCMI-II items are changed. The item weighting procedure was reduced. Items were no longer given a 1–3-point rating, but were simply given 1 or 2 points. Finally, the number of items per scale was cut dramatically. Instead of having 35 to 45 items per scale as on the MCMI-II, there are often only 16 or 17 items per scale in the MCMI-III (Millon, 1994). Because of this, the 175 items are not keyed 953 times as in the MCMI-II, but only 440 times. This should result in far more specific scales.

Reliability

Table 1-2 presents the number of items per scale of the MCMI-III and each scale's Alpha reliability coefficient. The personality disorder scales have from 15 to 24 items. From a traditional psychometric viewpoint (Nunnally, 1978), this should be a sufficient number of items for psychometrically sound scales. The clinical syndrome scales have generally fewer items, 12 to 17. A potential problem are scales with the smallest number of items, Somatoform with 12 and Bipolar and Delusional Disorder with 13 each.

Scales should have reliabilities (specifically Cronbach Alpha internal consistency reliabilities) of .70 or greater (Nunnally, 1978). The Basic Personality Disorder scales generally have Alphas in the .80s, which are excellent. Narcissistic is low with a .67 and Compulsive is at a .66. The Severe Personality Disorder scales are also sound, with Alphas in the mid .80s.

The Basic Clinical Syndrome scales are also all in the .80s, with the exception of Bipolar at a .71, which could be related to its having only 13 items. Finally, the Severe Clinical Syndrome scales have excellent coefficients, ranging from .79 to .90.

In summary, the reliability coefficients are quite strong. The reliabilities of the MCMI-III scales, with the exception of perhaps one or two scales, are among the highest in the industry.

Base Rate Scores and Scale Interpretation

One of the most confusing things about the MCMI tests are their base rate scores. In order to fully understand what base rate scores are, it is necessary to appreciate that there are two types of referencing when it comes to tests. The more traditional type of referencing is referred to as *norm referencing*. Norm referencing is utilized in most psychological tests (Retzlaff, 1992). In normative-based tests, scores reflect an individual's relative position within the normative population. For example, with intelligence tests an IQ score of 100 reflects a performance at the population mean, a performance at the 50th percentile level.

TABLE 1-2 MCMI-III Numbers of Items Per Scale and Scale Reliabilities

Scales	N of Items	Alpha
Validity Scales		
Validity:	3	NA
Disclosure:	NA	NA
Desirability:	21	.86
Debasement:	33	.95
Basic Personality Disorders		
Schizoid:	16	.81
Avoidant:	16	.89
Depressive:	15	.89
Dependent:	16	.85
Histrionic:	17	.81
Narcissistic:	24	.67
Antisocial:	17	.77
Sadistic:	20	.79
Compulsive:	17	.66
Negativistic:	16	.83
Self-Defeating:	15	.87
Severe Personality Disorders		
Schizotypal:	16	.85
Borderline:	16	.85
Paranoid:	17	.84
Basic Clinical Syndromes		
Anxiety:	14	.86
Somatoform:	12	.86
Bipolar:	13	.71
Dysthymia:	14	.88
Alcohol Dependence:	15	.82
Drug Dependence:	14	.83
PTSD:	16	.89
Severe Clinical Syndromes		
Thought Disorder:	17	.87
Major Depression:	17	.90
Delusional Disorder:	13	.79

Criterion referencing, however, is less common in clinical psychology test instruments. Here it isn't important how far the patient is from the mean of the normal population. Instead, what is important is where the patient is in relation to a criterion. Criterion referencing attempts to model a disorder, syndrome, or diagnosis. If 10 percent of the population has major depression, is your patient part of that 10 percent?

Base rates reference the test scores to these diagnostic criterion rather than to the norm or the mean. Specifically on the MCMI, base rate scores of 85 identify most optimally the chance that an individual patient has that disorder. A 75 base rate score or greater means that the patient at least has features or symptoms of that disorder.

One of the attractive features of criterion referencing is that it does not force distributions to a normal curve, and it does not force us to accept constructs and domains as being normally distributed.

As an example of this in the MCMI-III, see Figure 1-1. In the top distribution (they are drawn as normal distributions to simplify comparisons between the two) is dependent personality disorder. It has a prevalence of 18 percent. What this means is that in the construction phase of the MCMI-III, 18 percent of the patients had dependent personality disorder as an Axis II disorder, and it was their primary disorder. There were, however, 39 percent of the sample who had at least dependent traits or features. Actually, there are two base rates. The first base rate is 18 percent and is indicative of the primary pathology. The second base rate is 39 percent and is indicative of at least some part of the symptom picture.

Base rate scores arbitrarily go from 0 to 115. The distribution of raw scores on Dependent is from 0 to 24 (16 items with either a 1 or 2 weight). These raw scores are counted down from the high end of the normative distribution until 18 percent of the subjects have been identified. For male norms, anyone having a raw score of 15 or greater is part of that 18 percent. Continuing on down the distribution to the 39 percent point gives us a raw score of 9. The 85 base rate score is nonlinearly set at a raw score of 15, and the 75 base rate is set at a raw score of 9. The result is that the base rate scores allow an optimized modeling of the diagnoses.

Compare the first distribution in Figure 1-1 with the second distribution. Sadistic personality disorder is found far less often. Indeed, the prevalence of having that as a primary diagnosis is only 1 percent. Having it as a primary *or* secondary diagnosis is only 6 percent. The base rates, again, vary between 0 and 115. The raw scores vary between 0 and 27. Now a raw score of 20 identifies the 1 percent of the subjects with a sadistic personality disorder. The 85 base rate score is mapped to that 20 raw score. Going down an additional 5 percent is a raw score of 15. The 75 base rate score is placed at that 15 raw score. Although Dependent and Sadistic scales have the same base rate cutoff scores of 85 and 75, representing a diagnosis and trait, respectively, these base rate scores lie at different points on the frequency distribution for the population. Thus, the base rate scores allow us to know whether or not a patient has a disorder without having to be aware of the specific prevalence or base rate of that disorder.

A brief comment on scores below 75. Whereas in most scoring techniques we look at the very high and very low scores, this is inappropriate with the MCMI-III. There is no interpretive difference between a base rate score of 0 and a base rate score of 60. These are both below the cutoff of 75 and as such

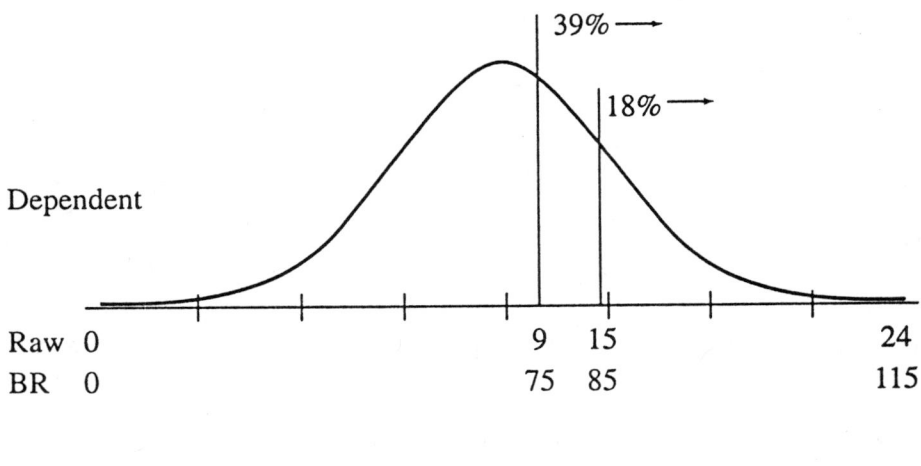
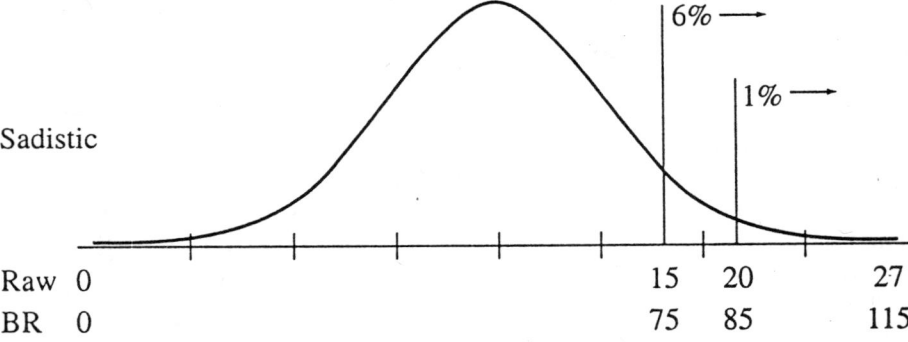

FIGURE 1-1 Base Rate Score Assignment for Dependent and Sadistic Scales

should be viewed as differentially uninterpretable. The reason for this is that in the pushing and pulling of the base rate scores, to have them map up with the raw scores, these scores lose their ratio measurement characteristics.

In summary, the first interpretation of interest is whether or not a patient scores between 75 and 84, which leads to an interpretation of the patient having that psychopathology at a trait or feature level. The second major interpretation is that if a patient has a score of 85 or greater, the psychopathology is at a disorder level and is probably impairing. The final interpretation is that scores of 74 or less imply that the patient does not have the pathology.

The response bias scales are scored somewhat differently and therefore interpreted differently. The validity scale does not have base rate scores. It simply is the raw score of 0 to 3. A raw score of 1 or more should be viewed as making the test potentially invalid.

The Disclosure scale is the only scale where both ends of the base rate distribution should be interpreted. The Disclosure scores can range from 0 to 100. If the score is 85 or more on the Disclosure scale, it should be seen as an overreport of symptoms. If there is a score of 35 or less on the Disclosure scale, it should be viewed as an underreport of psychopathology.

Both the Desirability and Debasement scales vary from 0 to 100. Theoretically, a score of 85 or more on these indicates high levels of that particular construct.

Internal Corrections

In order to better optimize the hit rates of the test, there are a number of internal corrections. In many ways these are similar to the use of the K correction on the MMPI, where a certain proportion of K is added to different scales to adjust for defensive reporting. While there are a couple of minor algorithms and variations involving recent hospitalization and Axis I diagnosis, the two major corrections in the MCMI-III are the disclosure correction and depression with anxiety correction.

A high Disclosure scale score results in all scales of the MCMI-III being reduced to some degree. Conversely, very low scores on the Disclosure scale result in additional base rate points for all scales on the MCMI-III. The logic here is that someone who overreports psychopathology will generally have artificially inflated scale scores across the entire test and this should be corrected. Similarly, profiles where underreporting occurred need to be corrected upward.

The high depression and anxiety correction algorithm is driven by high scores on Depression or Anxiety with a recent admission to a psychiatric hospital and leads to a downward adjustment in base rate scores on the Avoidant, Depressive, Self-Defeating, Borderline, and Schizotypal scales. This attempts to correct for situationally high affectively oriented personality disorder scale scores.

Validity

Operating Characteristics

As was stated earlier, the MCMI-III is not a traditionally norm-referenced test. Traditionally, after tests and scales are built, they are validated either by correlating them with an external scale of similar content or by comparing two or more groups. With criterion-referenced tests it is far more important to know what the criterion hit rates are. For these hit rates, the term *operating characteristics* is used (Retzlaff & Gibertini, 1994; Gibertini, Brandenburg, & Retzlaff, 1986). Table 1-3 shows the five operating characteristics: prevalence, sensitivity, specificity, positive predictive power, and negative predictive power.

The first operating characteristic, prevalence, answers the question "What is the percentage of patients in the group who have the disorder?" This is also the probability that an individual patient has a disorder prior to any knowledge of the case or clinical workup.

Sensitivity answers the question "How sensitive is this test to a particular disorder?" An example from the MCMI-III would be "Of all the antisocial personality disorder subjects in this group, how many have scores above 85?" This is a classic statistic that we might use in research to see how "good" a test is. Unfortunately, however, it requires us to know who is in the experimental and who is in the control group. It requires us to know *a priori* who is antisocial, because if you don't know who is antisocial, you don't know how many of them score above 85.

TABLE 1-3 Operating Characteristics

Prevalence
The proportion/percentage of patients in the group who have the disorder

Sensitivity
The proportion/percentage of patients who are known to have a disorder who are identified by the test as having it (e.g., of all the antisocials in this group, how many have scores above 85?)

Specificity
The proportion/percentage of patients who are known to *not* have a disorder who are identified by the test as *not* having it (e.g., of all the patients who are not antisocial, how many have scores below 85?)

Positive Predictive Power
The proportion/percentage of patients who are identified by a test as having a disorder who actually have the disorder (e.g., of all my patients who have a score above 85 on antisocial, how many actually are antisocial? What is the chance that the patient in front of me with the 90 on antisocial is actually antisocial?)

Negative Predictive Power
The proportion/percentage of patients who are identified by a test as *not* having a disorder who actually *don't* have it (e.g., what is the probability that this patient in front of me who has a 40 on antisocial is actually not antisocial?)

Specificity is the flip side of sensitivity. It asks, "How specific is this test to a single disorder *vis à vis* the other disorders?" For the MCMI-III it asks the question "Of all the patients who are not antisocial, how many have a score below 85 on the Antisocial scale?" In most research paradigms it would be "Knowing my control group of college freshmen, how many scored below 85 on my test of antisocial?" You obviously want the majority of the control group having low scores. Again, however, you must know the control group before testing.

The last two operating characteristics are of far more importance in clinical assessment. Positive predictive power asks, "Only knowing that this person has a high score on antisocial, what are the chances that they are really antisocial?" This is far more typical of what we find in clinical practice. We have no *a priori* knowledge of whether the person is in the antisocial group or the normal population group. Positive predictive power also can be viewed as answering the question "How confident are we in this diagnosis?" This is a type of statistic that is very rarely used in psychological testing.

On most psychological tests, what we get are validity statistics with, for example, correlations of .37 or T tests with P values of .001. Knowing a T test had a probability of .001 tells us little about the probability of an individual patient in our office having a particular diagnosis. Positive predictive power does that by indicating the probability that a patient with a base rate score of 85 or greater is antisocial. This is calculated by dividing the number of patients in the normative study who had a score above 85 and were diagnosed by the clinicians as having the disorder by the number of patients who simply had a score above 85 regardless of actual diagnosis.

Negative predictive power answers the question "Knowing that my patient had a score of less than 85, what are the chances that the patient doesn't really have this disorder?" If the patient has a score of 40 on the antisocial scale, what is the chance that he or she is really not antisocial? Surprisingly, these statistics are usually quite high, in the .90s, because negative predictive power capitalizes on the large prevalence of patients in general not being antisocial.

The MCMI-III

As this book comes to press, the positive predictive powers and other operating characteristics of the MCMI-III have not yet been developed. There are many reasons for this. The first is that these studies take large numbers of subjects. With 28 scales there needs to be a large number of subjects so that there are at least 30 or 40 of each diagnosis in order to properly model each of the diagnoses. There are also problems with obtaining reliable clinical diagnoses to generate the operating characteristics. While the MCMI-I and the

MCMI-II fairly nicely paralleled the *DSM*'s diagnoses, the MCMI-III contains a superset of diagnoses. Sadistic and Self-Defeating scales continue even though these diagnoses have been dropped from the *DSM-IV*. Therefore, it will be difficult in the validity studies to diagnose these conditions. Along this line, the diagnosis of depressive personality disorder has only been available for a short period of time, since the publication of the *DSM-IV*. Most clinicians have not seen the criteria for this nor have they started using this diagnosis. It will be several years before operating characteristic statistics are available for the MCMI-III. It will take many studies in a variety of clinical settings to adequately evaluate the validity of the MCMI-III.

As an interim statistic, however, Table 1-4 presents the positive predictive powers for the MCMI-II. As an example, for the MCMI-II the Schizoid Personality Disorder scale has a relatively low positive predictive power of .38. What this means is that if a patient has a score on Schizoid of greater than 85, there is only a 38 percent chance that the patient is indeed schizoid. A 38 percent chance is better than the underlying prevalence, but it is still probably at a point where most clinicians would feel uncomfortable with it. However, many of the other diagnoses, such as Avoidant and Dependent, enjoy positive predictive powers in the .60s and .70s. With these a clinician would be two-thirds certain that the patient had that disorder given a score of 85 or greater.

Looking at the clinical syndrome scales, what is found for the Anxiety and Dysthymia scales are respectable .70s. Somatoform has only .33. It should not be forgotten that this may largely be due to the difficulty in constructing items for this domain (e.g., "I have a hard time keeping my balance while walking"). Bipolar Manic has a positive predictive power of .53. Alcohol and Drug Dependence are both strong, in the high .70s to high .80s. Finally, Thought Disorder, Major Depression, and Delusional Disorder are relatively low, in the .30s to .50s. This is due to two problems. One is a relatively low prevalence of those disorders. The second is the difficulty in constructing items for very phenomenally specific domains such as thought disorder and delusional disorder.

An Interpretation Approach to the MCMI-III

There are a number of ways of interpreting tests. Usually, the fewer the scales on the test, the easier the interpretation. Unfortunately, with 28 scales on the MCMI-III, a more complex approach to interpretation is required. The interpretation of the Millon should use the blocking of the scales and be viewed as hierarchical, with the severe disorder scales dictating the interpretation of the basic disorder scales.

TABLE 1-4 MCMI-II Positive Predictive Powers for Base Rate Score >84

Scales	PPP
Validity	(NA)
Validity:	
Disclosure:	(NA)
Desirability:	(NA)
Debasement:	(NA)
Basic Personality Disorders	
Schizoid:	.38
Avoidant:	.72
Depressive:	(NA)
Dependent:	.70
Histrionic:	.48
Narcissistic:	.55
Antisocial:	.68
Sadistic:	.58
Compulsive:	.61
Negativistic:	.50
Self-Defeating:	.46
Severe Personality Disorders	
Schizotypal:	.47
Borderline:	.60
Paranoid:	.40
Basic Clinical Syndromes	
Anxiety:	.74
Somatoform:	.33
Bipolar:	.53
Dysthymia:	.72
Alcohol Dependence:	.88
Drug Dependence:	.78
PTSD:	(NA)
Severe Clinical Syndromes	
Thought Disorder:	.30
Major Depression:	.50
Delusional Disorder:	.40

Validity Scales

The first block of scales to look at are the validity scales. It is important to examine these response bias scales before looking at the content scales. The most fundamental of these is the Validity Scale. If the patient endorsed even one of the three extremely unlikely items as true, the test should be viewed as uninterpretable. Next, the patient's profile should be analyzed for disclosure. Is the patient, in general, underreporting or overreporting psychopathology? If the Disclosure scale is below 35 or above 85, the profile is, in most clinical settings, technically invalid. Finally, examine the Desirability and Debasement scales for general style.

Personality Disorder Scales

At this point, look at the Severe Personality Disorder scales. If there is a high Severe Personality Disorder scale, this should serve as an anchor for the rest of the personality disorders scales. A high Severe Personality Disorder scale will usually predispose a number of the Basic Personality Disorder scales to be high. If patients are schizotypal, it is highly likely that they will have high scores on Schizoid and Avoidant and perhaps one or two other basic personality scales. The primary personality interpretation should be on the severe personality scale, and that interpretation should be "colored" and "fleshed out" on the basis of the Basic Personality Disorders scales.

If there is not a high Severe Personality Disorder scales, then the high one or two point codes from the Basic Personality Disorder scales should be interpreted. Choca, Shanley, and Van Denburg's (1992) and Craig's (1993a, 1993b) books do a good job of providing common high point code (Retzlaff et al., 1994) interpretations as well as all others. Additionally, the other chapters of this book will give the reader a more thorough understanding of the interpretation of the scales from particular therapeutic approach perspectives.

Clinical Syndrome Scales

As with the personality scale interpretative process, the first step is to examine the Severe Clinical Syndrome scales. If there is a high scale score there, then it is the anchor or pivot point of the clinical syndrome scales interpretation. If there is a high scale score within this block, there are probably elevated Basic Clinical Syndrome scales. A patient who is high on Major Depression is probably additionally high on Anxiety and Dysthymia. This makes clinical sense and is consistent with the construction of the MCMI-III. These scales all being elevated is not contradictory but indeed complementary. If there is no high Severe Clinical Syndrome scale, then the high one or two Basic Clinical Syndrome scales should be interpreted.

Finally, it is common for profiles with elevated clinical syndrome scales to not only have elevated complementary clinical syndrome scales, but also to have some high personality disorder scales. For instance, if PTSD is high, one might expect Anxiety and Dysthymia to be high, as well as possibly Alcohol Dependence. This interpretive process involves considering also what personality constellation makes up the PTSD syndrome (e.g., Hyer, 1994). It might include Schizoid, Avoidant, Antisocial, Sadistic, or Negativistic, as well as in severe cases, Borderline. Again, multiple high point scales are not necessarily contradictory, but, instead, are hierarchical and convergent.

The final point in interpretation is to always integrate what you have learned from the MCMI-III with the patient and clinic history. What is the patient's chief complaint? What is his or her age, sex, and particular psychopathology history? Clinical interpretation also needs to consider the clinical setting in which one works. What type of patient does the clinic normally attract? What are the diagnostic biases within your particular clinic or diagnostic group?

Summary

This chapter orients the reader to the MCMI-III. There are 28 scales including Response Bias, Basic Personality Disorder, Severe Personality Disorder, Basic Clinical Syndrome, and Severe Clinical Syndrome scales. By looking at individual items, scales were discussed as having good concordance with both Millon's theory and *DSM-IV*. The construction history of the MCMIs was provided to give the reader an appreciation of the sophistication and complexity of the development of this test. The construction included elements of content, statistical, and empirical construction techniques. The internal consistencies of the MCMI-III scales are remarkably high. The development of base rate scores was examined. The base rate scores do not reference the mean of the scales but are an optimized score that models the diagnostic criterion of each scale. The importance of operating characteristics and, specifically, the positive predictive power of the individual scales was covered. Finally, general interpretive guidelines were presented.

This foundation should aid the reader in considering George Everly's discussion (Chapter 2) on the theory of the domains, as well as the subsequent chapters that cover theory-specific interventions and therapeutic techniques for specific MCMI-III–derived diagnostic conditions.

References

American Psychiatric Association. (1980). *Diagnostic and statistical manual of mental disorders* (3d ed.) Washington, DC: Author.

American Psychiatric Association. (1987). *Diagnostic and statistical manual of mental disorders* (3d ed., rev.) Washington, DC: Author.
American Psychiatric Association. (1991). *DSM-IV options book: Work in progress.* Washington, DC: Author.
American Psychiatric Association. (1994). *Diagnostic and statistical manual of mental disorders* (4th ed.). Washington, DC: Author.
Choca, J., Shanley, L., & Van Denburg, E. (1992). *Interpretative guide to the Millon Clinical Multiaxial Inventory.* Washington, DC: American Psychological Association.
Craig, R. J. (1993a). *Millon Clinical Multiaxial Inventory: A clinical research information synthesis.* Hillsdale, NJ: Erlbaum.
Craig, R. J. (1993b). *Psychological screening with the MCMI-II.* Odessa, FL: Psychological Assessment Resources.
Gibertini, M., Brandenburg, N., & Retzlaff, P. (1986). The operating characteristics of the Millon Clinical Multiaxial Inventory. *Journal of Personality Assessment, 50,* 554–567.
Gibertini, M., & Retzlaff, P. (1988). Factor invariance of the Millon Clinical Multiaxial Inventory. *Journal of Psychopathology and Behavioral Assessment, 10,* 65–74.
Hyer, L., and Associates (1994). *Trauma victim: Theoretical issues and practical suggestions.* Muncie, IN: Accelerated Development.
Millon, T. (1969). *Modern psychopathology.* Philadelphia: Saunders.
Millon, T. (1977). *Millon clinical multiaxial inventory* Minneapolis, MN: National Computer Systems.
Millon, T. (1981). *Disorders of personality.* New York: Wiley.
Millon, T. (1986a). Personality prototypes and their diagnostic criteria. In T. Millon & G. Klerman (Eds.), *Contemporary directions in psychopathology: Toward* DSM-IV. (pp. 639–669). New York: Guilford Press.
Millon, T. (1986b). A theoretical derivation of pathological personalities. In T. Millon & G. Klerman (Eds.), *Contemporary directions in psychopathology: Toward DSM-IV.* (pp. 671–712). New York: Guilford Press.
Millon T. (1987). *Millon clinical multiaxial inventory-II: Manual for the MCMI-II.* Minneapolis, MN: National Computer Systems.
Millon, T. (1990). *Toward a new personology.* New York: Wiley.
Millon, T. (1994). *Manual for the MCMI-III.* Minneapolis, MN: National Computer Systems.
Nunnally, J. C. (1978). *Psychometric theory.* New York: McGraw-Hill.
Retzlaff, P. (1992). Professional training in psychological testing: New teachers and new tests. *Journal of Training and Practice in Professional Psychology, 6,* 45–50.
Retzlaff, P., & Gibertini, M. (1987). Factor structure of the MCMI basic personality scales and common item artifact. *Journal of Personality Assessment, 51,* 588–594.
Retzlaff, P., & Gibertini, M. (1994). Neuropsychometric issues and problems. In R. Vanderploeg (Ed.), *Clinician's guide to neuropsychological assessment.* Hillsdale, NJ: Erlbaum.
Retzlaff, P., Ofman, P., Hyer, L., & Matheson, S. (1994). MCMI-II high-point codes: Severe personality disorder and clinical syndrome extensions. *Journal of Clinical Psychology, 50,* 228–234.

Retzlaff, P., Sheehan, E., & Fiel, A. (1991). MCMI-II report style and bias: Profile and validity scales analysis. *Journal of Personality Assessment, 56,* 466–477.

Retzlaff, P., Sheehan, E., & Lorr, M. (1990). MCMI-II scoring: Weighted and unweighted algorithms. *Journal of Personality Assessment, 55,* 219–223.

Suen, H. K. (1990). *Test theories.* Hillsdale, NJ: Erlbaum.

2

Domain-Oriented Personality Theory

GEORGE S. EVERLY, JR.

No study of abnormal human behavior would be complete without an investigation into the construct of human personality and its disorders. With the advent of the multi-axial *DSM-III* (APA, 1980), the recognized role that personality and personality disorders play in abnormal behavior was raised to a new prominence. Not only were personality disorders given their own diagnostic axis (Axis II) in the multi-axial *DSM-III*, but inquiry into the role that subclinical personality traits and personality disorders play in general patterns of mental illness was rekindled. This renaissance of interest in personologic research has yielded what may be new insights into the fundamental role that personality plays in patterns of mental illness. As a result of the new *DSM* format, psychiatric diagnoses include not only the patient's current symptom presentation, via Axis I, but also the personality traits that represent enduring, deeply embedded patterns of dysfunction, recorded on Axis II. The *DSM* multi-axial system requires that symptoms no longer be viewed as isolated monoliths of aberrant behavior; rather, the broader context of the person is now allowed to be considered by way of Axis II.

Regardless of the specific role that one sees personality and personality disorders playing in the general mental health schema, it is clear that disorders of personality are certainly prevalent. In an investigation of the epidemiology of personality disorders, Merikangas and Weissman (1986) concluded the following: "Nearly one in every 10 adults in the general population, and over one-half of those in treated populations, may be expected to suffer from one of the personality disorders" (p. 274). Let us take a closer look at personality and its disorders.

Personality and Personality Disorders

Personality may be thought of as an undergirding framework that gives coherence, provides a structure, and creates an intrinsic order to what may otherwise be perceived as a multitude of discrete psychological and behavioral actions. As Hall and Lindzey (1957) noted, the construct of personality provides an "order and congruence to all the different kinds of behavior in which the individual engages" (p. 9). To extend this notion a bit, it may be suggested that the construct of personality serves as the psychological equivalent of the body's biological system of structures and functions. With this biological analogy in mind, personality may be thought of as the integrated sum of consistent thoughts, emotions, and patterns of behavior that persist temporally and reach functionally across situations; hence, they reveal themselves to be more an intrinsic component of the individual than a force determined situationally. This psychological system that we refer to as personality is a deeply embedded system of inclinations and psychological characteristics that are not easily altered—as the Greek philosopher Heraclitis asserted, "A man's fate is his character."

Given this construct of personality, let us now turn to the nature of personality disorders and of mental illness in general. As an aberrant gene may create a defect in a system of biological structures and functions, so too can dysfunctional learning create a defect in personological styles. As a pathogen may attack a biological system, dysfunctionally altering it or its subsystems, so too can neglect, abuse, or trauma dysfunctionally alter personologic subsystems. Thus, by definition, a personality disorder represents a condition wherein the personality no longer serves to functionally integrate thoughts, feelings, and behaviors in a flexible and adaptive manner. Thus, a personality disorder is a condition wherein the personality becomes maladaptive so as to cause functional impairment in social or occupational activities or otherwise result in significant distress (APA, 1994).

From a systems perspective, personality disorders (*DSM-IV*, Axis II) and even the more florid clinical psychiatric syndromes (Axis I) may be viewed as manifestations of failures in the core personality's ability to competently adapt to adversity. In concert with this view, Drake and Vaillant (1985) argued that "Axis II disorders may well refer to extremes of normal personality that are distributed continuously without clear boundaries between normal and abnormal..." (p. 553). Similarly, Millon (1981) said that Axis I disorders are best thought of as pathological extensions of dysfunctional personality constituents. Extending these notions somewhat, Everly (1987) in his formulation of "personologic primacy" has noted that the most important factor in understanding consistent patterns of human behavior and most florid psychiatric illnesses is the construct of personality. Everly argues that personality weaves an undergirding psychological infrastructure such that premorbid and subclinical personality patterns serve as the best single predictors of patterns of (1) Axis I psychiatric syndromes, (2) psychotherapeutic responsiveness, (3) psychopharmacologic responsiveness, and (4) the overall course of psychiatric illness.

Spawned by the advent of the multi-axial structure of the *DSM*, we enter the 1990s with a growing appreciation that the florid Axis I clinical syndromes reside less as discrete monolithic syndromes of aberrant behavior, and more as what may be dysfunctional points on psychological continua that are ultimately anchored in personological substrates. With such a thought in mind, let us turn to an analysis of personality disorders.

Millon's Model of Personality Disorders

The study of the construct of human personality may be approached from many perspectives. In an attempt to integrate some of the great traditions in personologic speculation (e.g., Freud, Murray, Murphy) with more modern bio-social formulations of personality, Millon (1990) has proposed that personality be conceived from a theoretical framework, not a descriptive one alone. And, secondly, to ensure that the theory be consonant with established systems of biologic thought, it should be organized from an evolutionary perspective. It has been said that "there is nothing so practical as a good theory" (Lewin, 1936). If this is so, then it seems a worthwhile endeavor to review such an integrative theory, especially if it enables us to bridge what may appear on the surface to be unconnected fields of inquiry.

Important to understanding Millon's integrative theory of personality is viewing personality in the context of three polarities. Somewhat similar to what Freud (1915) described as the "great polarities that govern all of mental life," Millon (1969) initially constructed a bio-social learning model that sought to integrate both normal personality styles and abnormal personality disorders.

Central to this schema was the concept of reinforcement, operationalized through the use of three functional polarities: Positive vs. Negative, representing the potential types of reinforcement the individual may seek; Self vs. Other, representing the potential sources from which the individual may seek reinforcement; and Active vs. Passive, representing the potential instrumental processes employed in gaining positive and avoiding negative consequences. This approach to categorizing personality disorders rejects the notion that personality disorders are best categorized by their florid symptom patterns and adopts instead a more complex perspective from which personality disorders are seen as functional styles of adaption and coping. Millon notes, "By framing our thinking in terms of what reinforcements the individual is seeking, where he is looking to find them, and how he performs, we may see more simply and more clearly the essential strategies which guide [his life]" (Millon, 1969, p. 193).

In later writings, Millon (1988, 1990) brought evolutionary theory to bear on his reinforcement model. From this added perspective the three personality polarities were extended as follows. The Positive vs. Negative type of reinforcement polarity was conceived as representing the *aims* of survival polarity, that is, the pursuit of Pleasure vs. the avoidance of Pain. The Self vs. Others source of reinforcement polarity was reframed as the *focus* of survival polarity, that is, relying upon and promoting Self vs. depending upon and nurturing Others. Finally, the Active vs. Passive instrumental processes mode was viewed as the evolutionary *mode* of survival polarity, that is, an Active modifying and controlling mode of behaving vs. a more Passive, accommodating, and reactive mode of behaving.

The Prototypal Model

While Millon's theory of personality was grounded in the concept of the three polarities as described in the previous section, Millon's theoretical formulations took a "quantum leap" with his introduction of the prototypal model and its constituent prototypic domains.

Cantor and colleagues (1980) note that the "classical approach" to psychiatric diagnosis relies upon the identification of diagnostically necessary or sufficient pathognomonic features. In contrast, the prototypal approach to diagnosis merely requires that sets of pathognomonically correlated features be constructed. More succinctly, "a prototype consists of the most common features or properties of members of a category and thus describes a theoretical ideal or standard against which real people can be evaluated" (p. 575). From the perspective of the prototype, no one property is necessary nor sufficient for membership in the category. As a result, it is possible that no one individual would actually be a perfect match to the theoretical prototype. Individuals would, therefore, represent the prototype in varying degrees. The greater the number of prototypic features the individual possesses, the closer the match to the prototypic ideal.

The greatest value of the prototypal model with its constituent prototypal domains appears to be its sensitivity to capturing the heterogeneity of patients diagnosed with the same personality disorder. Cantor et al. (1980) assert, ". . . clinicians can now be trained to expect heterogeneity among patients" (p. 192).

A similar value of the prototypal model applied to diagnosis may be that, given the probabilistic nature of diagnosis, a clinician will be able to determine the confidence of a given diagnosis based upon the "goodness of fit" with the prototypic ideal.

In sum, the employment of a prototypal model of diagnosis underscores the probabilistic nature of the diagnostic process and embraces the "real-world" heterogeneity of patients possessing personality disorders. It may be suggested that inherent to the prototypal model is an intrinsic gauge of diagnostic confidence based upon any given patient's degree of prototypality.

Clinical Prototypal Domains of Personality

In the previous sections we have reviewed the foundations of Millon's theory of personality and personality disorders. The concept of the prototypal model was introduced as an important aspect of Millon's formulation. As Millon notes, individuals show differences in the degree to which their behaviors display pervasiveness and durability. Those behaviors that are indeed pervasive, durable, and otherwise resistant to situational influences and other sources of acute variability are the features of interest here, and are referred to as personality.

There are eight domains of personality. Initially, they may be broken down by the classical schools of psychopathology including behavioral, cognitive, psychoanalytic, and biological. Millon (1967) refers to this approach as the "data" level. It is largely a function of the approach of the therapist as opposed to anything inherent in the particular psychopathology. See Table 2-1 for a breakdown of the domains.

TABLE 2-1 The Domains of Psychopathology

Behavioral Domains
Expressive Acts—functional
Interpersonal Conduct—functional

Phenomenological Domains
Cognitive Style—functional
Object Representations—structural
Self-Image—structural

Intrapsychic Domains
Regulatory Mechanisms—functional
Morphologic Organization—structural

Biophysical Domain
Mood/Temperament—structural

Behavioral Domains

See Table 2-2 for detailed clinical definitions of the behavioral domains.

Expressive Acts
The behavioral appearances of expressive acts are readily observable by others. Observations of overt behavior enable the clinician to deduce, through inference, valuable qualities of the patient's overall characterological presentation.

Interpersonal Conduct
While clearly a behavioral expression, interpersonal conduct, that is, the way one relates to others, allows the clinician to deduce qualities of personal competence, self-esteem, and affiliative drives *vis à vis* the most dynamic factor in the patient's world—other individuals.

Phenomenological Domains

See Table 2-3 for clinical definitions of the phenomenological domains.

Cognitive Style
Styles of information processing, focusing of attention, informational organization, and patterns of communication are critical elements in understanding how a patient will respond trans-situationally. In that there simply is no such thing as objective reality (i.e., all of what we experience is ultimately prey for cognitive filtering mechanisms), understanding the cognitive style of a patient becomes a critical analytic element.

Object Representations
Important experiences from the past leave intrapsychic imprints, a structural "residue" that affects how one relates to the world with its ongoing series of

TABLE 2-2 Clinical Definitions of the Behavioral Domains

Expressive Acts (Functional)
The observables of physical and verbal behavior can be readily identified by clinicians. These data enable us through inference, to deduce either what patients unknowingly reveal about themselves or, conversely, what they wish us to think or to know about them. The criteria for this clinical attribute consist of both of these presented behavioral variants.

Interpersonal Conduct (Functional)
Patients' styles of relating to others can be captured in a number of ways, such as the manner in which their actions impact on others, intended or otherwise; the attitudes that underlie, prompt, and give shape to these actions; the methods by which they engage others to meet their needs; or their way of coping with interpersonal tensions and conflicts.

TABLE 2-3 Clinical Definitions of the Phenomenological Domains

Cognitive Styles (Functional)
For the clinician, the cognitive styles domain includes some of the most useful indices in identifying patients' distinctive ways of functioning. Here, it is learned how patients perceive events, focus their attention, process information, organize their thoughts, and communicate their reactions and ideas to others. The criteria for this clinical attribute represent some of the more notable styles in this functional realm.

Object Representations (Structural)
Significant experiences from the past leave an inner imprint, a structural residue composed of memories, attitudes, and affects that continue to serve as a substrate of dispositions for perceiving and reacting to life's ongoing events. Both the character and content of these internalized representations of the past are evaluated.

Self-Image (Structural)
Each person builds a perception of himself or herself as an identifiable being, an "I" or "me." Most people have a consistent sense of "who they are," but differ in the clarity of their introspections into self and/or in their ability to articulate the attributes comprised in this image. Clinical ratings, therefore, are likely to be somewhat speculative.

---

dynamic events. Such memories, in the aggregate, form a matrix of dispositions for perceiving and reacting to life's ever-changing journey of experience.

Self-Image

Each individual possesses an evaluation of oneself. External experiences are filtered through the "lens" of the self-image. The sense of self, once developed, remains remarkably stable, yet there is a wide range of variability with regard to self-introspectiveness.

Intrapsychic Domains

See Table 2-4 for clinical definitions of the intrapsychic domains.

Regulatory Mechanisms

Mechanisms of self-defense, self-protection, need gratification, and conflict resolution represent important internal processes that may serve to matrix all other functional domains in some form of unobservable self-protective fabric. Such an over-arching or otherwise unifying function becomes of critical clinical importance in understanding the overall character style.

Morphologic Organization

The overall configuration of intrapsychic fabrics that serves as a framework for all that one experiences may be thought of as an intrapsychic morphologic

TABLE 2-4   Clinical Definitions of the Intrapsychic Domains

Regulatory Mechanisms (Functional)
This clinical attribute represents internal and often unconscious processes that are difficult to discern and evaluate. Nevertheless, they are important in that they show how patients deny or distort painful feelings or incompatible thoughts, often setting into motion a sequence of events that intensify the very problems they may have sought to circumvent.

Morphologic Organization (Structural)
The overall configuration of elements making up the mind's interior world may display weakness in organizational cohesion, or exhibit deficient balance and coordination, or possess rigidities or pressures. It is the structural strength, interior congruity, and functional efficacy of this intrapsychic system to which this clinical attribute pertains.

---

organization. This organization of all the mind's critical elements may possess or develop systematic deficits or weaknesses. This clinical domain, therefore, reflects the overall organizational qualities of the mind.

Biophysical Domain

See Table 2-5 for a clinical definition of the biophysical domain.

Mood/Temperament

The mood/temperament domain is one of the most important of the clinical domains. Characterological mood pervades virtually every aspect of an individual's existence, dramatically coloring relationships and all other self–environment interactions.

Structure and Function

Having briefly reviewed the domains for analyzing the prototypic personality, we may view these same eight domains somewhat differently to gain even more analytic insight. Again, while the preceding organization is brought to the clinical situation by the therapist's philosophy, the organization of the domains without the clinical bias is somewhat different. The core personologic features that demonstrate durability can be categorized into two types of characteristics: (1) the individual's structural characteristics and (2) the individual's functional characteristics. These domains can be thought of as possessing the greatest clinical relevance to any process of personologic analysis.

Structural characteristics of personality may be viewed as deeply embedded and relatively enduring memories, attitudes, emotions, needs, conflicts, et cetera. These form an intrapsychic network of memories, affect, drives, and

TABLE 2-5   Clinical Definition of the Biophysical Domain

Mood/Temperament (Structural)
The meanings of extreme affective states are easy to decode. Not so with persistent moods and subtle feelings that have and continue to insidiously color a wide range of patients' relationships and experiences. No matter how clear the criteria for this clinical attribute may be, the data base for their deduction may call for more information than may be available observationally, especially during acute emotional periods.

---

conceptions of self and others that serves as the foundation for person–environment interactions.

There exist four structural domains that are relevant to the appraisal of personality disorders: the object relations, self-image, morphologic organization, and mood/temperament domains. Fourteen prototypic variations, one for each personality disorder, exist for each of the four structural domains.

There exist four functional domains that are inherently relevant to the study of personality disorders: the expressive acts, interpersonal conduct, cognitive style, and regulatory mechanisms domains. These functional domains represent the dynamic processes used to manage environmental relationships and the person–environment interaction. Once again, 14 prototypic variations, one for each personality disorder, exist for each of the four functional domains.

Treatment and Domain-Related Theory

Fundamentals

As noted earlier, the concept of the personologic prototype, as delineated via a domain-related system of description, not only "explains" the variability within the actual real-life presentations of theoretically homogenous personality disorders, but also is a useful tool to refine diagnostic conceptualizations and formulate treatment protocols.

More simply stated, "real patients" fail to conform to textbook diagnostic descriptions in the ideal sense; and, given the complexity of the human experience, no two human beings, no matter what their diagnosis, are likely to be exactly the same in how they see and interact with their respective environments.

The domain-based prototypic formulation of personality disorders allows the clinician to analyze, more finitely, the most dysfunctional aspects of the patient's characterological amalgam and to formulate both brief and long-term interventions designed to readily attend to the most dysfunctional aspects of the patient's presentation.

Such an analytic and formulatory approach is consistent with the extant interactive psychotherapy movement (Norcross & Goldfried, 1992; Millon, 1988; Millon, Everly, & Davis, 1993). Briefly, the integrative psychotherapy of personality disorders can be conceived of as an integrated configuration of historically diverse psychotherapeutic strategies and tactics in which a combination of interventions can be serially or simultaneously directed toward the most salient dysfunctional domains of any given personality disorder. Only through domain-related conceptualization can such formalities be applied. Using the categorical alignment of domains as aggregated in Table 2-1, it becomes possible to create a personologic prototype of each of the personality disorders in the *DSM*, wherein each of the domains represents a piece of "ideal," or prototypic, characterologic structure.

As an exemplar, Table 2-6 is a tabular presentation of a prototypic avoidant personality disorder. Such a formulation can be constructed for each of the personality disorders and reveals a penetrating "goodness of fit" for any patient *vis à vis* the prototype. Here, for the avoidant, the various aspects of the prototype emerge. Behaviorally, the patient will be fretful and uneasy. Interpersonal behavior will seem aversive, with a distancing from social activities. From a phenomenological perspective, the patient will be cognitively distracted in the present. He or she will have difficulty with conflicted and vexatious object relations. And the self-image will be one of alienation due to a sense of social ineptness and inferiority. The intrapsychic level of symptoms will include fantasy as a primary defense mechanism. The underlying organization of psychic elements is fragile and incomplete. Finally, the biophysical mood is anguished due to the underlying conflict between needing others and fearing them. In summary, from a prototypical perspective, the avoidant patient may have all or some subset of these symptoms. Some may be more relevant given the particular situation or chief complaint. Given that these domains exist, the clinician can look for several of the symptoms to confirm a diagnosis. All are interrelated and suitable as the target of psychotherapeutic intervention.

Treatment Planning

Counseling, psychotherapy, and other interventions designed to change behavior, whether such behavior is overt and observable or covert and stealthy, are clearly numerous, historically and phenomenologically diverse. Consistent with the so-called "medical model," a synonym for Cartesian-Pasteurian separatism, disparate behavior change technologies have historically stood juxtaposed and mutually exclusive when any treatment plan was formulated.

TABLE 2-6 Domains of the Avoidant Personality

Behavioral Level
(F) Expressively Fretful (e.g., conveys personal unease and disquiet, a constant timorous, hesitant and restive state; overreacts to innocuous events and anxiously judges them to signify ridicule, criticism, and disapproval).

(F) Interpersonally Aversive (e.g., distances from activities that involve intimate personal relationships and reports extensive history of social pan-anxiety and distrust; seeks acceptance, but is unwilling to get involved unless certain to be liked, maintaining distance and privacy to avoid being shamed and humiliated).

Phenomenological Level
(F) Cognitively Distracted (e.g., warily scans environment for potential threats and is preoccupied by intrusive and disruptive random thoughts and observations; an upwelling from within of irrelevant ideation upsets thought continuity and interferes with social communications and accurate appraisals).

(S) Vexatious Objects (e.g., internalized representations are composed of readily reactivated, intense, and conflict-ridden memories of problematic early relations; limited avenues for experiencing or recalling gratification and few mechanisms to channel needs, bind impulses, resolve conflicts, or deflect external stressors).

(S) Alienated Self-Image (e.g., sees self as socially inept, inadequate, and inferior, justifying thereby his or her isolation and rejection by others; feels personally unappealing, devalues self-achievements, and reports persistent sense of aloneness and emptiness).

Intrapsychic Level
(F) Fantasy Mechanism (e.g., depends excessively on imagination to achieve need gratification, confidence building, and conflict resolution; withdraws into reveries as a means of safely discharging frustrated affectionate, as well as angry, impulses).

(S) Fragile Organization (e.g., a precarious complex of tortuous emotions depends almost exclusively on a single modality for its resolution and discharge, that of avoidance, escape, and fantasy, and, hence, when faced with personal risks, new opportunities, or unanticipated stress, few morphologic structures are available to deploy and few back-up positions can be reverted to, short of regressive decompensation).

Biophysical Level
(S) Anguished Mood (e.g., describes constant and confusing undercurrent of tension, sadness, and anger; vacillates between desire for affection, fear of rebuff, embarrassment, and numbness of feeling).

The concept of eclecticism was an attempt on the part of therapists to acknowledge that there was no one "best" therapy without consideration of the idiosyncratic needs of the patient. While eclecticism was the first sign of flexibility in therapeutic posturing, it too often remained an "either-or" decision-making process. The advent of integrative psychotherapeutic formulations represented a major breakthrough in treatment planning, for it recognized the value in serial and concomitant combining of otherwise conceptually diverse behavior change tactics within the treatment plan for a single patient.

Millon's concept of personologic prototypes and their constituent eight domains represents a major facilitative thrust for the strategic planning phase of any integrative psychotherapeutic formulation. Millon's domains provide eight phenomenologically unique targets for psychotherapeutic/behavior-change technologies. Table 2-7 shows how psychotherapeutic/behavior-change strategic formulations can be aligned, focused, or targeted upon the eight prototypic domains.

Clinicians interested in the behavioral acts of patients will want to target the maladaptive behavior of each personality disorder with the classic behavioral techniques of, perhaps, social skills training, assertiveness training, or operant conditioning, for example. Interpersonally oriented therapists might

TABLE 2-7 Domain-Targeted Interventions

Behavioral Domains

Expressive Acts

Counterconditioning; social-skills training; assertiveness training; behavioral rehearsal; operant conditioning

Interpersonal Conduct

Group therapy; family therapy; social-skills training; humanistic therapy approaches; anger management; interpersonal therapy

Phenomenological Domains

Cognitive Style

Reframing methods; cognitive-behavioral approaches; existential therapies

Object Representations

Dream analysis; object-relations analysis

Self-Image

Client-centered therapy; self-oriented analysis; assertiveness training

Intrapsychic Domains

Regulatory Mechanisms

Ego-oriented analysis; hypotherapy; psychoanalytic psychotherapy

Morphologic Organization

Transference; classical psychoanalysis; psychoanalytic psychotherapy

Biophysical Domain

Mood temperament

Psychopharmacologic agents; relaxation training; counterconditioning; experiential therapy look at the interpersonal conduct and apply group techniques, family therapy, or anger management.

Cognitive therapists will want to look at the dysfunctional cognitive patterns of the disorders and correct them through a number of techniques including reframing or cognitive-behavioral techniques. Object relations therapies or dream analysis may aid patients' dysfunctional objects and their interactions. The difficulties of the self may be remediated through self therapies or client-centered therapy.

The intrapsychic domains are amenable to psychoanalytic psychotherapy. The regulatory defense mechanisms might also benefit from ego-oriented psychotherapy or hypnotherapy. The organization of the intrapsychic elements may also be treated with classical psychoanalysis.

Finally, the affectively oriented mood and temperament aspects of the personality disorders may be treated through psychopharmacologic agents, perhaps antianxiety or antidepressant agents. Alternatively, experiential therapy directed toward these affects may be appropriate. While the preceding techniques as well as those presented in Table 2-7 are by no means to be considered an exhaustive list of possible therapies, they do represent an initial starting point in the understanding of domain-oriented psychotherapies. Indeed, chapters 2 through 10 of this book each take a specific treatment approach and apply it to each of the personality disorders.

Integrative Psychotherapy

Amalgamating the concepts presented in Table 2-6 and Table 2-7, it is possible to see how a domain-oriented therapeutic plan can be formulated for the prototypic avoidant personality disorders, for example, or any other personality disorder (see Table 2-8).

In Table 2-8, the domain-specific symptoms of the avoidant are presented with possible domain-specific treatment techniques. While obviously the simultaneous use of all these techniques for a single patient would be inappropriate and counterproductive, the integrative psychotherapist could select from the symptoms and treatments a coordinated group of three or four. For example, by targeting for therapy the fretful behavior, aversive interactions, alienated self, and anguished mood, the therapist could put together a package of therapeutic techniques that could primarily and secondarily target all these symptoms. Group-based psychotherapy, for instance, could be used as a platform for not only the interpersonal problems of this patient but also as a vehicle for social-skills and assertiveness training. An additional group agenda could be the counterconditioning of the anguished mood. For the benefit of the patient, the systematic understanding of the symptoms across domains allows for a package of integrated therapies to be brought to bear to better address the systemic interactions across those domains.

Similar strategic therapeutic planning exercises can be performed for all

TABLE 2-8 Domain-Specific Therapies for the Avoidant Personality

Behavioral Domains
Expressive Acts:
Fretful behaviors: | Social-skills training

Interpersonal Conduct:
Aversive interactions: | Group therapy

Phenomenological Domains
Cognitive Style:
Distracted cognitive style: | Mindfulness meditation

Object Representations:
Vexatious representations: | Object-relations analysis

Self-Image:
Alienated self: | Assertiveness training

Intrapsychic Domains
Regulatory Mechanisms:
Fantasy preoccupation: | Ego-based therapy

Morphologic Organization:
Fragile organization: | Psychoanalysis

Biophysical Domain
Mood Temperament:
Anguished mood: | Counterconditioning

---

of the *DSM* personality disorders based upon a prototypic analysis such as that above.

Salient Pathologies

It can be argued that a comprehensive prototypic analysis and intervention, as done above, need not be performed on all of the *DSM* personality disorders because each domain within each disorder is not equally dysfunctional. Embracing such a notion, domain-based analysis makes it easier to identify the most pathognomonically salient features (domains) of each *DSM* personality disorder and allows, alternatively, a more discretely targeted intervention process.

For example, in Table 2-9, it is the behavioral acts of the antisocial that come to clinical attention. Therefore, behavioral therapies are probably the

TABLE 2-9 Domain-Specific Therapy for the Most Salient Pathologies

Personality Disorder	Most Pathogonomic Domain
Schizoid:	Mood/temperament
Avoidant:	Self-image
Depressive:	Mood/temperament
Dependent:	Interpersonal conduct
Histrionic:	Interpersonal conduct
Narcissistic:	Self-image
Antisocial:	Expressive acts
Sadistic:	Mood/temperament
Compulsive:	Cognitive style
Negativistic:	Self-image
Self-Defeating:	Mood/temperament
Schizotypal:	Expressive acts
Borderline:	Interpersonel conduct
Paranoid:	Self-image

most appropriate if only a single therapy is used. It is the self-image of the narcissist that results in much of the social and occupational dysfunction. As such, self-oriented or client-oriented therapies are probably most efficacious. Finally, for example, it is the discontented self-image of the negativistic patient that is most salient and should probably be addressed through therapy. Table 2-9 is only one approach; others may find differing solutions to the domain-based analysis.

Such an approach may prove immensely useful in the formulation of symptom-oriented, brief psychotherapeutic interventions as have come into vogue recently. Nevertheless, it is the bias of this author that a comprehensive prototypic analysis yields far greater understanding of the patient and thus is a more powerful therapeutic intervention.

Summary

Domain-related personality theory brings a new analytic tool to bear upon the challenge of psychotherapeutic intervention with personality disorders. Such an approach yields new insights into their overt and subtle phenomenology and new hope for their treatment.

Domain-oriented personality theory allows us to reconcile the extreme variability seen within diagnostic categories. As noted earlier, domain-oriented analysis is an effective tool for embracing the natural heterogeneity within personality disorders.

The greatest advantage of this system based upon domains may be its ability to result in highly specific interventions targeted toward the most salient features within the pathognomonic presentations while also allowing comprehensive insight into the total clinical picture. Thus, both the obvious and the stealthy can be integrated to yield greater clinical efficacy. Lastly, the domain-oriented system is consistent with and facilitative of an integrative psychotherapeutic approach.

References

American Psychiatric Association. (1980). *Diagnostic and statistical manual of mental disorders* (3d ed.). Washington, DC: Author.

American Psychiatric Association. (1994). *Diagnostic and statistical manual of mental disorders.* (4th ed.). Washington, DC: Author.

Cantor, N., Smith, E., French, R., & Mezzich, J. (1980). Psychiatric diagnoses as prototype categorization. *Journal of Abnormal Psychology, 89,* 181–193.

Drake, R., & Vaillant, G. (1985). A validity study of Axis II of *DSM-III. American Journal of Psychiatry, 142,* 553–558.

Everly, G. S. (1987). The principle of personologic primacy and personologic psychotherapy. In C. Green (Ed.), *Proceedings of the Conference on the Millon Inventories.* Minnetonka, MN: NCS.

Freud, S. (1915). The instincts and their vicissitudes. In *Collected papers* (vol. 4). London: Hogarth.

Hall, C., & Lindzey, G. (1957). *Theories of personality.* New York: Wiley.

Lewin, K. (1936). *Principles of a topographical psychology.* New York: McGraw.

Merikangas, K. R., & Weissman, N. M. (1986). Epidemiology of *DSM-III* Axis II personality disorders. In A. J. Frances & R. E. Hales (Eds.), *Psychiatry update* (vol. 5, pp. 258–278). Washington, DC: American Psychiatric Association.

Millon, T. (1969). *Modern psychopathology.* Philadelphia: Saunders.

Millon, T. (1981). *Disorders of personality.* New York: Wiley.

Millon, T. (1988). Personologic psychotherapy. *Psychotherapy, 25,* 209–219.

Millon, T. (1990). *Toward a new personology.* New York: Wiley.

Millon, T., Everly, G., & Davis, R. (1993). How can knowledge of psychopathology facilitate psychotherapy integration. *Journal of Psychotherapy Integration, 3*(4), 331–352.

Norcross, J., & Goldfried, M. (1992). *Handbook of psychotherapy integration.* New York: Basic Books.

3

Use of the MCMI-III in Behavior Therapy

DENNIS DONAT

The *expressive domain* refers to the observable aspects of physical and verbal behavior. This domain focuses on what a person actually does and says. In the context of a more comprehensive theory of personality, it allows the clinician to deduce other attributes (e.g., cognitive style, mood) that can enhance understanding of the patient's condition and that may provide important information to guide clinical interventions. When focusing on the behavioral domain, the obvious techniques to emphasize are those of behavior therapy. This chapter will focus on behavioral methods and how they can be employed, in the context of Millon's biosocial learning theory, to assist clients in effecting behavior change.

Behavior Therapy

Probably more than any other mental health profession, clinical psychology has sought to integrate scientific research and clinical care. This goal has been fostered by a belief that sustainable advances in clinical care are more likely if methods of treatment are grounded in sound scientific research and theory. The applied area of behavior modification and therapy began as the use of experimentally established principles of learning for the purpose of changing unadaptive behavior (Wolpe, 1973). It was expected that, through the use of interventions based on the experimentally established principles of learning, unadaptive habits are weakened and eliminated while more adaptive habits are initiated and strengthened (Wolpe, 1973). Stimulated by the observations and theoretical principles derived from laboratory research by scientists such as Bekhterev and Pavlov, psychologists such as J. B. Watson and Rosalie Rayner conceptualized and tested applications for clinical problems during the 1920s (Watson, 1978). Additional research conducted in the laboratories of Thorndike, Hull, Skinner, and others extended the principles of behavior and guided applications conducted by scientist-practitioners such as Paul and Lentz (1977).

Classical Conditioning

The laboratory research of Ivan Pavlov conducted during the early 1900s stimulated the development of the classical conditioning school of learning theory. This approach focuses on the influence of environmental conditions as stimuli to evoke behavior. On the basis of his research, Pavlov developed a theoretical model that states that learning occurs when a neutral stimulus is repeatedly paired with a stimulus (unconditioned stimulus) that consistently elicits a specific, or unconditioned, response. Through repeated pairings, a previously neutral stimulus will begin to produce the response despite the absence of the unconditioned stimulus. Conditioned responses have been established for a variety of subjects (including humans) and a wide variety of involuntary responses.

The principles of classical conditioning have given rise to interventions for a variety of clinical problems. For example, Wolpe (1958) developed the procedure of reciprocal inhibition to counter severe anxiety responses to specific situations. Other examples of the application of classical conditioning principles to clinical problems include flooding (Turner & Michelson, 1984), *in vivo* desensitization (Becker, 1985), aversive counterconditioning (Marshall, 1985), and covert sensitization (Cautela, 1985b). Many more examples can be found in Bellack and Hersen (1985).

Operant Conditioning

Classical conditioning does not involve the establishment of new responses or behaviors, but rather the ability of a new stimulus to elicit responses that previously were involuntarily elicited by other stimulus conditions. Operant conditioning, on the other hand, focuses on how new "voluntary" behaviors are established and maintained according to their impact on the environment. This approach, based primarily on the work of B. F. Skinner, holds that most complex behaviors are emitted by the organism according to how they "operate" on the environment. That is, the behaviors are more or less likely to occur according to the consequences that they evoke from the environment. Behaviors that produce consequences that are pleasurable for the organism will increase the likelihood of that behavior in the future, while behaviors that produce aversive consequences will be less likely to occur. Thus, through the identification and systematic manipulation of such consequences, behavior can be changed.

Probably the most striking clinical application of operant methods of behavior change is the token economy (Kazdin, 1977). The development of a token economy forces treatment staff to identify and prioritize the specific adaptive behaviors they want to increase and, to a lesser extent, maladaptive behaviors that they want to decrease for their patients. They must also identify and assess the strength of possible reinforcers for their patients. They can then work to establish a contingent relationship between the relevant behaviors (such as attending group therapy) and the administration of tokens or points that can later be exchanged for tangible reinforcers such as foods or other items. If necessary, tokens can be taken away for certain maladaptive behavior such as threatening other patients. Structuring a treatment program this way has repeatedly been demonstrated to improve patient (and staff) behavior. Additional examples of the application of operant principles include the procedures of shaping (Lovaas, 1966), contingency contracting (Dowd & Olsen, 1985), time out (Forehand, 1985), response cost (Axelrod, 1985), overcorrection (Foxx & Bechtel, 1982), and differential reinforcement (Homer & Peterson, 1980). Many other examples of behavioral techniques can be found in Bellack and Hersen (1985).

Research continues to deepen our understanding of how learning and behavior change take place (Rescorla, 1988). As the results from this research are integrated into theoretical models, the traditional understanding of classical and operant principles may change. It is likely that such changes will also have implications for improving clinical care.

Recent Trends in Behavior Therapy

Consistent with their heritage of basing interventions on principles derived from laboratory research, practitioners of behavior therapy have placed a high value on the ability to reliably observe and quantify the behavior that is to be assessed and changed. There traditionally has been relatively little acceptance of subjective feelings, internal states, or unconscious mechanisms as determinants of behavior.

More recently, many behavioral practitioners have become more receptive to the inclusion of such constructs as emotions or thoughts as long as these constructs can somehow be made observable and measurable. The use of subjective distress scales (Wolpe, 1973) or electronic equipment designed to monitor and transduce physiological variables has allowed for the quantification of physiological arousal. This has fostered the development of intervention methods such as relaxation training (Borkovec & Sides, 1979) and biofeedback training (Blanchard & Epstein, 1978) that apply learning principles to alter these variables.

Similarly, thoughts can be conceptualized as "self-talk" and made observable and measurable by verbal or written report by the client. These can then be modified through behaviorally based techniques such as self-statement modification (Dowd, 1985), thought stopping (Wisocki, 1985), or covert positive reinforcement (Cautela, 1985a). The inclusion of such variables for assessment and modification has expanded the breadth of clinical problems that are amenable to behavior therapy. The impact of the inclusion of "cognitive behavior" in conceptualizing problems and formulating treatment plans is highlighted by the consideration, in 1993, by the Association for the Advancement of Behavior Therapy to change its name to the Association for Behavioral and Cognitive Therapy.

A major innovation in the clinical application of behavioral principles has been the involvement of clients to actively assess and change their own behavior through the systematic application of behavioral technology. This approach places an emphasis on training clients to understand and apply behavioral methods themselves with the therapist acting as an educator/advisor. Most behavioral procedures with outpatients now have a strong self-management emphasis.

Techniques of Behavior Therapy

With the established principles of learning as a base, a broad variety of behavioral intervention techniques have been developed. The specific techniques vary in their relative reliance on classical versus operant theory as well as the modality of behavior (overt behavior, physiological behavior, cognitive/verbal behavior) that they attempt to alter. Bellack and Hersen (1985) identified no less than 150 behavioral intervention techniques that represent different methods of applying learning principles to clinical problems.

Generally, interventions based on classical conditioning principles rely on "counterconditioning," which seeks to substitute a response that is incompatible with the undesired response when the relevant stimulus conditions occur. Interventions based on the principles of operant conditioning focus on manipulating the consequences that follow behavior to increase adaptive behavior and/or decrease maladaptive behavior. These interventions are typically called "contingency management."

The most popular behavioral procedures, and perhaps the most relevant for dysfunctional personality traits and disorders, are the self-management procedures (Gross, 1985). These procedures focus on involving the client as an active participant in identifying the behaviors to change, assessing factors which influence those behaviors, and in implementing the procedures to effect change. While self-management programs may vary considerably, they typically involve the application of several behavioral techniques that are employed regardless of the specific behavior on which the plan focuses.

Self-management programs typically begin with an assessment procedure, implemented by the client, called self-monitoring (Kazdin, 1974). This procedure involves the observation, recording, and evaluation of one's own behavior. Self-monitoring is conducted in a systematic, deliberate manner and typically involves the identification of a clinically relevant behavior to monitor, discriminating when the behavior occurs and recording the concurrent environmental (situational) circumstances, self-statements (thoughts), and subjective estimation of emotional distress (physiological arousal). The self-monitoring procedure often provides the client and therapist with clear information regarding the nature and magnitude of the problem. In fact, the process of self-monitoring will often result in a temporary reduction of the problem behavior simply by focusing attention to it.

The self-monitoring procedure also is helpful in clarifying what alternative behavior may be preferred to the current problem behavior. Consequently, the results will not only identify behavior to be reduced but also help to identify alternative behavior that can be increased.

The identification of circumstances in which the problem behavior occurs allows for the detection of stimulus control (Schreibman, 1985) for that behavior. For example, the problem may occur primarily at certain times of the day, with certain people, or in association with certain thoughts or emotions. The identification of these stimulus conditions helps to predict when the problem behavior will occur. Those stimulus conditions can then be avoided or altered in the future, or alternative behaviors can be promoted when the stimulus conditions occur.

The identification of consistent self-statements (or thought patterns) associated with the problem behavior allows for an assessment regarding whether such statements contribute to the maintenance of the problem. A review of the self-statements may reveal unrealistic expectations about the outcome of a situation, unnecessarily self-critical statements, an inability to take credit for personal strengths, or many other variations in self-talk that can maintain a problem. The procedure of self-statement modification (Dowd, 1985) can be employed to replace self-statements that promote maladaptive behavior with statements that promote preferred behavior.

A subjective units of distress (SUDS) estimate (Wolpe, 1973) allows for an assessment of the possible involvement of bodily arousal as part of the problem. If physiological arousal is involved in maintaining the problem or inhibiting change to preferred behavior, relaxation training (Borkovec & Sides, 1979) or biofeedback training (Blanchard & Epstein, 1978) can be employed to help the client voluntarily counteract such arousal.

Finally, an explication of the client's overt behaviors following the stimulus conditions allows for an assessment as to whether they serve to maintain or ameliorate the identified problem. This may allow for the application of problem-solving training (Marchione, 1985) or other specific skills training, such as assertion or communication skills, to effect more acceptable alternatives to the current overt behavior and, thereby, ameliorate the problem.

For problem behaviors that are not neatly circumscribed by specific stimulus conditions, as should be expected for persons with dysfunctional personality traits and disorders, it is often useful to combine techniques from the different modalities (overt, cognitive, physiological) to fashion an intervention that is most appropriate for the client's identified problem. A variety of such "multicomponent packages" have been developed for common clinical problems that occur in a variety of stimulus conditions. These include impulse-control training (Camp et al., 1977), stress-inoculation training (Meichenbaum, 1985), anger-control therapy (Novaco, 1985), anxiety-management training (Suinn and Deffenbacher, 1988), assertion training (Gambrill, 1985), communication/conversational/social skills training (Curran & Monti, 1983), problem-solving training (D'Zurilla, 1986), depression management (Lewinsohn, Biglan, & Zeiss, 1976), and systematic desensitization (Wolpe, 1985). These packages differ in their relative emphasis on different aspects of overt, cognitive, and physiological behavior.

Behavior Therapy and Millon's Personality Theory

The failure of clinical psychology and psychiatry to closely consider the scientific integrity of theories of human behavior has led to many theories that, while alluring in their ability to explain behavior, are not testable and do not promote the development of hypotheses by which to plan and evaluate clinical interventions. These past failures played a major role in the development of the current psychiatric diagnostic system (American Psychiatric Association, 1980) as an avowedly "atheoretical" nosology. In a sense, the current nosology parallels a behavioral approach in its attempt to focus on observable phenomena in the process of classifying mental disorders. An atheoretical approach, however, fails to capitalize on the potential benefits of good theory or stimulate the critical examination and further development of such theory. In this regard, such an approach could retard the scientific understanding of psychopathology development and its attendant benefits for treatment.

Millon's theoretical model of the development of personality traits and disorders was an attempt to cull and integrate the best that the various scientific perspectives had to offer in explaining personality and psychopathology (Millon, 1969). He specifically attempted to conceptualize why dysfunctional personality styles develop, how they are maintained, and how compensatory experiences can be introduced to moderate and change them.

He sought to do this in a way that would facilitate the development of testable hypotheses.

Given the strong tie between scientific research and behavioral approaches to treatment, it is not surprising that behavioral constructs are a strong influence on Millon's theory. The explication of instrumental methods to seek pleasure (positive reinforcement) and avoid or minimize pain (negative reinforcement) and the clarification of sources of reinforcement are major components of the Millon theory. To the extent that these and other components of Millon's theory are based on sound scientific research, the theory holds the promise of being an approach that will facilitate the scientific examination and understanding of the development and maintenance of personality pathology as well as providing implications for treatment.

Behavioral Expressions of Personality

Personality traits represent enduring patterns of perceiving, relating to, and thinking about the environment and oneself and are exhibited in a wide variety of social contexts (American Psychiatric Association, 1980, 1994). Individuals are considered "disordered" when the personality traits are inflexible and maladaptive and contribute to either significant functional impairment or subjective distress. Personality traits and disorders, therefore, represent relatively stable patterns of overt, cognitive, and physiological behavior that exhibit relatively little variation across the many situations encountered.

The distinction between personality traits and disorders places considerable importance on the appropriateness of behavior in the situational context. The same behavior may be more appropriate in one situation than in another. This section will focus on describing the overt, cognitive, and affective behaviors commonly encountered with the varieties of personality traits and disorders. A summary table of Millon's expressive domain for the personality disorders is provided in Table 3-1.

Schizoid

The schizoid personality is relatively quiet, socially isolated, and restricted in the expression of behaviors associated with emotional experience and as such is best viewed as *impassive*. Such persons will appear to be relatively detached from the interpersonal issues and involvements that are so important in other people's lives. At a more pathological level, they are lethargic, apathetic, and disinclined to involve themselves with the concerns of others. They demonstrate little inclination to instrumentally achieve the affection and recognition of other people that are such strong reinforcers for most other people. They

TABLE 3-1 Expressive Acts Domain

Schizoid Personality
Expressively Impassive (e.g., appears to be in an inert emotional state, lifeless, undemonstrative, lacking in energy and vitality; is unmoved, boring, unanimated, robotic, phlegmatic, displaying deficits in activation, motoric expressiveness, and spontaneity)

Avoidant Personality
Expressively Fretful (e.g., conveys personal unease and disquiet, a constant timorous, hesitant, and restive state; overreacts to innocuous events and anxiously judges them to signify ridicule, criticism, and disapproval)

Depressive Personality
Expressively Disconsolate (e.g., appearance and posture convey an irrelievably forlorn, somber, heavy-hearted, woebegone, if not grief-stricken quality; irremediably dispirited and discouraged, portraying a sense of permanent hopelessness and wretchedness)

Dependent Personality
Expressively Incompetent (e.g., withdraws from adult responsibilities by acting helpless and seeking nurturance from others; is docile and passive, lacks functional competencies, and avoids self-assertion)

Histrionic Personality
Expressively Dramatic (e.g., is overreactive, volatile, provocative, and engaging, as well as intolerant of inactivity, resulting in impulsive, highly emotional, and theatrical responsiveness; describes penchant for momentary excitements, fleeting adventures, and short-sighted hedonism)

Narcissistic Personality
Expressively Haughty (e.g., acts in an arrogant, supercilious, pompous, and disdainful manner, flouting conventional rules of shared social living, viewing them as naive or inapplicable to self; reveals a careless disregard for personal integrity and a self-important indifference to the rights of others)

Antisocial Personality
Expressively Impulsive (e.g., is impetuous and irrepressible, acting hastily and spontaneously in a restless, spur-of-the-moment manner; is short-sighted, incautious and imprudent, failing to plan ahead or consider alternatives, no less heed consequences)

Sadistic (Aggressive) Personality
Expressively Precipitate (e.g., is disposed to react in sudden abrupt outbursts of an unexpected and unwarranted nature; recklessly reactive and daring, attracted to challenge, risk, and harm, as well as unflinching, undeterred by pain and undaunted by danger and punishment)

Compulsive Personality
Expressively Disciplined (e.g., maintains a regulated, highly structured and strictly organized life; perfectionism interferes with decision making and task completion)

Continued

TABLE 3-1 *Continued*

Negativistic Personality
Expressively Resentful (e.g., resists fulfilling expectancies of others, frequently exhibiting procrastination, inefficiency, and obstinate, as well as contrary and irksome, behaviors; reveals gratification in demoralizing and undermining the pleasures and aspirations of others)

Self-Defeating Personality
Expressively Abstinent (e.g., presents self as nonindulgent, frugal, and chaste; is reluctant to seek pleasurable experiences, refraining from exhibiting signs of enjoying life; acts in an unpresuming and self-effacing manner, preferring to place self in an inferior light or abject position)

Schizotypal Personality
Expressively Eccentric (e.g., exhibits socially gauche and peculiar mannerisms; is perceived by others as aberrant, disposed to behave in an unobtrusively odd, aloof, curious, or bizarre manner)

Borderline Personality
Expressively Spasmodic (e.g., displays a desultory energy level with sudden, unexpected, and impulsive outbursts; abrupt, endogenous shifts in drive state and inhibitory controls; not only places activation and emotional equilibrium in constant jeopardy, but engages in recurrent suicidal or self-mutilating behaviors)

Paranoid Personality
Expressively Defensive (e.g., is vigilantly guarded, alert to anticipate and ward off expected derogation, malice, and deception; is tenacious and firmly resistant to sources of external influence and control)

---

appear to lack a desire or capacity to experience positive or negative reinforcement. While this may be partly due to an environment that was impoverished in encouraging the development of such motives, it is also likely that such persons have a constitutional deficit in affectivity that predisposes them to be less likely to experience consequences as either pleasurable or aversive and, therefore, less likely to be influenced by external events.

In therapy such clients will have difficulty focusing on the relevant behaviors requiring intervention. They will be disinclined to adopt and sustain an active role in pursuing self-management goals. Often, external sources of influence, such as concerned relatives, will be required to prompt behavior change and to identify and provide consequences to sustain efforts for behavior change. The identification of consequences that can serve as reinforcers for behavior change will be a major challenge for therapists working with such individuals.

Typically such clients will require very clear direction from the therapist and ongoing guidance and support from other people in carrying out such a behavioral plan. The clients' and families' expectations must accommodate the restrictions that the constitutional deficit in affectivity places on the inclination to persevere at behavior change efforts. With this limitation in mind, most schizoid persons can benefit from social-skills or similar (communications skills, conversational skills, assertion skills) training.

Avoidant

The avoidant personality will also tend to be quiet and socially distant but is considered to experience an intense approach-avoidance conflict in the presence of most other people. Avoidant persons see a closer relationship with other people as potentially rewarding but experience heightened physiological arousal with associated dysfunctional self-statements (anxiety) when near them. This makes them appear *fretful*. They will feel more comfortable (negatively reinforced) by avoiding most interpersonal contacts. At a more pathological level, they watch for anticipated aversive interpersonal experiences. Innocuous interpersonal events are more likely to be misinterpreted as indicative of disdain or ridicule by others. Because they are so apprehensive, they fail to seek out or fully appreciate potential positively reinforcing experiences of relationships with other people.

Therapists must make an extra effort to establish satisfactory rapport with avoidant persons. They are inclined to feel nervous and to exhibit deficits in self-disclosure. Because they often recognize that interpersonal relationships are reinforcing for most other people, however, there often is motivation for change. They will be less likely to engage in escape behavior if the therapist exhibits a patient, nonthreatening, and sympathetic demeanor toward them.

Self-monitoring will help avoidant persons to identify variation in their inclination to avoid certain people or social situations, as well as the negative, self-deprecatory self-statements and associated emotional arousal that interfere with the development and maintenance of new social relationships. The principles of anxiety-management training are usually most relevant for such persons. In addition, past avoidant behavior may have resulted in a failure to acquire critical social skills. Consequently, some attention to social skills, communication skills, conversational skills, or assertion skills may also be relevant. Because of the strong anxiety tied to social interactions, the identification of differences in reactions according to the identity of the other person will likely be important in identifying people or classes of situations for which success is most likely. Early successes will likely be important in sustaining and expanding efforts to counteract past avoidant tendencies.

Depressive

The depressive personality shares many characteristics with the avoidant personality but is more *disconsolate*. The depressive personality will typically be quiet and socially distant. These persons also experience a strong approach-avoidance conflict in the presence of most other people and will feel more comfortable (negatively reinforced) by avoiding most interpersonal contacts. They remain aware, however, that other people seem better able to interact and develop relationships that are positively reinforcing. They often become acutely aware that something is missing in their lives and are discouraged that they are not able to effect the behaviors necessary to realize such relationships.

For depressive personalities the promise of establishing more satisfactory relationships with other people can be a strong reinforcer for continued effort in a self-management program. Because interpersonal anxiety is a prominent feature, an initial focus on anxiety management is usually most appropriate. Biofeedback training can be very useful since some channels, such as EMG, are easy to master and provide a quantified record of progress across sessions. This starts therapy on a reinforcing note. As with avoidant personalities, self-monitoring can be employed to identify variation in their avoidant behavior across situations, as well as the dysfunctional self-statements that impede the efforts at developing new social relationships. With success in managing anxiety, attention can turn to social-skills training to counter impairments in this area. Role plays with frequent compliments from the therapist will be very relevant in developing and transferring relevant skills. Early successes in the implementation of new social skills will be important.

Dependent

The dependent personality lacks initiative in asserting personal feelings and beliefs, often appearing *incompetent*. Dependent persons typically fail to recognize or self-reinforce for extant personal strengths and typically underestimate their own capabilities. In contrast to avoidant persons, however, they are positively reinforced to develop strong attachments to certain other people whom they view as relatively more self-confident and competent than themselves. At a more pathological level, they become strongly dependent on certain other people for provision of nearly all interpersonal reinforcement and for confirmation of self-worth. The unconditional regard of such individuals also helps to avoid any aversive consequences that may result from a personal failure to act competently. They suppress personal desires and any behavioral inclinations that might upset other people and instigate possible criticism.

Because they wish to avoid evoking critical responses from others, such persons will avoid asserting personal desires and be inclined to suppress problems. They will frequently present themselves for therapy when their attempts to maintain the positive regard from significant others are failing and the dependent relationship is in danger of being lost.

While the initial issue in therapy is often delimited to interactions with one or two other people, self-monitoring will be helpful in identifying a general inclination to avoid asserting themselves or to self-reinforce when opportunities present themselves. Often modification of self-talk will be required to counteract dysfunctional self-statements regarding self-worth or personal competencies and replace them with more accurate statements. Social skills/assertion training with role play practice will likely be helpful in effecting the willingness to emit and accurately assess new social behavior. As with the avoidant personality, it is very important to set initial goals to maximize the likelihood of success and to raise these goals slowly to maintain the opportunity for continued success. The therapist will likely become an important source of interpersonal reinforcement as the relationship builds. The therapist can assist the client to more accurately identify and self-reinforce for personal competencies and to accept compliments from others as legitimate. As successes are realized, the client becomes less reliant on the therapist for confirmation of self-worth.

Histrionic

The histrionic personality will often appear, on initial contact, to be gregarious, charming, and emotionally expressive if not *dramatic*. As with the dependent personality, frequent interpersonal contact with and expressions of positive regard from others are strong positive reinforcers. In contrast to the dependent personality, however, histrionic persons are not inclined to limit themselves to a small number of people as sources of reinforcement and will, instead, actively seek out new and interesting people and experiences. At a more pathological level, such individuals define their personal worth in terms of their ability to actively seek out and achieve compliments and other expressions of positive regard from others. They become affected and theatrical in an attempt to manipulate circumstances and realize expressions of positive attention from others. While they may, for extended periods of time, appear confident and self-assured, they are strongly dependent upon others for indications of self-worth and become quite anxious and/or depressed at the possibility of criticism or social disapproval.

Therapists should be aware that such individuals will often be more concerned with presenting an impressive appearance rather than with the practical issues associated with identifying and resolving problems. An initial period of apparent motivation and cooperation is likely to be followed by poor dependability in following through on homework that is part of behavioral self-management, such as self-monitoring assignments. Initially such clients will likely be most responsive to interventions that are directed toward relieving acute emotional distress. This may involve a form of relaxation training, problem-solving strategies, or both. Sustained efforts directed at altering interpersonal behavior are not likely, however. Involvement in therapy can be reinforced by initially focusing on the acute distress that instigated the presentation for therapy. Through initial successes in assisting with acute distress, the therapist can become an important source of support and, therefore, a strong positive reinforcer. Over time the focus can be shifted to more general interpersonal issues. With such a focus, impulse-management and problem-solving training can be employed to identify and counteract impulses to seek out new sources of reinforcement. The client can be taught to identify and more accurately self-reinforce for objective personal strengths regardless of whether these are recognized by others.

Narcissistic

The narcissistic personality emits self-statements indicating high self-worth and self-confidence acting in a *haughty* manner. Narcissistic persons are relatively resistant to modification according to discordant experience. This helps to make them resistant to emotional distress and the disabling effect that such distress can have on behavior. The beneficial effect of emotional arousal is also relatively absent, however, and any desire to guide personal behavior according to the responses of others is minimized. Such individuals are often able to easily establish personal priorities but are inclined to disregard the priorities of other people (such as therapists) in guiding their own behavior. Consequently, their self-directedness and self-assuredness can frustrate and disappoint others due to an appearance of being indifferent to their concerns. At a more pathological level, such individuals become intensely self-involved and arrogant. They exhibit little inclination to engage in behaviors to validate their self-confidence and self-assuredness for other people.

Their natural self-assuredness makes such individuals resistant to identifying personal problems and to exerting any effort to correct them. Extremely distressing circumstances, such as rejection by a lover or spouse, will likely be necessary to motivate them to seek help. In most cases the therapist should maintain a focus on such distress since the distress is likely to rapidly decrease and, with it, motivation for continued involvement in therapy. Continued involvement allows for the possibility of identifying similar, but less severe, situations in the client's life that may require similar changes in behavior. If such individuals agree on the definition of the problem, they will likely be motivated to follow a treatment plan that they feel will ensure their wellbeing.

The therapist can reinforce progress by stating admiration for the wise and beneficial steps being taken. Such individuals will likely benefit from training designed to accurately identify and respond to the concerns of other people, such as training in communication and empathic skills. Adherence to therapy tasks will be stronger if the end result can be viewed as some form of personal gain. If such clients can be impressed with the critical importance of following a treatment plan to avoid physical or mental blemishes, they will often do so very carefully.

Antisocial

The antisocial personality will often initially appear socially facile, energetic, and self-confident. Over time, however, such persons will tend to be strong-willed and to dominate others. They often are quick to recognize how other people can be influenced to cooperate with their own personal priorities. They strongly value the freedom to set their own priorities and are relatively disinclined to seek or accept direction from other people. At a more pathological level, they are impetuous, restless, and inclined to engage in *impulsive* actions. They fail to recognize and evaluate the potential consequences of different courses of action and, consequently, will often arouse more problems for themselves. They will be inclined to react quickly and strongly with frustration to people or circumstances that block their attainment of self-defined goals. They are unlikely to engage in protracted self-criticism under such circumstances and will, instead, see the behavior of other people as the source of the problem.

While such individuals experience a strong aversion for taking guidance from others, they are often very responsive to the concept of practical behavioral training that focuses on "self-control." If initial training can be directed toward ameliorating legitimate sources of frustration, the acceptance of the therapist as a "coach" or advisor is more likely. They are typically most responsive to such training if it can be presented as a strategy for achieving an ultimate personal gain, such as impulse or anger management being useful for preventing personal behaviors that provoke aversive consequences (such as trouble with the police or the court). In many cases it may be helpful to train such individuals to detect and respond to the concerns and desires of other people to avoid arousing problems with others that will ultimately impinge on their own freedom of action.

Sadistic

The sadistic/aggressive personality shares many characteristics of the antisocial personality. These individuals are strongly reinforced by experiences of challenge and risk and are relatively persistent in pursuing personally defined goals. Often, however, goals are poorly defined and actions are *precipitate*. Such individuals are less sensitive and less likely to be deterred by experiences that would be aversive for most people. They strongly value willpower and will contest external sources of control for primacy. They experience strong positive reinforcement in the defeat of competitors and may engage in behavior that is considered cruel or unnecessary by others, such as ridiculing those who have contested and lost.

The strongly competitive inclination of the aggressive personality makes them disinclined to seek help from other people. As with the antisocial personality, they can be assisted, however, to calculate the potential advantages of cooperating with other people versus the problems that may result from continuing to contest with them. They often find the prospect of training directed toward enhancing "self-control" abilities to be appealing. The principles of impulse and anger management, as well as proper assertion, are relevant for these individuals and can be presented as "smart" strategies to avoid arousing hassles from other people.

Compulsive

The compulsive personality will tend to be dependable and orderly. While such people may behave respectfully toward others, they go to extremes to avoid disruptive interactions by maintaining a tight control over their emotions. They will dislike an impulsive and emotionally unrestrained style of behavior, as would frequently be emitted by the histrionic personality. They are reinforced to achieve order and predictability in their lives. At a more pathological level, their desire to avoid strong frustration, discouragement, and anxiety reinforces an active conformity to the perceived expectations of others. They will strongly suppress the expression of any discordant feelings. Relative to other people, they become overly conformist and restrained and behave in an overly *disciplined* and perfectionistic manner.

The compulsive personality has difficulty exploring emotional issues and their link to overt behavior. Thus, they will not find "talk" therapies to be reinforcing. They are likely to be responsive to the prospect of "self-control" training, however, and will diligently follow instructions of the therapist if enhanced control of emotional distress is a possible consequence. Thus, they are likely to find training for emotional (anxiety, anger, or discouragement) management to be attractive. The concept of managing emotional distress by "sharing" or discussing emotions with other people, however, will be more difficult for them to accept. As success in the control of some emotional distress is achieved, the inclination to discuss emotional issues can be reinforced and this ability can be slowly enhanced. Training that focuses on the ability to recognize early stages of emotional distress and the implementation of strategies to avoid the embarrassment of a sudden and extreme loss of emotional control is negatively reinforcing for these clients.

Negativistic

The negativistic personality is notable for inconsistent behavior with other people. Negativistic persons may for short periods of time appear friendly, cooperative, and desirous of complying with the desires of others. However, they will over a longer period of time be inclined to view other people as insufficiently concerned about their priorities, become frustrated with the other people, and begin to act in a stubborn, contrary, and *resentful* fashion. This contrast between cooperative and contrary behavior has the predictable effect of engendering confusion and frustration in the other people. This will influence the other people to act critically, which only exacerbates the situation. In many cases the resulting conflict simply breeds more frustration and contributes to interpersonal conflict. The end result is a series of failed interpersonal relationships and an attitude that "they just never fit in."

Since negativistic clients are desirous of achieving the positive regard of people, the instrumental behaviors necessary to achieve that regard from others are strongly reinforced with episodes of success. The principles of anxiety and anger management, as well as assertion training, are very appropriate for such persons. The idea of self-management training may not be immediately accepted by such clients, who often view such a recommendation as implying that interpersonal difficulties are their own fault. They typically desire to avoid interpersonal strife, however, and, if an initial period of ambivalence and blaming of other people can be tolerated, they will become more receptive, particularly as they experience success after applying anxiety-management and assertion skills.

The interpersonal issues engendered by the negativistic personality's behavior will often intrude into the relationship with the therapist. Such clients should be expected to be ambivalent and inconsistent in following through with behavioral treatment recommendations. They may openly state doubts about the worth of therapy. It is important that the therapist continue to recognize objective strengths and indicants of success and positively reinforce these. The therapist must avoid being drawn into a contest of criticism and counter-criticism with such clients. These clients will usually progress much slower than an objective assessment of their capabilities would indicate. Until they can reduce personal anxiety with the therapist and adopt a more consistent interpersonal demeanor, progress outside of therapy will be minimal.

Self-Defeating

The self-defeating personality may appear benignly friendly and compliant for short periods of time. Over longer periods of time, however, self-defeating persons are found to be quietly self-critical and lacking in initiative to the point of being *abstinent*. An objective analysis of their capabilities and strengths by the therapist will often identify very significant strengths. The patient, however, does not recognize these strengths, fails to self-reinforce, and, consequently, appears to not experience positive reinforcement from personal effort and accomplishment. The resulting lack of initiative will also impair the patient's ability to develop the skills necessary to acquire such reinforcers. Thus, such individuals may not be able to achieve reinforcers even if they can be identified.

Individuals who attempt to reach out and help such persons will often become frustrated and conclude that they "don't really want to get better." Such clients require assistance to identify potential reinforcers, identify how personal strengths can be employed to instrumentally achieve such reinforcers, set attainable goals for early attempts, and provide reinforcement for the effort that is being expended. The process of setting the stage for social reinforcement of objective indicants of progress, no matter how modest, is an important challenge in working with these clients. Therapists and other caregivers must remain patient and not allow the apparent discrepancy between the patient's objective capabilities and motivation to use those capabilities to influence them to push the client faster than he or she can tolerate.

In addition, the behavior of collaterals must be considered in modifying behavior of the self-defeating personality. It is likely that collaterals have become an important factor in maintaining this style of behavior. Collaterals must begin to discriminate between situations in which unconditional support is indicated and other situations in which corrective feedback should be supportively and consistently provided. They must negotiate a thin line between being a source of support and being more conditional in providing interpersonal reinforcement for the client's efforts.

Schizotypal

The schizotypal personality is a decompensated form of the detached (schizoid and avoidant) personalities. As such, persons become increasingly detached from contact with other people and the benefits that such contact offers in testing personal assumptions about reality. They become increasingly unconventional in their behavior. They drift into social isolation and become more and more aberrant in overt and cognitive behavior. Eventually they are viewed by others as odd or *eccentric*. Such individuals must be assisted to become more aware of how their behavior affects other people and moderate their eccentric inclinations. As with the schizoid personality, the identification of relevant reinforcers is an important challenge when working with such clients. A focus on training in basic social skills is usually most appropriate for such clients.

Borderline

The borderline personality is a decompensated form of the negativistic personality characteristics. Borderline persons experience dramatic dysregulation of overt behavior and physiological arousal. Their precipitate shifts of behavior and emotions appear *spasmodic* and provoke inconsistent interpersonal behavior. This often frustrates other people and is likely to provoke critical behavior toward the client, further exacerbating the interpersonal turmoil that ambivalent personalities experience. As this process progresses, the client will experience increasingly severe emotional distress with a greater likelihood of associated thoughts of self-injurious behavior.

The development of an ability to maximize affective regulation is an important initial therapeutic task for such clients. Anxiety-management, anger-management, or other forms of emotional management training are often a necessary initial task for the therapist and client to pursue. The therapist must clearly identify and reinforce progress in developing these skills since the client is unlikely to recognize such progress or self-reinforce. As with the dependent and self-defeating personalities, the behavior of collaterals will be very important in facilitating and maintaining behavior change. As the client improves with regard to emotional stability, the focus can turn to assertion skills or similar behavioral skill training to develop alternative methods of interacting with significant others.

Paranoid

The paranoid personality represents a decompensation of the independent personality styles. Paranoid individuals maintain a vigilant mistrust of others and remain on guard against anticipated criticism and deception by others. They will blame others for disappointments and problems that they encounter and will typically fail to recognize the contribution of their own behavior in precipitating such problems. They are *defensive* and vigorously resist perceived efforts of external influence and control, and they place a high value on self-management capability and "willpower."

Such individuals often respond positively to interventions designed to enhance self-control capability. It is important that the therapist adopt the role of an instructor or "coach" rather than acting as an agent of external control. To achieve such an "alliance," the therapist may have to avoid confrontation during early sessions and even tolerate the possibility that such patients will misperceive that the therapist agrees with them when they place blame on others. The major challenge faced by the therapist is to indirectly guide paranoid clients to decide that the desired behaviors are in their own interest. Having made such a decision, they will often be energetic in their efforts to develop the skills to attain these goals. For example, the therapist may have to emphasize the distinction between an aggressive interpersonal style and an assertive interpersonal style by providing examples of how while aggressive behavior may result in short-term satisfaction, it will usually backfire in achieving goals. The development of assertion skills can then be presented as the smarter way of getting what you want. The patient's application of impulse-management skills to tolerate situations where the goal is not immediately forthcoming can also be reinforced as the smarter way of doing things.

CASE STUDY

The following case study is intended to provide an example that can highlight many of the points that have been discussed.

Patient History

DM is a 43-year-old white, divorced male who was admitted to the psychiatric unit of a private psychiatric hospital for detoxification. The police had been contacted by a concerned neighbor and found the patient in his bedroom with a loaded gun and many empty beer cans and vodka bottles in the room. Because he was unemployed and had no insurance coverage, he was transferred to a public psychiatric hospital for care after detoxification.

DM had been divorced several years earlier and his wife desired no further contact. Shortly after the divorce, he was fired from his job as a factory worker due to absences that were attributed to the effect of alcohol abuse. He had completed approximately two years of college.

Psychiatric History

DM reported a long history of alcohol abuse dating back to his teen years. While he had made frequent initial contacts for counseling, he never attended more than three sessions. He reported intermittent contact with Alcoholics Anonymous but had not been able to sustain this involvement. He reported that he had not exceeded greater than 3 months sobriety during the previous 20–25 years. A year earlier he had been hospitalized at the state hospital for depression related to drinking and was discharged after a stay of 13 days.

Medical History

The patient had a history of several severe physical complications including liver failure and gastrointestinal bleeding. At the time of this admission, however, there were no significant medical problems.

Previous Neuropsychological Assessment

Neuropsychological assessment during the previous admission revealed intelligence in the average range (VIQ=110; PIQ=98; FSIQ=104). Attention/concentration, visuospatial reasoning, and visuomotor capabilities were all within the average range, as were reading comprehension and word recognition. No significant cognitive deficits were noted.

Data from the MMPI-II, also administered during the previous admission, revealed "clinically significant symptoms of depression and anxiety in the form of dysthymia. Feelings of low self-esteem, low energy, guilt, acute loneliness, negative self-attitudes, and tension characterize this profile."

Discussion

Neuropsychological test data acquired during the current admission were similar to those of the previous admission. The MCMI-III profile for this patient is outlined in Table 3-2. As expected, the Alcohol Dependence scale was an evident peak scale. Consistent with the MMPI-II results acquired during the previous admission, relatively high scores were also found on the Anxiety Disorder and Dysthymia scales. Relative to other personality scales, high scores were noted on the Compulsive, Dependent, and Self-Defeating personality scales.

On the basis of data from the MCMI-III personality scales and our previous research (Donat, Geczy, et al., 1992; Donat, Walters, & Hume, et al., 1991), we anticipated that DM would rapidly stabilize and begin to behave in a relatively friendly, cooperative, and compliant manner. We hypothesized that this benign and friendly demeanor served to avoid arousing the intense concern and scrutiny of other people and, therefore, served to maintain a comfortable distance from them. We expected that the apparently cooperative demeanor was unlikely to translate to durable changes in behaviors needed to realize long-term progress.

On the basis of the personality assessment results, the ward staff were informed to expect that DM would rapidly stabilize and act in a friendly and cooperative manner. They were warned to not equate this compliant behavior with true progress and to expect that hospitalization will likely be longer than may seem immediately apparent (in an overstressed environment such as this, staff are often reinforced to discharge patients as quickly as possible). A small number of staff who had experience in substance abuse treatment programs quickly criticized DM's interpersonal style as "people-pleasing" behavior. They were cautioned to avoid trying to confront or "break through" his superficial veneer of sociability. Staff were directed to act friendly and congenial in return but to be alert for circumstances that DM broaches when he is willing to discuss personal problems, anxieties, or discouragements. They were instructed to be differentially attentive to such conditions.

In individual meetings with the psychologist the early goal was to effect success by focusing on problems that the patient was willing to share.

TABLE 3-2 MCMI-III of the Case Study

MCMI-III Inventory		Base Rate
	Validity	0
X	Disclosure	60
Y	Desirability	70
Z	Debasement	61
1	Schizoid	24
2A	Avoidant	12
2B	Depressive	0
3	Dependent	80*
4	Histrionic	50
5	Narcissistic	49
6A	Antisocial	38
6B	Aggressive (Sadistic)	26
7	Compulsive	89**
8A	Negativistic	38
8B	Self-Defeating	78*
S	Schizotypal	20
C	Borderline	65
P	Paranoid	36
A	Anxiety	75*
H	Somatoform	66
N	Bipolar: Manic	48
D	Dysthymia	75*
B	Alcohol Dependence	83*
T	Drug Dependence	62
PT	PTSD	60
SS	Thought Disorder	60
CC	Major Depression	65
PP	Delusional Disorder	0

*BR 75–84
**BR 85–94

Our initial focus was on building efficacy in managing anxiety/depression, a problem that DM readily admitted to on the MCMI-III. Consequently, the initial focus was on biofeedback training because patients seldom fail to successfully lower EMG activity across sessions. The availability of quantified evidence of success in physiological management allowed for a very clear demonstration of efficacy on a task that the patient viewed as related to the self-management of anxiety/depression. This success in personal efficacy provided a legitimate opportunity for the therapist and other staff to provide social reinforcement for personal effort, perseverance, and success at dealing with a relevant problem area.

While the staff continued to show respect for the patient's guardedness regarding most personal issues, this initial success helped to "break the ice" for the therapist to slowly shift the focus to situations (employment, dissolution of marriage, difficulty in sustaining AA and therapy involvement) that contribute to the experience of anxiety and discouragement as well as drinking episodes. These are also situations that cannot be easily resolved and for which the patient must rely on interpersonal support to tolerate. DM's behavioral inclination, however, was to avoid upsetting other people with his problems by adopting his benign and friendly style. We set daily goals to broach these and other perceived issues with sustaining recovery to other group members or certain ward staff. SUDS ratings decreased as he became more experienced at bringing up problems in group and other settings. At the same time, the therapist and other staff, as well as other patients in the program, were encouraged to discuss situations in which they actively coped with anxiety to model the process of actively coping. As these and other difficult situations and dysfunctional cognitions were identified, principles of anxiety management and assertion training were employed to effect changes in cognitive and overt behavior that also could be reinforced by ward staff.

During this entire period the staff were encouraged to observe for any evidence of the application of anxiety-management strategies or improved assertion (particularly requesting advice and support from others) and to compliment (socially reinforce) these behaviors. It was emphasized for both the patient and staff that recovery from substance dependence is very difficult, particularly for an individual with a history and life situation like DM's. Consequently, they were instructed to prepare for possible relapses as a normal expectation of the course of recovery. It was hoped that this would dampen the disappointment experienced by the patient and staff if such a relapse occurred.

At this time DM is still in the hospital. As discharge approaches, the therapist will emphasize that the skills he has developed to realize progress on the ward parallel the skills necessary to negotiate challenges that will be faced in using outpatient resources and AA in the community. The patient has chosen a "home" AA group, acquired an AA sponsor, and has begun visiting an outpatient therapist at the local community mental health center.

The manner in which behavioral methods were employed in this case was influenced by the data acquired with the MCMI-III and the research/theory that underlie its development. The use of behavioral methods for this case can be contrasted with the management of cases with different personality features discussed in McKeegan, Geczy, and Donat (1992). We believe there is considerable potential for the development of differential treatment approaches, using behavioral techniques, that vary according to the prominent personality features of the client.

Summary

Because behavior therapists have emphasized the importance of focusing on observable behavior, behavioral techniques are excellent tools for intervention in the expressive domain. Behavior therapists have benefited from a close tie between their intervention techniques and principles derived from laboratory research. This tie has also contributed to a conservatism regarding the use of inferred constructs, such as cognitions and personality, in theory and practice. This conservatism has limited the scope of problems for which behavioral methods have been applied. Behaviorally oriented clinicians can often benefit from exposure to theoretical models that attempt to integrate scientific findings from other areas of study, such as developmental and social psychology. Millon's biosocial learning approach, as applied with the MCMI-III, provides a possible avenue for behaviorally oriented clinicians to expand the boundaries of their practice.

In this chapter we've reviewed some ways that the integration of behavior therapy and personality theory can enhance clinical care. In our experience, the inclusion of the MCMI-III results, in the context of Millon's theory, helps to guide the application of behavioral methods in both individual and group therapy as well as in consulting to direct care treatment staff.

References

American Psychiatric Association. (1980). *Diagnostic and statistical manual of mental disorders* (3d ed.). Washington, DC: Author.

American Psychiatric Association. (1994). *Diagnostic and statistical manual of mental disorders* (4th ed.). Washington, DC: Author.

Axelrod, S. (1985). Response cost. In A. S. Bellack & M. Hersen (Eds.), *Dictionary of behavior therapy techniques* (pp. 183–184). New York: Pergamon Press.

Bartsch, T. W., & Hoffman, J. J. (1985). A cluster analysis of Millon Clinical Multiaxial Inventory (MCMI) profiles: More about taxonomy of alcoholic subtypes. *Journal of Clinical Psychology, 54,* 707–713.

Becker, R. E. (1985). *In-vivo* desensitization. In A. S. Bellack & M. Hersen (Eds.), *Dictionary of behavior therapy techniques* (pp. 142–143). New York: Pergamon Press.

Belar, C. D., & Perry, N. W. (1992). National conference on scientist-practitioner education and training for the professional practice of psychology. *American Psychologist, 47,* 71–75.

Bellack, A. S., & Hersen, M. (1985). *Dictionary of behavior therapy techniques.* New York: Pergamon Press.

Blanchard, E. B., & Epstein, L. H. (1978). *A biofeedback primer.* Reading, MA: Addison-Wesley.

Borkovec, T. D., & Sides, J. K. (1979). Critical procedural variables related to the physiological effects of progressive relaxation: A review. *Behavior Research and Therapy, 17,* 119.

Camp, B. W., Blom, G. F., Herbert, F., & van Doornick, W. J. (1977). "Think Aloud": a program for developing self control in young aggressive boys. *Journal of Abnormal Clinical Psychology, 5,* 157–169.

Cautela, J. R. (1985a). Covert positive reinforcement. In A. S. Bellack & M. Hersen (Eds.), *Dictionary of behavior therapy techniques* (pp. 95). New York: Pergamon Press.

Cautela, J. R. (1985b). Covert sensitization. In A. S. Bellack & M. Hersen (Eds.), *Dictionary of behavior therapy techniques* (pp. 96–100). New York: Pergamon Press.

Choca, J. P., Shanley, L. A., & Van Denberg (1992). *Interpretive guide to the Millon Clinical Multiaxial Inventory.* Washington, DC: American Psychological Association.

Curran, J. P., & Monti, P. M. (Eds.). (1983). *Social skills training: A practical handbook of behavior modification and therapy.* New York: Guilford Press.

DeJong, C. A., van den Brink, W., Harteveld, F. M., & van der Weilen (1993). Personality disorders in alcoholics and drug addicts. *Comprehensive Psychiatry, 34,* 87–94.

Donat, D. C. (1988). Millon Clinical Multiaxial Inventory (MCMI) clusters for alcohol abusers: Further evidence of validity and implications for medical psychotherapy. *Medical Psychotherapy, 1,* 41–50.

Donat, D. C., Geczy, B., Helmrich, J., & LeMay, M. (1992). Empirically derived personality subtypes of public psychiatric patients: Effect on self-reported symptoms, coping inclinations, and evaluation of expressed emotion in caregivers. *Journal of Personality Assessment, 58,* 36–50.

Donat, D. C., & McKeegan, G. F. (1990). Behavioral knowledge among direct care staff in an inpatient psychiatric setting. *Behavioral Residential Treatment, 5,* 37–53.

Donat, D. C., Walters, J., & Hume, A. (1991). Personality characteristics of alcohol dependent inpatients: Relationship of MCMI subtypes to self-reported drinking behavior. *Journal of Personality Assessment, 57,* 335–344.

Dowd, E. T. (1985). Self-statement modification. In A. S. Bellack & M. Hersen (Eds.), *Dictionary of behavior therapy techniques* (pp. 200). New York: Pergamon Press.

Dowd, E. T., & Olson, D. H. (1985). Contingency contracting. In A. S. Bellack & M. Hersen (Eds.), *Dictionary of behavior therapy techniques* (pp. 70–73). New York: Pergamon Press.

D'Zurilla, T. J. (1986). *Problem solving therapy: A social competence approach to clinical intervention.* New York: Springer.

Forehand, R. (1985). Time out. In A. S. Bellack & M. Hersen (Eds.), *Dictionary of behavior therapy techniques* (pp. 222–227). New York: Pergamon Press.

Foxx, R. M., & Bechtel, D. R. (1982). Overcorrection. In M. Hersen, R. M. Eisler, & P. M. Miller (Eds.), *Progress in behavior modification* (volume 13, pp. 227–288). New York: Academic Press.

Gambril, E. (1985). Assertiveness training. In A. S. Bellak & M. Hersen (Eds.), *Dictionary of behavior therapy techniques* (pp. 7–10). New York: Pergamon Press.

Gross, A. E. (1985). Self-control therapy. In A. S. Bellack & M. Hersen (Eds.), *Dictionary of behavior therapy techniques* (pp. 192–195). New York: Pergamon Press.

Grove, W. M., & Andreasen, N. C. (1986). Multivariate statistical analysis in psychopathology. In T. Millon & G. Klerman (Eds.), *Contemporary directions in psychopathology* (pp. 347-362). New York: Guilford Press.

Homer, A. L., & Peterson, L. (1980). Differential reinforcement of other behavior: A preferred response elimination procedure. *Behavior Therapy, 11,* 449–471.

Kazdin, A. E. (1974). Self-monitoring and behavior change. In M. J. Mahoney & C. E. Thoresen (Eds.), *Self-control: Power to the person* (pp. 218–246). Monterey, CA: Brooks-Cole.

Kazdin, A. E. (1977). *The token economy: A review and evaluation.* New York: Plenum.

Korchin, S. J. (1976). *Modern clinical psychology.* New York: Basic Books.

Lewinsohn, P. M., Biglan, A., & Zeiss, A. M. (l976). Behavioral treatment of depression. In P.O. Davidson (Ed.), *The behavioral management of anxiety, depression, and pain* (pp. 91–146). New York: Brunner/Mazel.

Lorr, M., & Strack, S. (1990). Profile clusters of the MCMI-II personality disorder scales. *Journal of Clinical Psychology, 46,* 606–612.

Lovaas, I. O. (1966). A program for the establishment of speech in psychotic children. In J. K. Wing (ed.), *Early childhood autism.* (pp. 115–144). New York: Pergamon Press.

Marchione, K. (1985). Problem solving training. In A. S. Bellack & M. Hersen (Eds.), *Dictionary of behavior therapy techniques* (pp. 167–169). New York: Pergamon Press.

Marshall, W. L. (1985). Aversive conditioning. In A. S. Bellack & M. Hersen (Eds.), *Dictionary of behavior therapy techniques* (pp. 15–21). New York: Pergamon Press.

Mayer, G. S., & Scott, R. J. (1988). An exploration of heterogeneity in an inpatient male alcoholic population. *Journal of Personality Disorders, 2,* 243–255.

McKeegan, G. F., Geczy, B., & Donat, D. C. (1993). Applying behavioral methods in the inpatient setting: Patients with mixed borderline and dependent traits. *Psychosocial Rehabilitation Journal, 16,* 55–64.

Meichenbaum, D. (1985). *Stress inoculation training.* New York: Pergamon Press.

Millon, T. (1969). *Modern psychopathology: A biosocial learning approach.* Philadelphia: Saunders.

Novaco, R. (1985). Anger control therapy. In A. S. Bellack & M. Hersen (Eds.), *Dictionary of behavior therapy techniques* (pp. 1–4). New York: Pergamon Press.

O'Sullivan, J. J., & Quevillon, R. P. (1992). Forty years later: Is the Boulder Model still alive? *American Psychologist, 47,* 67–70.

Paul, G. L., & Lentz, R. J. (1977). *Psychosocial treatment of chronic mental patients: Milieu versus social learning approaches.* Cambridge, MA: Harvard University Press.

Persons, J. (1993). Why are there so few scientist-practitioners? A modest proposal. *The Behavior Therapist, 16,* 34.

Rescorla, R. A. (1988). Pavlovian conditioning: It's not what you think it is. *American Psychologist, 43,* 151–160.

Schreibman, L. (1985). Stimulus control. In A. S. Bellack & M. Hersen (Eds.), *Dictionary of behavior therapy techniques* (p. 209). New York: Pergamon Press.

Suinn, R. & Deffenbacher, J. (1988). Anxiety management training. *The Counseling Psychologist,* 16(1), 31–49.

Turner, S. M., & Michelson, L. (1984). Obsessive-compulsive disorders. In S. M. Turner (Ed.), *Behavioral theories and the treatment of anxiety* (pp. 239–277). New York: Plenum.

Watson, R. I. (1978). *The great psychologists.* New York: Lippincott.

Wisocki, P. (1985). Thought stopping. In A. S. Bellack & M. Hersen (Eds.), *Dictionary of behavior therapy techniques* (pp. 219–222). New York: Pergamon Press.

Wolpe, J. (1958). *Psychotherapy by reciprocal inhibition.* Stanford, CA: Stanford University Press.

Wolpe, J. (1973). *The practice of behavior therapy.* Stanford, CA: Stanford University Press.

Wolpe, J. (1985). Systematic desensitization. In A. S. Bellack & M. Hersen (Eds.), *Dictionary of behavior therapy techniques* (pp. 215–219). New York: Pergamon Press.

4

Interpersonal Psychotherapy and MCMI-III–Based Assessment

ROBERT J. CRAIG

In their influential book on clinical psychology, Sundberg and Tyler (1962) reserved the last chapter to muse about future directions within the field. They envisioned that clinical psychologists might become specialists in medical psychology, psychological treatment or human relations. In the intervening decades, we have learned that clinical psychologists are specialists in all of the above. If psychologists specialize in human relations while providing psychological services and treatment, then I believe it is a natural extension to practice a form of therapy and intervention that has as its core an emphasis on human relationships.

In this chapter I shall present the historical roots of interpersonal psychotherapy, provide clinical examples of its key concepts, illustrate the domain approach to understanding personality disorders, and discuss what an interpersonal approach to the treatment of those disorders needs to specifically address and what problems there may be for the therapist while treating those disorders. The chapter concludes with a case example illustrating pre- and post-MCMI (II/III)–based assessment and how that is used to formulate the therapeutic approach in the case.

Interpersonal Psychotherapy

Historical Roots

The derivations of interpersonal psychotherapy can be traced to the seminal contributions of Sigmund Freud and the development of psychoanalysis. Although usually Freud's theory is considered an individually oriented psychology that focused on psychosexual stages, fixations, and developmental arrests, several of his intrapsychic mechanisms and process either directly or indirectly pertained to relational concepts. However, Freud emphasized the analysand's meaning and interpretation of these events (dreams, free associative material, distorted perceptions influenced by unconscious processes, derivative behaviors, etc.) to help understand and resolve the patient's problems rather than addressing the relational components involved in the events.

In fact, Freudian concepts of mental representation, transference, and countertransference can be considered early theories of relationship processes that evolved into what would be subsequently termed relationship-oriented psychotherapy by subsequent therapists. A mental representation is the combination of objective reality that exists in the external world with an internal template or image of that object in the internal (or imagined) world. This representation has an associated affective component that has the power to influence a person's emotion and behavior. For example, if a child views a parent as bad (perhaps because of physical or sexual abuse), then it is possible that many adult caregivers and authority figures might be rejected because of a mental representation that views all such "objects" as bad.

While there are many other psychoanalytic concepts that have some relational component, the concepts of transference and countertransference are two that specifically are relational and have received extensive coverage in the psychoanalytic literature. Simply, transference is the process whereby a patient projects attitudes, beliefs, feelings, and fears from some historical figure in their personal life onto the therapist and then relates to the therapist accordingly. Of course, this is all unconscious, and the traditional techniques of psychoanalysis were designed to uncover and analyze these transferences. Countertransference is merely the transference of the therapist projected onto the patient. Psychoanalytic supervision often deals with countertransference reactions in the therapist so that the analysis of the patient's transference can proceed unimpeded and uncontaminated.

The psychiatrist Adolf Meyer at Johns Hopkins and his associate, Harry Stack Sullivan, popularized the interpersonal approach within psychiatry, while Carl Rogers was instrumental in developing this approach for clinical psychology.

Meyer (1957) considered his theory a psychobiology theory and viewed mental illness as an attempt of the person to adapt to the environment, which was replete with psychosocial features. Meyer was himself influenced by the renowned psychologist William James and by the philosophy of pragmatism, which had gained ascendance in contemporary philosophical thought. This interpersonal focus evolved into the study of civilization, urbanization, stress, social class, and the structure of mental hospitals (Klerman et al., 1984).

While Meyer brought an interpersonal study to American psychiatry, it was the psychiatrist Sullivan (1953) who popularized this notion and considered psychiatry to be the study of interpersonal relations. He then developed a theory regarding the development of psychiatric disorders and interpersonal influences. Coexisting with Sullivan's applications of social thinking to psychiatry was the emergence of social roles as a major concept within the study of sociology. These concepts were blended by Sullivan and provided the framework within which he intervened in patient problems.

Carl Rogers (1942, 1965) developed a client-centered, nondirective approach to counseling and psychotherapy and emphasized the processes of genuineness, unconditional positive regard, and acceptance as necessary to promote individual development. He and his students placed this approach on an empirical footing and actively researched the notion that it was the relationship between therapist and client that made the critical difference as to whether there would be growth and development or personal and emotional stagnation.

The influence of social concepts was eventually extended within psychiatry to the study of the role of social and familial factors in the transmission of schizophrenia (Bowen, 1960; Lidz, Fleck, & Corneliason, 1965; Wynne & Singer, 1963). The interpersonal approach to psychotherapy was later extended and applied to many disorders. Currently it has specifically become popular, along with the cognitive-behavioral approach, in the treatment of depression.

Interpersonal Psychotherapy Parameters

Interpersonal psychotherapy (IPT), sometimes also referred to as relationship-oriented psychotherapy, has the following features (Klerman et al., 1984).

Time-Limits
IPT is usually designed to be given within a framework of 9 to 12 months. IPT believes that it is possible to resolve immediate problems and many symptomatic states by focusing on the interpersonal processes that produce maladaptive patterns of functioning. Doing so accelerates patient improvement. While there is less evidence to substantiate the belief that it is impossible to change basic personality patterns and long-term maladaptive interpersonal functioning without long-term therapy, interpersonal psychotherapy may yet prove beneficial in these areas as well.

Focus

IPT is directed to one or two specific content areas, and the focus of therapy is the resolution of problems in these specific areas. Many forms of psychotherapy promote and even require the use of free association or "stream of consciousness" as the essential part of the therapeutic process, in the belief that such material is an avenue to the unconscious. This technique necessitates a long-term approach, where the ultimate goal is personality reconstruction rather than symptom removal or explicit behavior change. In contrast, IPT only uses free association as it pertains to the resolution of specific problems.

Present Behavior

IPT focuses on present, rather than past, relationships and addresses the patient's immediate social context as influencing symptom formation. Although the therapist does inquire about past relationships, early family relationships, other significant relationships, and their behavior and reactions to significant emotional events, the ultimate focus is on the patient's present behavior. The rationale for this is that, if the patient can learn new ways of coping and behaving within a certain relationship or within a specific type of social context, then there could be transfer or generalization of this new learning to similar relationships or environments.

Interpersonal Foci

IPT generally eschews intrapsychic functioning. IPT therapists do not focus on the patient's inner mental life. While defense mechanisms are recognized and respected, IPT therapists do not try to help patients understand how their present functioning is a reaction to some internal conflict. Rather, the conflict is addressed in terms of the individual's interpersonal relations.

Clinical Example. One example of this is how dreams are used within an IPT session compared to an intrapsychic approach. While dreams are usually not the focus of IPT, when a patient reports a dream as part of the therapy, the IPT therapist interprets the dream with an interpersonal rather than with an intrapsychic focus. An example of this is the following dream of a male dealing with a mid-life crisis and its aftermath. His wife learned he was having an affair, and this precipitated their entry into marital and individual therapy.

> "I was shopping in some kind of store which sells ammo for slingshots during the Civil War. I am making a last-ditch attempt to win. Somebody (I think me) is looking for pebbles and steel balls. I moved behind circular racks of something while employees carefully watched me. I think I was trying to hide. Then I was at a pro shop at a country club.

Some woman, who I felt was a spy-assistant in a shawl, holds up the counter clerk, demanding a variety of ammo including a radioactive pebble. The clerk either finds a terra-cotta colored one among grey particles, or a grey one among terra-cotta particles. We moved through the restaurant in the country club. With me is a distinguished gentleman. I sing "Mammy" like in the Al Jolson version. We then headed out to the golf course, which is not fenced in, where I intend to sling shots over the houses towards the railroad tracks."

An intrapsychic focus would interpret the sexual and aggressive components in the dreams, the defense mechanisms associated with this content, and the conflict resolution apparent in the dream. Sexual content is seen in the patient looking for "steel balls," which may reflect his search for lost masculinity and/or sexual adequacy, and hiding behind a "circular rack," which may be interpreted as a vaginal symbol. The woman demanding a "radioactive pebble" could be interpreted as castration anxiety, and singing "Mammy" could be thought of as a symbolic reference to the mammary glands and suggesting further emasculation. The defenses seen in this dream are withdrawal and escape (hiding behind a circular rack), and the conflict is one of acting out his aggressive impulses ("I intend to sling shots over the houses") versus containing them.

An intrapsychic orientation might consider this dream as representative of the individual's basic psychology, where the internal conflict (control of aggressive drives vs. acting them out) is viewed as a derivative of the Oedipal conflict. The patient might be seen as re-enacting this conflict in his present behavior.

An interpersonal foci would recognize these intrapsychic elements but view them as secondary in importance in contrast to the interpersonal elements contained in the dream. These elements are as follows:

Marital conflict, represented by his dreaming of the "Civil War"
Deference to a female, as represented by him singing "Mammy"
A feeling of being closely observed, suggested by "employees watch me carefully"
A feeling of being emasculated by such close observation—"looking for steel balls" and "demanding . . . radioactive pebbles"

An interpersonal interpretation of this dream would address this patient's concern over his marital troubles, his awareness that he is now under close observation since people have discovered his affair, his feeling emasculated by such scrutiny, and his feeling of loss of sexual adequacy as a male. The fact that this patient desires retaliation ("I intend to sling shots over the house") would also be framed by an interpretation that he really doesn't intend to hurt anyone inside the house, since, in the dream, he shoots "over" the house. This interpersonal focus and interpretation would then be related to the specific presenting complaint and precipitating event in an effort to gain insight and change his feelings and behavior toward his wife. The intrapsychic conflict would probably not be dealt with using IPT.

Personality in Relationship to Others

IPT does not always focus on or address the patient's personality. When this occurs, it is usually done so in relationship to another person. It is recognized that personality might predict outcome of psychotherapy, affect the patient–therapist relationship, and even detrimentally affect the patient's ability to solve problems, and as such it must be addressed in therapy. However, when such matters become the focus of therapy, they are usually addressed in terms of how the patient functions in such relationships.

Clinical Example. A male was seen in outpatient therapy for aftercare services following a brief psychiatric hospitalization for major depression. The precipitating event was the announcement by his wife that she was leaving him. The patient became depressed and suicidal and required inpatient psychiatric care. During his hospitalization his wife did leave him, and, in therapy, his focus was trying to find ways of behaving differently so that she would want to return to the marriage.

The patient was essentially neurotic, with severe dependency and a number of perceived inadequacies. For example, on one occasion during their separation, he and his wife had made a date to go to the beach in a neighboring state. Several days before the actual event the patient drove to the beach alone, learning the route, so he would not demonstrate ineptness at being able to find the park. His explanation of his behavior in therapy was that he wanted his wife to see him as knowledgeable, confident, and adequate, even though internally he felt weak and inadequate. During their separation another man moved in with her. Although the patient complained about this arrangement, in therapy he continually rationalized her behavior as "exploratory" and denied there was anything sexual in the relationship. Later he discovered she had been using cocaine, which she continued to deny despite being confronted with the evidence. He cried in therapy, professing an inability to deal with this problem and expressing a desire to resolve it. His therapist suggested an "Intervention," a behaviorally rehearsed family confrontation technique used in substance abuse treatment to engage a patient to receive help. The patient reacted angrily to the suggestion. He said he had wanted the therapist to be this direct all along and essentially wanted to be told how to deal with the myriad of problems and dependent behaviors presented over many therapy sessions. He said it was clear the therapist knew how to handle this situation and he was angry at the thought that the therapist probably also had known how to resolve the other matters presented in therapy but had chosen to "withhold" the resolution from him.

A psychodynamically oriented approach to this vignette might involve trying to get the patient to see the transference reaction inherent in this episode and then exploring early childhood relationships, particularly with authority figures, and uncovering the source of this patient's underlying dependency. An IPT focus would recognize the transference inherent in the story and have the patient focus on how he behaved toward the therapist and how he behaved toward his wife. With both people he was placing himself in a dependent, helpless position and asking for someone else to take control of his life. The relationship-oriented therapist would assess (a) what has contributed to this patient's problem right here and now, (b) what are his current stresses, (c) who are the key figures in producing the stress, (d) how is the patient learning to cope with the problem, (e) what are the patient's strengths, (f) how can the patient ventilate painful emotions surrounding his inadequacies, (g) how can the patient achieve a more satisfactory relationship with the significant people in his life, and (h) what needs to be done to redress any miscommunications so that alternative problem-solving behaviors can be considered without the patient's neurosis and dependency getting in the way of successful problem resolution. Throughout, the focus would be on this patient's behavior in relationships, whether it be with his wife, with his therapist, or with others.

Goals and Tasks of Interpersonal Psychotherapy

Klerman et al. (1984) provide a basic outline of how to conduct IPT with clients who are depressed. They suggest that in the first session the therapist evaluates the symptom picture, provide the patient with the diagnosis, evaluate the need for medication, and explain how the syndrome will be treated. In the early sessions the therapist must review current and past relationships and how they affect the development of symptom formation. The major problem areas must be identified, and the therapist provides the patient with an understanding of the problem, a process that has been described as "feedback, within the structure of the interview" (Craig, 1989) but which has its roots in Sullivan's (1954) ideas for psychiatric interviews. Treatment goals should then be agreed upon, and the administrative aspects of therapy (scheduling, fees, setting a treatment contract) should then be addressed.

In the intermediate sessions the therapist helps the patient re-establish interest in relationships, redresses faulty communication, and helps the patient negotiate and resolve interpersonal problems and disputes. New roles are promoted when required, social isolation is reduced, and the formation of new relationships is encouraged.

These goals and tasks are accomplished with a therapist who is very active within the therapeutic hour. Following are some techniques used by IPT therapists and some clinical examples:

1. Advice: A 35-year-old, single, white female alcoholic in recovery was in psychotherapy to help her understand and resolve her self-defeating behaviors with men. She considered a career change and questioned whether or not she should begin dating again, particularly since members in AA had told her to make no changes for 1 year. Her previous boyfriend was alcoholic, and she was faced with a decision to end this relationship and begin another with a nonalcoholic who had asked her out. Her therapist encouraged her to return to school and both pursue and prepare for her new career. She was also advised to begin dating when she felt comfortable in doing so, rather than place an artificial time limit on her feelings.

2. Suggestion: A 45-year-old, married white female was in therapy for post-traumatic stress disorder following her witnessing a traumatic event within her home. Her husband had made a suicide attempt after being seriously depressed for an extensive period of time. Following another suicide attempt, he moved in with his son after his release from the hospital. His son eventually grew tired of his father's lack of energy and apparent lack of motivation and demanded that he leave. The man wanted to return to his wife, who asked her therapist if this was a good idea. She remained fearful of him. Her therapist suggested that he get an apartment and they "date" for a while, until she is assured that he has returned to normal.

3. Setting Limits: A 40-year-old, separated, white male came for marital therapy, although his wife had recently left him. He was alcoholic and unwilling to discuss his alcoholism. His only reason for coming to therapy was to get his wife back. She was being seen individually by another therapist in a group practice. The patient's alcoholism was the source of the marital difficulties, and he was often physically abusive toward his wife. The patient refused to allow the therapist to conduct a proper assessment of his alcoholism, refused to complete objective psychological tests, and even came toward the therapist in a menacing and threatening manner when the therapist attempted to conduct a more thorough assessment of his problematic drinking. While the therapist realized that these were probably the very behaviors with which the patient's wife had to deal daily, the therapist had to retain control of the therapeutic hour. He told the patient to sit, that he had to allow the therapist to do his job, and that he had to agree to be properly assessed; otherwise, therapy could not proceed because of a lack of a therapeutic alliance between patient and therapist.

4. Education: A middle-aged, white female was in therapy to deal with problems associated with her husband's psychiatric illness. His diagnosis was major depression, recurrent, with psychotic features. After several sessions during which it became apparent that she had unrealistic expectations regarding rate of recovery, the therapist explained the symptoms of depression to her, the personality such patients often show (usually excessive dependency), and the typical course of the illness with treatment.

5. Direct Help: Advice, education, and suggestions are sometimes given by a relationship-oriented therapist when such efforts would advance the process of therapy. A 38-year-old female was in an abusive relationship with an alcoholic husband. She needed to be empowered and to take control of her life, yet she was fearful of doing so. Her therapist suggested that she take pictures of her husband whenever he came home drunk and destroyed the home. She was told to have pictures of herself taken whenever she received a beating that left visible marks. She should call the police and file charges against him (she did subsequently call the police and make out reports, which were kept on file, but she was reluctant to actually file charges). She should leave the house, before he came home, whenever she anticipated another beating. (Parenthetically, these suggestions were all implemented, and the case was subsequently successful, as her husband discontinued drinking and hence the violence stopped.) This can be construed as direct help because it empowered the patient to become assertive and take control of her life.

Empirical Findings

Ultimately, any form of psychotherapy must have empirical verification of its effectiveness. In particular, for which types of problems and patients is therapy brand X the treatment of choice and where is it contraindicated? There have been some empirical studies with relationship-oriented psychotherapy.

Some early reports of IPT's effectiveness dealt with the treatment of depression (DiMascio et al., 1979; Weissman et al., 1979), but a major evaluation of relationship-oriented psychotherapy occurred in the NIMH's collaborative study of treatment for depression (Elkin et al., 1989). A total of 250 patients with major depression were randomly assigned to one of four 16-week treatment conditions consisting of either IPT, cognitive behavioral psychotherapy, imipramine hydrocloride plus clinical management, and placebo plus clinical management. Recovery rates were better for patients seen either in IPT or the antidepressant therapy groups.

Short-term IPT was compared to low-contact treatment for psychiatric disorders among opiate addicts. Seventy-two opiate addicts were randomly assigned to either the therapy group, consisting of weekly psychotherapy for 6 months, or to a low-contact group, consisting of one brief meeting a month for 6 months. All patients were also on methadone maintenance. Results showed that both treatment groups experienced significant improvement in outcome measures, with the interpersonally treated group demonstrating improvement in locus-of-control measures (Rounsaville et al., 1983).

While this study suggested some benefit of providing IPT to addicts on methadone maintenance, more positive results were obtained in another, similar study. One hundred and ten patients on methadone maintenance were assigned to drug counseling alone, to supportive-expressive psychotherapy (a relationship-oriented technique) plus drug counseling, or to cognitive-behavioral psychotherapy plus drug counseling. Outcome measures included standardized psychological tests, observer ratings, and urine tests. While all treatment groups showed improvement, addicts receiving the psychotherapies showed improvement in more areas and to a greater degree than addicts receiving only drug counseling. Patients receiving supportive-expressive therapy did better on measures of psychological functioning and employment, while addicts receiving cognitive-behavioral therapy did well with resolution of legal problems (Woody et al., 1983).

Not all results have been positive. Depressed patients with personality disorders had worse outcomes in terms of recovery from depression and showed less improvement in social functioning compared to depressed patients without personality disorders. The specific treatments (cognitive-behavioral therapy, IPT, and antidepressant medication with clinical management) had similar outcomes with respect to the personality-disordered group. The patients were treated for up to 12 weeks; it is quite probable that improvement in interpersonal functioning for patients with personality disorders would require longer and perhaps more intense treatment (Shea et al., 1990).

In another study, 42 outpatient cocaine abusers were randomly assigned to either a relapse prevention treatment or to IPT. For patients whose substance abuse was classified as severe, the relapse prevention group achieved higher rates of abstinence and recovery. For patients classified as lower in severity, outcome was comparable for both treatment groups (Carroll, Rounsaville, & Gawin, 1991).

These recent studies suggest that relationship-oriented psychotherapy may deliver benefits to substance abusers over and above those usually obtained with drug abuse counseling and methadone maintenance therapies.

It is important to realize that providing a certain kind of focused therapy, such as IPT, does not preclude the combined use of other therapies, such as cognitive-behavioral, or pharmacotherapy, used sequentially or concurrently. The real issue is what method(s) of intervention can best help the patient.

Relationship-Based Assessment and Millon's Theory

Millon argues that the structure of a clinical science consists of (1) theory, which provides an explanation of the phenomenology of what is being studied as well as providing concepts and hypotheses to be tested; (2) a taxonomy or classification scheme, which categorizes the clinical features that correspond to the theory; (3) instrumentation, which provides the tools for identifying and quantifying what is being observed; and (4) intervention techniques and strategies that try to help make changes. In studying personality and personality disorders, an area referred to as personology, Millon speaks of his theory of personology, his biopsychosocial theory of the development of personality disorders (1986b); his theory of organizing and categorizing those styles and disorders into a conceptual framework (1984, 1986a); his tests, such as the MCMI and its subsequent revisions designed to assess those disorders (1987); and, finally, domain-specific intervention techniques (1988), as part of a therapy designed to ameliorate those disorders.

The domain-oriented psychotherapy naturally follows his domain-oriented description of personality disorders. Millon (1984, 1986a) provides each disorder with clinical domain criteria that present functional and structural criteria used to understand and describe the disorder. Chapter 2 in this volume presents a detailed explanation of this approach.

Every personality disorder can be described with each of these criteria or elements. Since this chapter deals with relationship-oriented psychotherapy, MCMI-based assessment of personality disorders has direct relevance to the behavioral domain of interpersonal conduct. Table 4-1 presents Millon's overall schemata for characterizing prototypical interpersonal conduct according to each personalty disorders. This categorization further predicts the specific behavior and problems that are likely to be encountered by a therapist treating patients with this disorder.

Following is a brief description of the interpersonal conduct that must be addressed if the disorder is to be ameliorated, interpersonal therapeutic suggestions, and common impediments within each disorder that complicate the process for the therapist.

Schizoid

Schizoid patients have difficulty forming and maintaining interpersonal relations. They are generally *unengaged* and likely to relate to a therapist in an emotionally bland manner with little interaction.

They are unlikely to begin a discussion or to address a topic of significant importance. These patients generally wait for the therapist to initiate therapeutic activity and then are usually verbally succinct and terse in response to therapeutic inquiry. The patients' indifference and overall reluctance to engage in more healthy interpersonal relations and general lack of a positive treatment alliance with the therapist will impede the progress of therapy.

The therapist will probably be required to lead the discussion and introduce the content of therapy. The IPT therapist will elicit those key relationships in the patient's life that have been problematic, focusing on the patient's

TABLE 4-1 Interpersonal Conduct Domain

Schizoid Personality
Interpersonally Unengaged (e.g., seems different and remote, rarely responsive to the actions or feelings of others, chooses solitary activities, possesses minimal "human" interests; fades into the background, is aloof or unobtrusive, neither desires nor enjoys close relationships, prefers a peripheral role in social, work, and family settings)

Avoidant Personality
Interpersonally Aversive (e.g., distances from activities that involve intimate personal relationships and reports extensive history of social pan-anxiety and distrust; seeks acceptance, but is unwilling to get involved unless certain to be liked, maintaining distance and privacy to avoid being shamed and humiliated)

Depressive Personality
Interpersonally Defenseless (e.g., owing to feeling vulnerable, assailable, and unshielded, will beseech others to be nurturant and protective; fearing abandonment and desertion, will not only act in an endangered manner, but seek, if not demand, assurances of affection, steadfastness, and devotion)

Dependent Personality
Interpersonally Submissive (e.g., needs excessive advice and reassurance, as well as subordinates self to stronger, nurturing figure, without whom may feel anxiously alone and helpless; is compliant, conciliatory, and placating, fearing being left to care for onself)

Histrionic Personality
Interpersonally Attention-Seeking (e.g., actively solicits praise and manipulates others to gain needed reassurance, attention, and approval; is demanding, flirtatious, vain, and seductively exhibitionistic, especially when wishing to be the center of attention)

Narcissistic Personality
Interpersonally Exploitive (e.g., feels entitled, is unempathic, and expects special favors without assuming reciprocal responsibilities; shamelessly takes others for granted and uses them to enhance self and indulge desires)

Antisocial Personality
Interpersonally Irresponsible (e.g., is untrustworthy and unreliable, failing to meet or intentionally negating personal obligations of a marital, parental, employment, or financial nature; actively intrudes upon and violates the rights of others, as well as trangresses established social codes through deceitful or illegal behaviors)

Sadistic (Aggressive) Personality
Interpersonally Abrasive (e.g., reveals satisfaction in intimidating, coercing, and humiliating others; regularly expresses verbally abusive and derisive social commentary, as well as exhibiting vicious, if not physically brutal, behavior)

Compulsive Personality
Interpersonally Respectful (e.g., exhibits unusual adherence to social conventions and proprieties, as well as being scrupulous and overconscientious about matters of morality and ethics; prefers polite, formal, and correct personal relationships, usually insisting that subordinates adhere to personally established rules and methods)

TABLE 4-1 *Continued*

Negativistic Personality
Interpersonally Contrary (e.g., assumes conflicting and changing roles in social relationships, particularly dependent and contrite acquiescence and assertive and hostile independence; conveys envy and pique toward those more fortunate, as well as actively concurrently or sequentially obstructive and intolerant of others, expressing either negative or incompatible attitudes)

Self-Defeating Personality
Interpersonally Deferential (e.g., distances from those who are consistently supportive, relating to others where one can be sacrificing, servile, and obsequious, allowing, if not encouraging them to exploit, mistreat, or take advantage; renders ineffectual the attempts of others to be helpful and solicits condemnation by accepting undeserved blame and courting unjust criticism)

Schizotypal Personality
Interpersonally Secretive (e.g., prefers privacy and isolation, with few highly tentative attachments and personal obligations; has drifted over time into increasingly peripheral vocational roles and clandestine social activities)

Borderline Personality
Interpersonally Paradoxical (e.g., although needing attention and affection, is unpredictably contrary, manipulative, and volatile, frequently eliciting rejection rather than support; frantically reacts to fears of abandonment and isolation, but often in angry, mercurial, and self-damaging ways)

Paranoid Personality
Interpersonally Provocative (e.g., not only bears grudges and is unforgiving of those of the past, but displays a quarrelsome, fractious, and abrasive attitude with recent acquaintances; precipitates exasperation and anger by a testing of loyalties and an intrusive and searching preoccupation with hidden motives)

---

emotional reactions to key people (usually fear manifested by behavioral indifference), and seek ways for the patient to relate to other people more naturally. This process needs to start with the therapeutic relationship itself, and the patient needs to practice changes in relating to people by changing the way he or she relates to the therapist.

Avoidant
These patients may be distrustful and distancing or relate socially, but beneath this veneer is a devastating fear of experiencing rejection and disapproval. They find social interaction generally *aversive.*

Their fear of social encounters where they are likely to be judged and rejected can inhibit the process of therapy. They will tend to resist changes that eventually result in increased social encounters, yet this is exactly what must occur.

An interpersonal focus to the avoidant personality would address the specific relationships in the person's life that had resulted in this "burnt child" reactivity to relationships, look for interpersonal experiences that had been rewarding, help the patient to distinguish between the two, and help the patient to gradually change his or her expectations in such relationships.

Depressive

These patients, even when not clinically depressed, are gloomy, pessimistic, passive, indecisive, self-critical, self-reproaching, and self-derogatory. They are preoccupied with anticipating negative social events and appear *defenseless*. Any move by the therapist to change these behaviors and thoughts will likely be met with a sense of futility, pessimism, fear of failure, and hopelessness.

IPT argues that relationships, past and present, have been responsible for creating this pattern in the patient. Therefore, the focus needs to be on those relationships at the present time that are precipitating this type of behaviors in the patient. The patient needs to practice new and more cheerful responses in the context of people and situations that evoke negative responses.

Dependent

These patients are *submissive* interpersonally. They will quickly form an attachment to a therapist and expect that this powerful figure will guide their lives, solve their problems, and maintain their need for security.

They will resist therapeutic strategies designed for more independent functioning and will occasionally express hostility at the therapist, which is quickly followed by guilt, remorse, and apologies. They will likely form a rapid attachment to the therapist but resist movement toward independence.

Behavioral change is likely to be quite slow. The IPT therapist needs to focus on each significant relationship in the patients' lives, demonstrating the patients' reactions and roles in the relationship, and getting them to suggest ways in which they would like to relate differently to those people. The therapist needs to discuss specific situations and ways of changing how they behave in each relationship and make recommendations for ways of behaving differently. Patients need to be gradually coaxed into taking more independent actions, without having them become dependent on the therapist.

Histrionic

These patients are flirtatious, dramatic, and *attention-seeking*. They also actively seek praise and approval. They may be seductive in manner or dress.

These patients are also prone to impulsive behaviors, angry tirades, and explosive comments that keep others at bay.

Much of this behavior is outside the awareness of the patients, so any attempt at introspection will likely result in denial, resistance, and unwillingness to introspect. An additional problem for the therapist is that these patients are often engaging and charming, so the therapist may experience a transference reaction to this behavior whereby much of the patients' dramatic flair might go unchallenged, since it is perceived as "enjoyable." Also, quixotic emotionality can be expected in the sessions.

An IPT focus with these patients is often on the concrete problems they are having with specific people—for example, "My husband spends all his free time riding his motorcycle and only uses me for sex. He never paid me much attention so I started having an affair." Therapy will help the patient explore possible reasons for her husband's behavior, explore the wife's basic needs in a relationship, determine what attracted her to this specific man, and try to get her to relate in a less needy way to important relationships in her life.

Narcissistic

These patients are so self-centered that they do not experience life's problems as emanating from anything they have done. They are *exploitive* in relationships and use others to bring them attention and admiration. Often it is their egocentricity in relationships that others find objectionable, yet which they find quite reinforcing.

Therapy can be impeded by their unwillingness to look at themselves and their effect on others critically and objectively. Also, these patients are prone to narcissistic injuries when they experience a perceived blow to their self-esteem or if their narcissistic supplies are not repeatedly replenished.

The IPT therapist will eventually try to reduce the patients' self-centeredness and focus on how others are responding to the patients. The needs and reactions of other significant people in their lives will be discussed, and then the sessions are refocused on what the patients are getting out of these relationships compared to what they are giving to the relationships. Techniques such as practicing active listening and empathic responses may be helpful.

Antisocial

These patients are quite *irresponsible,* manipulative, and exploitive. They are unreliable and have superficial relationships. They may make a good impression at first, because they have a certain degree of charm, but their essential motive is to deceive and/or dominate others through intimidation, threat, and exertion of power.

There are four main impediments to therapy: (1) The therapist's main problem will be to get them to continue in therapy, since their behavior is ego-syntonic (it is unlikely that such patients voluntarily enter therapy unless under some duress); (2) they tend to say one thing in therapy and do something else outside of therapy; (3) the therapist needs to work hard to promote an honest therapeutic alliance; and (4) these patients will try to intimidate and control the therapy and the therapist.

Because these patients expect to be intimidated and controlled themselves, the therapist needs to teach them a new way of being. The therapist cannot "play games," must talk straight with the patients, and must relate totally honestly. Once trust has been established, the ways the patients relate to others can be discussed, though the task is not an easy one.

Sadistic

These patients tend to be cruel, angry, aggressive, intimidating, humiliating, controlling, verbally abusive, and *abrasive*. The main impediment to successful therapy is that these are the very behaviors that will likely be displayed toward the therapist.

The main target of therapy is to reduce cruel and aggressive behaviors by reducing the emotional reactions and the interpersonal events that precipitate them and to help the patients understand their need to control people though aggressive behaviors. The patients need to focus on each event, beginning with the most current one, and explore how their behavior escalated into aggression. Looking at relationships they could not control might help the patients discover qualities in people they find admirable or detestable. This helps to create an interpersonal focus.

Compulsive

Depending on the degree of the disorder, these patients will relate in a *respectful* and orderly way to others. They suppress any felt interpersonal hostility and are proper and conventional.

Rigid behavior patterns and a fear of disapproving authority figures are the main impediments to therapy.

The therapist can use their tendency to be obedient toward authority figures to gradually shape their behavior toward resolution of the problems that brought them into therapy. For example, the patient needs to explore what reactions are expected from others if things are not perfect. Then the patient might sit down with the "problematic" person and elicit what reactions the person is likely to have if the patient makes a mistake. Discrepancies between perceptions, expectations, and realities can then serve as the content of the therapy session.

Negativistic

These patients will either be passive-aggressive with a therapist, expressing their anger and hostility obliquely but resistingly, or else behave in a petulant, oppositional, and *contrary* manner.

They enter a relationship believing that conflict will result, so they become querulous yet later contrite. This keeps others, including the therapist, off balance with a feeling that relating to them is like walking on eggs, because one never knows how they are going to behave that day. The projection of negative feelings onto the therapist can be expected.

IPT focuses on their reactions and behaviors to specific people in their life. The patients need to reflect on how they learned to behave as they do by first examining how they behave with important relationships. The patients must come to understand the constancy of their behavior before a plan of action is initiated to redress it.

Self-Defeating

These patients are self-abasing and tend to blame themselves for all the troubles they experience. They are interpersonally *deferential* to the point of allowing others to abuse them, emotionally and/or physically.

This adoption of causation for interpersonal troubles is unconsciously designed to defeat attempts to change behavior and leave the therapist exasperated with clients who resist changing their behavior about which they constantly complain.

The goal for these patients is to get them to take control of their lives, to empower them to resolve their problems and to become more independent. Because such behaviors always occur in an interpersonal context, the therapist can easily focus on those situations causing distress in the patients' lives and get them to try new behaviors with others that are likely to be maximally successful and thus slowly shape their behavior toward others.

Schizotypal

These patients appear "spacey" and withdrawn and have cognitive slippage and odd mannerisms with mild to severe relationship deficits. Interpersonally, they are *secretive*.

It will be difficult for the patients to actually express the source of their difficulties within a therapy session. They tend to not really relate to the therapist and act secretively.

This is a more dysfunctional variant of the schizoid personality style, and the therapeutic techniques previously discussed for the schizoid type are also applicable to the schizotypal disorder. The therapist will be required to use very direct techniques, such as guiding the content of the session.

Borderline

These patients vacillate between excessive overvaluation and undeserved devaluation of a strong authority figure. They are *paradoxical* and impulsive and have quixotic emotions, with particular difficulties in dealing with anger.

It has been described as essentially an identity disorder, but it may also be an attachment disorder as well. Separation issues are likely to intrude into the therapy, and the therapist may be seen as a combination savior and withholding figure, so that transference issues can dominate the therapy.

There is consensus in the clinical literature that the therapy of borderline conditions requires long-term treatment. Thus an IPT approach diverges somewhat, at least conceptually, and takes a longer-term approach, focusing almost exclusively on the issues of the patients' interpersonal attachments, helping them manage anger and depression and strengthening their self-identify by reducing dependent behaviors.

Paranoid

These patients can be *provocative*, belligerent, abrasive, confronting, and delusional, projecting inner fears and perceptions onto a therapist who is seen as malevolent and evil.

The lack of trust is the basic interpersonal process that can destroy the therapy. Also, they are likely to evoke strong transference reactions in the therapist.

The best approach with these patients is probably to slowly build up trust with the therapist, who may help them identify relationships in their life that were not malevolent.

Mixed Personality Disorders

Of course, these are pure cases that typically exist in textbooks only, whereas real-life patients often are a mixture of several of these disorders and will often meet official diagnostic criteria for two or three of them. In this case, the blend will need to be addressed. For example, a patient who meets the criteria for both antisocial and sadistic personality disorders will probably demonstrate an interpersonal conduct that is both irresponsible and abrasive. A patient who is both histrionic and narcissistic will show behavior that is both attention seeking and exploitative. A patient who is dependent and self-defeating will show combined interpersonal features, appearing submissive, deferential, acquiescent, passive, and masochistic.

CASE STUDY

We have been discussing these disorders as if they exist in a vacuum. However, while personality disorders are often the focus of therapeutic attention, they often coexist with an Axis I clinical disorder, which also requires treatment. A dependent personality disorder may co-exist with clinical depression; a person with an antisocial personality disorder is prone to develop a problem with substance abuse; a histrionic or narcissistic personality is prone to marital problems. The therapist is required to attend to the Axis I disorder within the context of the Axis II disorder, which is also often done with techniques emphasizing interpersonal processes.

The following represents a case example using the MCMI-II to assist in the initial assessment of the presenting complaint and a repeat MCMI-III to gauge the progress of therapy.

History

The patient, a 36-year-old, white male, initially sought psychological services for post-divorce adjustment counseling. He had been married for 14 years and had three children, but his wife was alcoholic and refused to receive help for it, so he had filed for divorce.

After he had been separated for about three years, he became involved with a woman. She had moved in with him but this lasted only 6 weeks. A few months later, at the time of the evaluation, he had met yet another woman with a history of victimization in abusive relationships, serious depression, several suicidal attempts requiring psychiatric hospitalizations, and possible seasonal affective disorder. She had been married twice and, shortly after the therapy began, moved in with the patient (and eventually married him).

Initial counseling goals were to (1) improve his post-divorce communication with his ex-wife so as to not use the children to work out their continuing anger toward each other, (2) improve his self-esteem, and (3) provide him with some support for his parenting problems, since he had been given custody to two of his children.

MCMI-II

As part of the continuing evaluation, the MCMI-II was given to the patient (see Table 4-2). The initial test results had highpoints on Negativistic, Avoidant, and Self-Defeating. This reflects a person who is oversensitive to perceived rejection, fearful, anxious, negativistic, disgruntled, querulous, and petulant. Such patients react to stress by emotionally acting out affect

TABLE 4-2 Case Study Initial MCMI

MCMI-II Inventory		Base Rate
	Validity	0
X	Disclosure	89**
Y	Desirability	62
Z	Debasement	71
1	Schizoid	67
2A	Avoidant	101***
3	Dependent	87**
4	Histrionic	64
5	Narcissistic	94**
6A	Antisocial	65
6B	Aggressive (Sadistic)	82*
7	Compulsive	54
8A	Negativistic	104***
8B	Self-Defeating	97**
S	Schizotypal	68
C	Borderline	63
P	Paranoid	65
A	Anxiety	66
H	Somatoform	53
N	Bipolar: Manic	53
D	Dysthymia	58
B	Alcohol Dependence	60
T	Drug Dependence	58
SS	Thought Disorder	67
CC	Major Depression	57
PP	Delusional Disorder	64

*BR 75–84
**BR 85–94
***BR 95 and above

and are prone to temper tantrums and explosive and angry outbursts. They tend to be filled with resentments and have conflicts over dependency issues, which is further substantiated by an elevated score on Scale 3 (Dependent) (Craig, 1993b). Much of his behavior has a repetitive and self-defeating aspect to it (Scale 8B). Also, the patient did not endorse items that reflected the presence of any clinical syndromes (e.g., Axis I disorders). The treatment focus was the patient's personality style itself.

With the addition of the MCMI-II test results an additional goal became apparent: To address this patient's dependent and self-defeating features, he needed to become more assertive and to take control of many aspects of his life. He needed to reduce his passive-aggressive approach to dealing with conflict by reducing the sources of stress in his life, by more adaptively coping with areas under his control, and by using the supportive relationships in his life without demonstrating excessive dependency on them.

IPT Course

Relationship-oriented therapy was used to help accomplish these tasks. During the course of therapy several events intervened and took precedence over the main goals. Yet, even here the main goals were still indirectly addressed. For example, he and his new wife experienced significant financial problems to the point where they were considering filing for personal bankruptcy. They were thinking of selling their home to help pay their debts, many of which were caused by his ex-wife's spending habits during their separation. However, to implement the goal of increased assertion, the patient was directed (an IPT technique) to negotiate with his major creditors (e.g., mortgage company, bank on a car loan of his ex-wife, etc.) so that a more reasonable payment plan could be worked out. He also was directed to seek legal counsel on matters pertaining to suing his ex-wife for required back payments. His interpersonal behavior was to act slowly on these suggestions, emanating some resistance but eventually complying.

Another issue that intervened was the possibility of physical and sexual child abuse, both with his wife's child (age 6) and with his own child (also age 6). Again, the therapist had the patient take a more proactive stance by getting both children in for an evaluation and by developing a specific plan of action following this evaluation. His interpersonal behavior was quite assertive in this instance and he immediately acted upon all suggestions.

During treatment their teenage son became suicidal and also needed treatment. Much of his behavior was a reaction to his ex-wife's alcoholic behavior during visitations. The therapist contacted the ex-wife and insisted she come in to address a matter relating to her son, but the eventual goal was to motivate her to receive treatment for her alcoholism. The patient agreed to periodic sessions with his ex-wife to reduce using the children to vent their own anger toward each other.

During each of these episodes, in addition to providing support, direction, and advice, the patient was asked to introspect on how he was relating to the people in his life, what was going through his mind during these crises, and what was the proper course of action he might have taken. With each impending crisis he was better able to deal with the myriad of problems extant in his life and was no longer dealing with his life with such oppositional, negativistic, and self-defeating manner.

Interpersonal therapy helped this patient to be more assertive in reacting to the many new problems that surfaced during his therapy.

Following a year of therapy of approximately 25 sessions, the MCMI-III was administered, as shown in Table 4-3.

TABLE 4-3 Case Study Follow-up MCMI

MCMI-III Inventory		Base Rate
	Validity	0
X	Disclosure	70
Y	Desirability	70
Z	Debasement	70
1	Schizoid	72
2A	Avoidant	80*
2B	Depressive	0
3	Dependent	85**
4	Histrionic	42
5	Narcissistic	75*
6A	Antisocial	73
6B	Aggressive (Sadistic)	61
7	Compulsive	49
8A	Negativistic	90**
8B	Self-Defeating	79*
S	Schizotypal	70
C	Borderline	70
P	Paranoid	78*
A	Anxiety	80*
H	Somatoform	63
N	Bipolar: Manic	69
D	Dysthymia	68
B	Alcohol Dependence	65
T	Drug Dependence	62
PT	PTSD	68
SS	Thought Disorder	72
CC	Major Depression	63
PP	Delusional Disorder	89**

*BR 75–84
**BR 85–94

Several things are apparent: (1) The patient no longer demonstrates the self-defeating component to his character that was present a year ago (reduction in Scale 6B). (2) His tendency to express anger though inappropriate means has been reduced (reduction in Scale 6B). (3) He has become less self-centered (reduction in Scale 5). On the other hand, (4) his sensitivity to feelings of rejection remain. (5) His essential character style of dependent and negativistic remains unchanged, perhaps because of so many intervening crises that the therapist could not give sufficient attention to this, or because changing basic behavior patterns and styles of relating takes more time.

Summary

Taking an interpersonal approach to intervention seems logical since interpersonal processes and events are largely responsible for many patients' presenting problems. Using the MCMI-III to assist in the evaluation of personality disorders adds an objective dimension to interpersonal assessment and conveys patients' interpersonal styles, which helps refine the therapeutic goals and the direction for treatment.

References

Bowen, M. (1960). A family concept of schizophrenia. In D. Jackson (Ed.), *The etiology of schizophrenia*. New York: Basic Books.

Carroll, K. M., Rounsaville, B. J., & Gawin, F. H. (1991). A comparative trial of psychotherapies for ambulatory cocaine abusers: Relapse prevention and interpersonal psychotherapy. *American Journal of Drug and Alcohol Abuse, 17*, 229–247.

Craig, R. J. (1989). The clinical process of interviewing. In R. J. Craig (Ed.), *Clinical and diagnostic interviewing*. Northvale, NJ: Aronson.

Craig, R. J. (1993a). *Millon Clinical Multiaxial Inventory: A clinical research information synthesis*. Hillsdale, NJ: Erlbaum.

Craig, R. J. (1993b). *Psychological screening with the MCMI-II*. Odessa, FL. Psychological Assessment Resources.

DiMascio, A., Weissman, M. M., Prusoff, B. A., Neu, C., Zwilling, M., & Klerman, G. L. (1979). Differential symptom reduction by drugs and psychotherapy in acute depression. *Archives of General Psychiatry. 36*, 1450–1456.

Elkin, I., Shea, M. T., Watkins, J. T., Imber, S. D., Sotsky, S. M., Collins, J. F., Glass, D. R., Pilkonis, P. A, Leber, W. R., Docherty, J. P., & Parloff, M. B. (1989). National Institute of Mental Health treatment of depression collaborative research program: General effectiveness of treatments. *Archives of General Psychiatry, 46*, 971–982.

Klerman, G. L., Weissman, M. M., Rounsaville, B. J., & Chevron, E. S. (1984). *Interpersonal psychotherapy of depression*. New York: Basic Books.

Lidz, T., Fleck, S., & Cornelison, A. (1965). *Schizophrenia and the family*. Springfield, IL: Thomas.

Meyer, A. (1957). *Psychobiology: A science of man*. Springfield, IL: Thomas.

Millon, T. (1984). On the renaissance of personality assessment and personality theory. *Journal of Personality Assessment, 48*, 450–466.

Millon, T. (1986a). Personality prototypes and their diagnostic criteria. In T. Millon & G. Klerman (Eds.), *Contemporary directions in psychopathology: Toward* DSM-IV (pp 639–669). New York: Guilford Press.

Millon, T. (1986b). A theoretical derivation of pathological personalities. In T. Millon & G. Klerman (Eds.), *Contemporary directions in psychopathology: Toward* DSM-IV (pp 671–712). New York: Guilford Press.

Millon, T. (1987). *Millon Clinical Multiaxial Inventory-II: Manual for the MCMI-II*. Minneapolis, MN: National Computer Systems.

Millon, T. (1988). Personologic psychotherapy: 10 commandments for a posteclectic approach to integrative treatment. *Psychotherapy, 25,* 209–219.

Rogers, C. R. (1942). *Counseling and psychotherapy*. Boston: Houghton-Mifflin.

Rogers, C. R. (1965). *Client-centered therapy*. Boston: Houghton-Mifflin.

Rounsaville, B. J., Glazer, W., Wilber, C. H., Weissman, M. M., & Kleber, H. D. (1983). Short-term interpersonal psychotherapy in methadone-maintained opiate addicts. *Archives of General Psychiatry, 40,* 629–636.

Shea, M. T., Pilkonis, P. A., Beckham, E., Collins, J. F., Elkin, I., Sotsky, S. M., & Docherty, J. P. (1990). Personality disorders and treatment outcome in the NIMH Treatment of Depression Collaborative Research Program. *American Journal of Psychiatry, 147,* 711–718.

Sullivan, H. S. (1954). *The psychiatric interview*. New York: Basic Books.

Sullivan, H. S. (1956). *Clinical studies in psychiatry*. New York: Norton.

Sundberg, N. D., & Tyler, L. E. (1962). *Clinical psychology. An introduction to research and practice*. New York: Appleton-Century-Crofts.

Weissman, M. M., Prusoff, B. A., DiMascio, A., Neu, C., Goklaney, M., & Klerman, G. L. (1979). The efficacy of drugs and psychotherapy in the treatment of acute depressive episodes. *Archives of General Psychiatry, 36,* 555–558.

Woody, G. E., Luborsky, L., McLellan, A. A., O'Brien, C. P., Beck, A. T., Blaine, J., Herman, I., & Hole, A. (1983). Psychotherapy for opiate addicts: Does it help? *Archives of General Psychiatry, 40,* 639–645.

Wynne, L., & Singer, M. (1963). Thought disorder and family relations of schizophrenia. *Archives of General Psychiatry, 9,* 191–198.

5

Cognitive Therapy and the MCMI-III

THOMAS E. WILL

The Stoic philosophers were the earliest progenitors of the philosophy that underlies cognitive therapy. In the *Enchiridion*, Epictetus wrote, "Men are disturbed not by things but by the views which they take of them." Other philosophical systems such as Buddhism and Taoism have made the point that emotions are based on cognitions. One can change one's emotions by changing one's cognitions.

Both Alfred Adler and Sigmund Freud contributed concepts that were compatible with and forerunners of current cognitive therapy thinking. Freud (1953) suggested that symptoms and affects may be the result of unconscious ideas. Adler (1931) advocated that humans give meaning to situations rather than the reverse. This fits well into the A-B-C paradigm of the cognitive approach. This model was advocated by Albert Ellis and was a principal construct motivating the development of cognitive-behavioral therapeutic approaches. The rational-emotive psychotherapy school that he developed attempts to make the patient aware of irrational belief systems and the consequent affective responses that are their sequelae.

Aaron T. Beck (Beck, 1976) is one of the leading forces in the current evolution of cognitive therapy. He has done considerable research in this area and is a powerful advocate, teacher, and evaluator of this therapeutic school. His approach has been quite effective in the treatment of depressive disorders, as well as other psychopathologic states.

Theoretical Assumptions and Clinical Techniques

The cognitive approach to psychotherapy makes the following assumptions regarding human behavior (Beck et al., 1979).

1. The process of perceiving and experiencing one's environment is an active process involving the patient utilizing both introspective and inspective data.
2. Cognitions that the patient experiences are in actuality a combination and integration of both internal and external stimuli.
3. The approach an individual takes when evaluating a life situation is manifest in the cognitions. These cognitions include both thoughts and visualizations.
4. The individual's phenomenological field or stream of consciousness is based on these cognitions. These cognitions reflect the individual's perspective of the past and future, as well as the conceptualization of the self and surrounding external environment.
5. It is hypothesized that changes in an individual's cognitive structure will affect that person's behavioral and affective life.
6. Cognitive distortions, which frequently fuel significant psychopathology, can be changed through the psychotherapy processes. This process involves making the patient aware of cognitive distortions and devising strategies to help change them. These strategies include both cognitive and behavioral techniques.

How does cognitive therapy differ from other psychotherapies currently available? Basically, there are two constructs that are different in this therapeutic approach. The first of these is the idea of *collaborative empiricism*, which is central to this therapeutic approach. This is quite different than the approach used in the more insight-oriented therapy techniques. In this interventional style the therapist is interactive with the patient on a continuing basis. The therapist elicits the patient's cooperation and participation in the therapy process. For patients with significant psychopathology the therapist may need to be quite directive at the outset in order to help the patient organize his or her behavioral and cognitive processes. The emphasis here is on actively engaging the patient in the therapeutic encounter.

This therapeutic approach also spends little time focusing on previous life events. The emphasis is on a *"here and now"* orientation, with the purpose being to help the patient deal functionally with current life stressors. Unconscious factors are not addressed in this therapeutic approach. The therapist and patient act much like a scientific team in that they investigate and test hypotheses about the patient's cognitions and feelings. In addition, this collaboration involves the patient in scheduling activities and doing homework assignments outside of the therapy venue.

Differentiation of cognitive therapy from behavioral approaches is based on the greater emphasis in cognitive therapy on the internal processes of the patient, which include the cognitions, attitudes, affective states, et cetera. The collaborative team of the patient and therapist investigates the automatic thoughts, assumptions, and conclusions of the patient and formulates these dysfunctional thoughts as hypotheses that can then be tested scientifically. If a patient believes that an individual met in the hallway at work is frowning because of dislike, this automatic assumption is tested by exploring alternate hypotheses for this same experience. These hypotheses may be tested by having the patient keep records of these problematic situations, as well as by directly ascertaining the causes for such frowns.

Dysfunctional Cognitive Functioning

One way of understanding the functional cognitions of the personality-disordered patient is by conceptualizing them in terms of primitive thinking versus mature thinking (Beck et al., 1979). Primitive thinking is most characteristic of children and reflects a lower level of cognitive development. Mature thinking, on the other hand, is more adaptive and functional. The pathologic individual may make one dimensional and global judgments of life events. Their interpretations of life events include responses that are judgmental, absolutist, moralistic, and invariant and contain elements of character diagnosis.

On the other hand, mature thinking is characterized by a multidimensional approach that integrates life circumstances into many dimensions. It is more quantitative than qualitative and is relativistic and nonjudgmental. In addition, this kind of thinking is characterized by behavioral diagnosis, as well as reversibility. In some ways this dichotomization of primitive thinking versus mature thinking may reflect an underlying biological substrate, as well as psychosocial characteristics of the personality-disordered patient. That is, these patients are frequently inflexible with regard to their cognitive styles and adaptive functioning. This inflexibility is often responsible for the vicious circles and self-destructive behaviors seen in this class of disorders.

Cognitive therapy, through its multimodal approach, seeks to move the patient along the continuum from primitive thinking to mature thinking. The techniques for this movement include multiple therapeutic techniques, as well as the identification of systematic errors in the thinking of the disordered individual.

Cognitive Interventions

Before embarking upon a course of cognitive therapy with a patient, it is important to explain to the patients what the therapist's definition of a cognition is, as well as how cognitions can affect behavior and mood. In this paradigm a cognition may be defined as a thought or visualization that the patients may not be aware of unless they focus their attention on its presence. Characteristically, cognitions can be described as automatic thoughts that are usual and idiosyncratic to the patients' thought processes. In most cases the patients view these cognitions as representative of their current life situation and as grounded in reality. In most cases the patients will not evaluate the veracity or validity of these cognitions. They will accept these as uncontested and basically truthful representations of reality.

In the cognitive therapy approach it is important that the patients understand and recognize the relationship between cognitions and subsequent behavior as a resulting effect. One way of demonstrating this to patients is to use clinical examples in a somewhat didactic fashion. This less threatening, psycho-educational approach provides the patients with some safety at the initiation of therapy.

Another way to demonstrate the linkage between thoughts and emotions is to have the patients get involved in some illustrative visualizations. These can include having the patients visualize an unpleasant situation and the attendant emotions to this situation. The therapist can then discuss with the patients their cognitions that mediated their emotional response to the unpleasant situation. Conversely, the therapist can also have the patients visualize a pleasant or happy situation and the emotions that attend to that occurrence. Once again, the therapist can illustrate linkage by discussing the cognitions that attend to the visualization of a pleasant situation.

After the patients understand this linkage, the therapist may wish to tackle the task of having the patients identify automatic thoughts. Frequently this is accomplished by having the patients keep a daily record of dysfunctional thoughts. These record sheets include the date of the occurrence, a description of the situation that led to automatic thoughts, the emotions that attended this situation, and the automatic thoughts or cognitions of the patients. In addition, the patients rate their belief in their automatic thoughts on a scale of 0 to 100, as well as provide a rational response to these automatic thoughts. Finally, the last column has the patients re-rate their belief in their automatic thoughts and specify and rate their subsequent emotions (Beck & Greenburg, 1974).

The examination and realty testing of automatic thoughts and visualizations are important aspects of the cognitive approach. It should not be assumed that all the patients' cognitions are in error, but, rather, they should be tested in a scientific fashion using the approach of collaborative empiricism delineated previously. The evidence for and against each cognition should be scrutinized rigorously and subjected to reality testing, with the therapist initially demonstrating this technique. This approach will fequently tease out the patients' most characteristic cognitive distortions. The applications of reality testing at this point in the therapy process can help patients correct these distortions. It is important, however, that the therapist not forget to explore the meaning to the patients of life occurrences and the distortions that attend that meaning. Not to attend to these meanings could result in the therapist missing important aspects that influences the patients' automatic thoughts.

After the patients begin data collection and have become somewhat skilled at recognizing and recording cognitive distortions, they may begin to note that some of these distortions occur much more frequently. In addition, there may be consistent variations on the themes that were initially brought to the therapist's attention. Simple awareness of these distortions is not sufficient for change to occur. The patients must be able to contest these distortions on the basis of reality and substitute more logical and reasonable inferences.

Another common technique used with cognitive therapy is reattribution. This technique is particularly effective with patients who tend to blame themselves excessively or assume exaggerated responsibility for any adverse life event. This technique does not attempt to absolve the patients of total responsibility, but to more fairly re-attribute, in a logical way, the responsibility that is truly theirs. This approach may not only help the patients feel less guilty about adverse life events and their part in these, but also help them solve problematic life situations that have previously been viewed as insolvable.

Conjoint Behavioral Techniques

Use of behavioral techniques in cognitive therapy has a long history. Its purpose, however, is different than that seen in the practice of the behaviorist. For the behaviorist the end point is reached once the behavior has changed. On the other hand, for the cognitive therapist the whole point of using behavioral techniques is to cause cognitive changes in the patients. That is, the hope is that the use of these techniques will produce changes in the patients' negative attitudes toward themselves, disprove certain erroneous hypotheses that they have about themselves (e.g., self-worth, inability to perform), and result in the patients' improved performance. To use the scientific metaphor for cognitive therapy, these behavioral techniques are simply experiments to test the validity of some of the negative assumptions the patients have about themselves. It is hoped that the introduction of these techniques will reality test these cognitive distortions, refute many of them, and result in patients whose cognitions are more reality-based and less detrimental and self-destructive. The hope is also to build a gradation of difficulty in these behavioral assignments so that as patients experience success on the simpler assignments they will be more likely to perform more complex and difficult behavioral tasks.

Beck (1973) recommends several steps in the application of behavioral techniques. He encourages a depressed patient to schedule activities as an initial assignment. Here the therapist, conjointly with the patient, may actually work out a weekly activity schedule in which the patient and therapist plan activities ahead of time and record whether or not those activities are actually completed by the patient. Once again, the patient begins with simple tasks, such as simply getting up and reading the newspaper, to performing more complex functions, such as interacting with more than a few individuals. It is important that the patient be educated about the rationale for performing this scheduling of activities tasks. As an example, a depressed patient who is sedentary may experience more distressful cognitions; thus, one rationale for increasing activity is to decrease these negative cognitions.

Cognitive Therapy and the Personality Disorders

Schizoid

Schizoid patients have an *impoverished* cognitive style that is often characterized by a vagueness in thought and defective perceptual scanning (Millon, 1981). These patients will miss the subtleties of life. Because of their cognitive styles, these patients will miss cues from their interpersonal milieu, which will result in emotional unresponsiveness. These patients may be characterized as being unemotional or intellectually unresponsive to stimuli that in most cases of "normal" behavior would elicit rage, anger, pleasure, or excitement.

To deal with the impoverished cognitions of schizoid patients, a number of cognitive therapy strategies may be beneficial. First of all, having the patients keep a dysfunctional thought record may help educate them in identifying their emotions (for the first time in many cases), as well as the gradations that these emotions contain. This should increase the patients' awareness of their feeling states and eventually the feeling states of significant others in their environment. Educational strategies may need to be basic with these patients and include listing both positive and negative emotions, as well as a continuum on which they are displayed. This record may also help the patients understand how others react to them when they are in specific emotional states, as well as to identify the possible emotional states of others with whom they come into contact. This might be the basis of developing empathy for the first time in this patient type. Ultimately, the astute clinician will want to enhance the patients' awareness of their impact on others, as well as the impact others have. This will enhance their ability to interact appropriately in social situations so that they can realize the positive reinforcements and pleasures that can be derived from social milieus (see Table 5-1).

Avoidant

The cognitive style of these patients is characterized as being *distracted* and preoccupied by unpleasant and perplexing inner thoughts. The schemas from

TABLE 5-1 Cognitive Style Domain

Schizoid Personality
Cognitively Impoverished (e.g., seems deficient across broad spheres of human knowledge and evidences vague and obscure thought processes, particularly about social matters; communication with others is often unfocused, loses its purpose or intention, or is conveyed via a loose or circuitous logic)

Avoidant Personality
Cognitively Distracted (e.g., warily scans environment for potential threats and is preoccupied by intrusive and disruptive random thoughts and observations; an upwelling from within of irrelevant ideation upsets thought continuity and interferes with social communications and accurate appraisals)

Depressive Personality
Cognitively Pessimistic (e.g., possesses defeatist and fatalistic attitudes about almost all matters, sees things in their blackest form and invariably expects the worst; feeling weighed down, discouraged, and bleak, gives the gloomiest interpretation of current events, despairing as well that things will never improve in the future)

Dependent Personality
Cognitively Naive (e.g., rarely disagrees with others and is easily persuaded, unsuspicious and gullible; reveals a Pollyanna attitude toward interpersonal difficulties, watering down objective problems and smoothing over troubling events)

Histrionic Personality
Cognitively Flighty (e.g., avoids introspective thought, is overly suggestible, attentive to fleeting external events, and speaks in impressionistic generalities; integrates experiences poorly, resulting in scattered learning and thoughtless judgments)

Narcissistic Personality
Cognitively Expansive (e.g., has an undisciplined imagination and exhibits a preoccupation with immature and self-glorifying fantasies of success, beauty, or love; is minimally constrained by objective reality, takes liberties with facts and often lies to redeem self-illusions)

Antisocial Personality
Cognitively Deviant (e.g., construes events and relationships in accord with socially unorthodox beliefs and morals; is disdainful of traditional ideals, fails to conform to social norms, and is contemptuous of conventional values)

Sadistic (Aggressive) Personality
Cognitively Dogmatic (e.g., is strongly opinionated and close-minded, as well as unbending and obstinate in holding to his or her preconceptions; exhibits a broad-ranging authoritartianism, social intolerance, and prejudice)

Compulsive Personality
Cognitively Constricted (e.g., constructs world in terms of rules, regulations, schedules, and hierarchies; is rigid, stubborn, and indecisive and notably upset by unfamiliar or novel ideas and customs)

Continued

TABLE 5-1 *Continued*

Negativistic Personality
Cognitively Skeptical (e.g., is cynical, doubting, and untrusting, approaching positive events with disbelief, and future possibilities with pessimism, anger, and trepidation; has a misanthropic view of life, is whining and grumbling, voicing disdain and caustic comments toward those experiencing good fortune)

Self-Defeating Personality
Cognitively Diffident (e.g., hesitant to interpret observations positively for fear that, in doing so, they may not take problematic forms, or achieve troublesome and self-denigrating outcomes; as a result, there is a habit of repeatedly expressing attitudes and anticipations contrary to favorable beliefs and feelings)

Schizotypal Personality
Cognitively Autistic (e.g., capacity to "read" thoughts and feelings of others is markedly dysfunctional, mixes social communications with personal irrelevancies, circumstantial speech, ideas of reference, and metaphorical asides; often ruminative, appearing self-absorbed and lost in daydreams with occasional magical thinking, bodily illusions, obscure suspicion, odd beliefs, and a blurring of reality and fantasy)

Borderline Personality
Cognitively Capricious (e.g., experiences rapidly changing, fluctuating, and antithetical perceptions or thoughts concerning passing events, as well as contrasting emotions and conflicting thoughts toward self and others, notably love, rage, and guilt; vacillating and contradictory reactions are evoked in others by virtue of one's behaviors, creating, in turn, conflicting and confusing social feedback)

Paranoid Personality
Cognitively Suspicious (e.g., is unwarrantedly skeptical, cynical, and mistrustful of the motives of others, including relatives, friends, and associates, construcing innocuous events as signifying hidden or conspiratorial intent; reveals tendency to read hidden meanings into benign matters and to magnify tangential or minor difficulties into proofs of duplicity and treachery, especially regarding the fidelity and trustworthiness of a spouse or intimate friend

---

which these inner thoughts derive include such cognitive distortions as "I don't fit in anywhere," "I'm defective," "I'm unlikable," and "I'm not an adequate individual." This conceptualization of self usually arises from childhood rejection by a significant other such as a parent, peer, or sibling (Beck et al., 1990). These patients make the fundamental error of thinking that others will react to them as that significant other did. They expect rejection and thus engender it. The interesting fact about these patients is that they may have many admirable qualities that make them quite likable and desirable as partners in interpersonal relationships. These, of course, are beliefs about themselves that they would never entertain.

It may be that these patients engage in distracted cognitive styles as a way of dealing with their low tolerance for dysphoria. They may seek diversion as a way of pushing out uncomfortable ideations from their consciousness. This distracted style then becomes reinforced because it reduces the patients' feelings of dysphoria and the attendant emotional consequences. It becomes apparent, therefore, that therapeutic interventions must address the cognitive distortions that these patients engage in with regard to their own sense of competency and self-worth. This can begin by identifying cognitive distortions that these patients hold as well as the origins of these distortions. Frequently these patients have no idea that others experience their disorder or that their distorted thinking is the result of dysfunctional and rejecting early interpersonal relationships. I will frequently go through the *DSM* criteria with these patients as a way of letting them know that they are not alone, and that others are grappling with the same difficulties they have.

Depressive

The depressive is *pessimistic* about all life events. The past is seen as a failure, and little that is adaptive or positive can be gleaned. Current situations are seen as hopeless in opposition to a helpless and overburdened personality. The future is rarely an issue. Automatic thoughts go immediately to the negative and the worst possible outcome of any situation. Interpersonal interactions are self-fulfillingly punishing. Attributions are always internalized and blaming. With little behavioral activity the chance for positive experience is minimal and the opportunity to test alternatives is diminished. The vicious cycle of limited action and increasingly bleak cognition moves quickly.

The cognitive treatment of this patient is more difficult than the cognitive treatment of a patient with a major depression. In the patient with a major depression there is a good chance that the underlying character structure includes elements that can be drawn upon. These elements might include the naiveté of the dependent or the social activity desire of the histrionic. In the depressive personality, little is available upon which to leverage therapy. The basics of cognitive (and behavior) therapy are still used, but with a more limited expectation. Whether activities are assigned or automatic thought logs are used, it will take much longer for the patients to benefit from these due to the characterlogical level of the cognitive disturbance.

Dependent

Cognitively the dependent is *naive* and seen as easily persuaded and gullible. These patients tend to view things in only positive terms, even events that others would consider significantly adverse or unpleasant. This cognitive naiveté of the patients may be used as a way of preventing estrangement in interpersonal relationships. Dependent patients frequently see themselves as inadequate and unable to deal with life's challenges without others. Thus, to smooth over potential difficulties with others, it may be that this cognitive style prevents unpleasant circumstances from arising in interpersonal relationships. It is as if dependent personality patients have decided they cannot handle the vicissitudes of life and thus must attach themselves to others in order to make it through a difficult and frightening world. They therefore attempt to find someone who will help them through life and protect them and also nurture them. As a consequence, they may subordinate their own will to that of others; it is in this situation that being cognitively naive may prove functional in a nonfunctional way.

The therapist must be careful not to fall into the trap of becoming just another individual upon whom the patients become dependent. Initially, the therapeutic work may engender some dependence on the patients' part, but the therapist must continually and gradually work to wean the patients from this dependency. The patients must continually be encouraged through the therapeutic process to perform homework assignments and present their own therapeutic agendas.

Histrionic

The cognitive style of histrionic patients is *flighty* and involves the avoidance of introspective thought. These patients are consumed with attention to superficialities in their environment and place little emphasis on their own internal life. Their total valuation is frequently invested in their appearance and the elicitation of external approval. Because they tend to focus so little on their internal life, they frequently have no sense of who they are apart from their identification with others. In some ways they may be seen as being incapable of focused cognitions, as well as lacking attention to details and specifics in their learning style. Most histrionics have memories that are diffuse and general with a tremendous lack of specificity in detail. Thus, their cognitive styles are vague and rather ambiguous and as a consequence often lead to emotional states that are undifferentiated and ambiguous as well (Shapiro, 1965).

Characteristic cognitive distortions seen in the histrionic personality as outlined by Beck and associates (1990) include an increased susceptibility to dichotomous thinking, in which patients will jump from one extreme conclusion to another. Thus, one acquaintance may be seen as wonderful after a brief introductory period, and another would be seen as quite negative after a short period of time. Additionally, these patients are subject to a distortion in their emotional reasoning in that they accept their emotions as evidence of truth rather than as simply their current emotional state. Because they feel it, it must be true.

Specific cognitive and behavioral therapy techniques should include the following strategies with these patients. First of all, because these patients have diffuse and scattered thought processes, it is important to teach them thought monitoring through such devices as keeping a dysfunctional thought record. This recording of thoughts can be useful in helping the patients become more specific in their cognitions, as well as identifying problematic cognitive distortions. These cognitive distortions can then be challenged through reality testing.

Narcissistic

The cognitive style of narcissists is characterized by an *expansiveness* of thought, with unbridled fantasies of success and achievement. These individuals are not constrained by objective reality, and they may lie to preserve their own feelings of self-esteem. Fantasy is very common with these individuals and may be a principal focus and preoccupation.

As one of my patients aptly put it, "Rules are for fools." This captures the quintessential attitude of narcissists toward the rules of society. In general, they feel that they should be exempted from these constraints. These patients are frequently found inspecting their therapist's credentials to ascertain if the therapist can handle such a "special patient." The therapist may be either overidealized or undervalued, and these patients may insult and attempt to manipulate the therapist.

The initial goal of therapy with these patients in the context of their cognitive style is to establish a cooperative relationship so that the therapist can teach them the cognitive model and approach to dealing with their problems. It is frequently difficult to establish a therapeutic rapport with these patients because of their tendency to not only question the therapist's credentials but also to compete with the therapist.

Inculcating the benefits of being a team player can be very beneficial as a way of decreasing these patients' drive for superiority. Therapy must address three characteristics of the narcissist: lack of empathy for others, hypersensitivity to any evaluative process, and overall feeling of grandiosity. In addition, because their cognitive style is frequently characterized by distortions of objective reality, it is important that these patients begin to develop skills in seeking accurate feedback from others, as well as learning how to accept such feedback when it is less than glowing. This ability to receive feedback is linked to decreasing the patients' grandiosity and increasing their empathy with others so as to engage in truly interactional dialogues with significant persons in their lives.

The shifting of automatic thoughts from an "I" focus to a focus on others can be enhanced by role playing and other similar therapeutic devices. This will help the patients realize that frequently other people are reacting to influences other than the patients (Beck et al., 1990).

Antisocial

Cognitive styles of antisocial patients can be characterized as *deviant* in that they prey upon others with little regard for anyone's welfare but their own. These patients usually present with a central schema that they are always right, and thus they have little motivation to question their cognitions. These cognitions are characterized by beliefs that are self-serving, untrusting of others, and predatory. These patients generally believe that future consequences will not result from current antisocial behaviors. Beck and associates (1990) delineate six self-serving beliefs that guide the behaviors of these patients:

1. My actions are justified by my desire to acquire or to avoid something.
2. My thoughts and feelings are completely valid because I have experienced them.
3. My choices are always correct.
4. I am right because I feel that way.
5. I don't take into consideration the views of others unless they directly control my immediate consequences.
6. Undesirable reactions to my behaviors and subsequent consequences either will not matter to me or will not occur.

Therapeutic strategies may include what has been termed a *choice-review exercise,* in which problems are outlined by the patients and then the advantages and disadvantages of various choices are delineated with these rated as to their desirability to the patients. This is one way of laying out, not only the patients' power in choosing various behaviors, but also the benefits that can accrue to them from choosing more adaptive behaviors that are also, at the same time, socially acceptable. In addition, this process teaches social empathy in that patients can begin to see how their choice of behaviors can result in various reactions from significant others. They might also begin to see that greater reciprocity with others can accrue benefits to them more in line with their desired goals. In my experience clinically I haven't attempted not so much to cure antisocial personality patients as to redirect their energy into more socially acceptable patterns. This is congruent with the idea of converting the "bad sociopath" to the "good sociopath." The good sociopath still has some of the same motivations as the bad sociopath but applies these drives in more socially acceptable ways.

Sadistic

The cognitive style of sadistic individuals is *dogmatic* and authoritarian. They hold strong opinions and are close-minded in their cognitive interactions. Behaviors that abuse, dominate, or control others are frequently engaged in. These individuals prefer pain as their way to relate to others.

The therapist must be cautious in dealing with this personality in that he or she may develop countertransferences, ranging from moralistic judgments to revulsion. The therapist would be wise to excuse himself or herself from a case if severe countertransferences arise. With regard to treatment strategies with these patients, much of what has been discussed for the antisocial personality disorder may be applied to these individuals as well. Because these individuals are frequently not likely to seek therapy voluntarily, they are more likely to be seen once they have been institutionalized or court-ordered into therapy. One carrot in therapy is helping the patients recognize how respecting the boundaries of others can be helpful to them. Thus, their psychopathology can be utilized in the service of the therapeutic process. In addition, developing greater empathy for others is a long-term therapy goal with these patients.

Compulsive

Compulsive patients construct a reality that is quite *constricted* and ruled by schedules and various hierarchical constructs. The new or novel situation is feared by these patients, so they avoid innovations in their lives. Co-morbid diagnoses for these patients include obsessive-compulsive disorder; affective disorders; phobic disorders; anxiety disorders; and, quite often, somatoform or psychosomatic disorders. Patients who somatize their life stresses frequently have significant obsessive-compulsive personality traits.

Establishing a therapeutic relationship with these patients can be quite difficult for many therapists. These patients present in a businesslike manner and are quite constricted affectively in their approach to the therapist. Initially this constrictive affective presentation should be respected, with therapy presented as something that may help the patients be more efficient and effective in their lives. The therapist must be careful not to become frustrated with these patients because they are focused on details and not able to note the nuances of interpersonal relationships.

Therapy needs to address the cognitive distortions that are so characteristic of this disorder. That is, these patients frequently see the world as black and white, with a need to avoid mistakes and imperfections. Frequently they think that being perfect is a realistic goal. I frequently approach these patients by encouraging them to see the implausibility of perfection as a goal in life. This strategy, of course, takes some time and is based on developing a trusting therapeutic relationship. One must be careful not to ask these patients to give up their compulsive lifestyles totally. The basic concept is that, with some modifications, these patients can live more functional personal lives and, perhaps, more productive work lives.

Negativistic

Cognitively these patients are characterized as *skeptical* in their cognitions in that they are untrusting and cynical in their approach to life. Positive life events are seen as inconsistent with their cognitive schemata. Thus, they constantly look for the vicissitudes of life to follow any good fortune they may have.

Typical automatic thoughts exhibited by negativistic patients include: "Things just don't work out for me in life," "I am taken advantage of by other individuals," "I'll do things my way," "I never get the credit I deserve for the good things I do in life," and "How dare they tell me how to perform a specific task." These patients live a life governed by unrealistic "shoulds" that are aimed at maintaining autonomy and are not goal-directed (Beck et al., 1990). It can easily be seen how the automatic thoughts of this patient population can interfere with work and social functioning. These patients fail to see the contribution of their behavioral and cognitive style to their life difficulties. Usually they blame others for their problems and do not accept any responsibility for themselves. This makes it particularly difficult to change behaviors in these patients.

The first step in the therapeutic process is to develop and engage in collaborative empiricism. It should be made clear to them that they are not being manipulated by their therapist and that they have the ability to make active choices through the therapy process. A decrease in their passive responses to life's problems and a need to be actively involved in their solutions are focuses that might be helpful for these patients.

Automatic thoughts or assumptions that these patients have can be tested as hypotheses with an experimental methodology. A record of their dysfunctional thoughts might be useful in this arena not only to identify automatic thoughts that have a negative consequence for them, but also to explore the realistic basis of such thoughts.

Self-Defeating

The cognitive style of these patients is characterized by *diffident* processes with a reluctance to interpret events as positive. Self-defeating individuals also experience a continual contrast in their emotions and thinking toward themselves and significant others.

Countertransference experienced with these patients includes (most frequently) the evocation of a protective parent and/or an attempt to save these patients from troublesome life events. In addition, these patients may elicit sadistic cognitions or affects in treating clinicians. It is important not to act on any of these countertransferences with these patients so as not to perpetuate previous dysfunctional patterns.

In dealing with these patients initially, it is vitally important to establish a collaborative, supportive therapeutic relationship. These patients will have a tendency to see the therapist as all-powerful and all-good, and thus they give much of their power away. Although some dependency is necessary in the early part of the therapeutic relationship, care must be taken to encourage the patients to see that they have strengths and competencies, as well. Often it is valuable to explore with the patients the vicious relationship circles in which they get involved. Frequently this cycle of exploitive relationships, where none of their needs get met, can be explicated and reified. Also, identifying automatic thoughts and their emotional sequelae may help these patients identify their inconsistency in cognitive processes.

Finally, encouraging these patients not to see themselves as victims, but as competent individuals who are capable of accomplishing much in life is a long-term goal in the therapy process. The key to therapy with these patients is the identification of vicious circles in which they engage, the reasons for these vicious circles, their interpersonal consequences, and cognitive and behavioral strategies that can address and remediate them.

Schizotypal

Schizotypal patients are characterized by bizarre, *autistic* ideation and significantly impaired social interactions. Their thinking is often paranoid and may contain magical thinking, as well as ideas of reference. Their speech may be odd and contain elements of circumstantiality and vagueness. Usually these patients are extremely isolated from their social milieu.

Because of the autistic nature of their cognitive style, it is important to emphasize initially the establishment of a sound psychotherapeutic relationship. This relationship can serve as the basis for reality testing for the patients because their lack of social interactions can result in losing contact with reality. Because of the disjointed nature of these patients' cognitions, it is important to structure therapy in a way that they can experience the successful achievement of at least one goal during the session. This will also help contain the patients' tendency to drift from one cognition to another in a tangential manner.

Bizarre cognitions can be treated as just another symptom that is the focus of therapy. Patients can be taught to respond rationally to bizarre ideations rather than in an emotionally or behaviorally inappropriate fashion. In addition, patients can be taught to disregard these cognitions. As an example, a patient who believed that a bomb was planted in her car and that it would explode if she started it was encouraged to examine her engine for objective evidence of such a device. After a number of times of examining the engine, this patient was able to disregard these cognitions by acknowledging that even though she had this belief, it didn't mean that it was a realistic fear.

Borderline

The cognitive style of the borderline personality is characterized by *capricious* thinking as well as antithetical perceptions or thoughts regarding current life situations. A common distortion that they experience in their thinking is described by Beck (1976) as dichotomous thinking. This is a tendency to evaluate experiences as either good or bad, successful or unsuccessful, et cetera. These individuals force rather extreme evaluations of life events as a consequence of their dichotomous thinking. The result is that their cognitive view leads to extreme emotional responses and actions because of their extreme evaluations of their current life situations or interpersonal relationships. In addition, these individuals frequently vacillate between a desire for intimacy and dependence and a fear of that situation. This makes them vacillate in their relationships with others between those two extremes. They frequently view the world as a dangerous and hostile environment. If they become dependent on others, they are at others' mercies.

Goals for working with these patients include the initial establishment of a therapeutic relationship. This can be difficult in that these patients can elicit countertransferences from therapists ranging from rejection to extreme rage. Also, these patients are prone to getting involved in power struggles with therapists over therapy agendas. It is important that the therapist understand that the countertransferences are normal responses to working with these kinds of patients. Once the hurdles of establishing a therapeutic relationship are overcome, areas for therapeutic intervention include the following. It is important to address the issue of dichotomous thinking, in that this cognitive distortion causes considerable difficulty in the lives of these individuals and their emotional responses. Being able to see life experiences more as shades of gray, as opposed to black and white, is essential for reality testing and improved emotional functioning.

Paranoid

The cognitive style of paranoid patients is characterized as *suspicious* and mistrustful of the motives of others. These patients often misconstrue environmental cues and see hidden meaning or conspiratorial intent in these occurrences. In addition, these patients have a strong tendency to cast blame on others when they experience interpersonal difficulties. They frequently fail to recognize their own contribution to these problems. Because of these patients' heightened levels of suspiciousness, they are likely not to divulge their thoughts to others; they will not enter the consultation room admitting to their suspiciousness. Frequently the ideation will become apparent when the therapist talks to significant others (including a spouse or partner) or after a therapeutic relationship is established with a patient.

The initial phase of treatment with these patients should focus on two basic strategies. First, do not challenge these individuals' central mistrust as being irrational. That is clearly a prescription for failure with this type of patients. Second, prove one's trustworthiness to these patients. Again, this is not accomplished by convincing the patients rationally that one is trustworthy, but by demonstrating that trait in a consistent relationship that is open and honest. It must be kept in mind that therapy is very stressful to these patients because of the problems they have with self-disclosure and openness. Hence, it must proceed at a judicious pace. Strategies that are normally undertaken must be carefully pursued so as not to threaten these patients.

A focus on the presenting complaint with these individuals will in most cases bring out the paranoid cognitive style that is disruptive to their interpersonal relationships. One must be careful, however, not to focus too much on this style initially, but rather to take nonthreatening behavioral and cognitive approaches. Gradually the patients may gain insight into their paranoid cognitions and self-fulfilling prophecies. Thus, the assumptions that other people are "out to get them" or are untrustworthy can be challenged and reworked with standard cognitive therapy techniques.

CASE STUDY

This patient (RS) presented to the author with a chief complaint of chronic headaches. She is a 20-year-old female who is a sophomore in college. Her father referred her to me because he was concerned about her problem with chronic headaches and hadn't been able to get help for her through standard medical and neurological assessments and interventions. She presented as a bright and very articulate young lady, who felt the only difficulty she was having was her headaches. Her mental status was well within normal limits. She already had had a thorough neurological workup that was negative for neurological etiology.

History

Her history revealed some indications of long-standing problems with depression, as well as issues related to abandonment by boyfriends. Before her most recent bout with headaches she had broken up with her boyfriend with whom she had lived while away at college. Currently she was living at home and spent many hours a day in bed asleep, generally avoiding social contacts. She did, however, maintain a B+ average at a local university. After an extensive history was taken, she revealed that she had been sexually assaulted while on a date in high school. Finally, she had a history of self-mutilation during periods of dysphoric moods.

MCMI-III

An analysis of her clinical syndrome scales indicates significant elevations on the Dysthymia and Anxiety scales. Additionally, there is a suggestive elevation on the Major Depression scale in the Severe Clinical Syndrome group of scales. These elevations certainly suggest an individual with significant problems with depression. In addition, she is evidencing clinical signs of a generalized anxiety disorder and appears somewhat agitated and apprehensive. Further, she reports physical discomforts such as headaches, gastrointestinal symptoms, fatigue, and insomnia. These are all consistent with her clinical presentation.

With regard to current personality functioning, this patient's profile is indicative of a mixed personality disorder with narcissistic, negativistic, and prominent borderline personality traits. These features are consistent with her clinical presentation as well as her past history of self-mutilation. Frequently borderline patients self-mutilate as a way of terminating extremely agitated and anxious states. In addition, patients with borderline personality traits frequently have problems with chronic pain syndromes. This patient's chronic headaches likely serve a variety of psychodynamic functions, such as distracting her attention from recent feelings of loss and emptiness, especially over matters of attractiveness. Thus, her bodily preoccupations may be a compensatory form of self-ministering, and her physical symptoms may also be useful in regaining the attention of significant others. Her headaches may also symbolically be a form of self-mutilation and rage turned inward.

This patient's MCMI-III results certainly indicate that initial treatment of her depressive disorder is warranted in that it is possibly playing a significant role in the etiology of her chronic headaches. Treatment with an antidepressant medication would probably be indicated in that this patient needs to be stabilized as quickly as possible. The beneficial effects of an antidepressant medication might also diminish the severity of her personality disorder. Often, once the Axis I diagnosis is adequately treated, personality-disordered patients experience some remission from the severity of their Axis II symptoms.

Finally, if the patient is able to be involved in a psychotherapeutic rela-

TABLE 5-2 Case Study MCMI

MCMI-III Inventory		Base Rate
	Validity	0
X	Disclosure	89**
Y	Desirability	75
Z	Debasement	85
1	Schizoid	10
2A	Avoidant	68
2B	Depressive	87**
3	Dependent	62
4	Histrionic	90**
5	Narcissistic	115***
6A	Antisocial	92**
6B	Aggressive (Sadistic)	84*
7	Compulsive	62
8A	Negativistic	115***
8B	Self-Defeating	86**
S	Schizotypal	64
C	Borderline	95***
P	Paranoid	78*
A	Anxiety	95***
H	Somatoform	76*
N	Bipolar: Manic	84*
D	Dysthymia	101***
B	Alcohol Dependence	57
T	Drug Dependence	69
PT	PTSD	68
SS	Thought Disorder	57
CC	Major Depression	77*
PP	Delusional Disorder	67

*BR 75–84
**BR 85–94
***BR 95 and above

tionship (and this might be difficult because of her significant personality traits), much effort will initially need to be expended in establishing rapport with her. Her self-confidence may be restored by allowing her to recall and relive her past achievements and successes. An important goal will then be to guide her in sensitivity to the needs of others and acceptance of the constraints and responsibilities of shared social living. This will involve strengthening this patient's ability to face her shortcomings frankly. Changing attitudes toward herself and others may be best initiated through procedures of cognitive reorientation. In addition, keeping track of her automatic thoughts and challenging these, especially as they relate to abandonment issues, is another significant therapeutic intervention.

Treatment Course

RS was initially treated with an antidepressant medication, and within 4 weeks she had a significant decrease in the frequency and severity of her chronic headaches. These headaches went from a severity of 9.5 and occurring on a daily basis to occurring approximately once every 2 weeks with a severity of 5.5 on a 10-point scale. As was predicted, as her depression resolved, her personality-disorder symptoms became less prominent. She became more social, and her naturally buoyant self-confidence returned. She discontinued therapy at the point that her self-confidence returned. She was seen a total of six times before discontinuing. From what can be gathered by contact with the family, this patient continues to function well on prophylactic dosages of antidepressant medication. No further psychological intervention has been sought by this patient.

Summary

The cognitive therapist hoping to develop a collaborative empiricism with patients will do well to look to the MCMI-III in order to differentiate the cognitive styles of the various personality disorders. These styles include cognitions, attitudes, beliefs, affects, and automatic thoughts. Certain styles can be expected in certain personality disorders, and cognitive interventions can be better tailored given this framework. Further, an understanding of the underlying personality and cognitive styles allows for more focused treatment of the Axis I disorders. This chapter has suggested the foundation for this type of cognitive analysis and treatment specificity.

References

Adler, A. (1931). *What life should mean to you*. New York: Blue Ribbon Books.
Beck, A. T. (1973). *The diagnosis and management of depression*. Philadelphia: University of Pennsylvania Press.
Beck, A. T. (1976). *Cognitive therapy and the emotional disorders*. New York: International Universities Press.
Beck, A. T., & Greenburg, R. L. (1974). *Coping with depression (a booklet)*. New York: Institute for Rational Living.

Beck, A. T., Rush, A. J., Shaw, B. F., & Emery, G. (1979). *Cognitive therapy of depression.* New York: Guilford Press.

Beck, A. T., Freeman, A., & Associates. (1990). *Cognitive therapy of personality disorders.* New York: Guilford Press.

Freud, S. (1953). *The standard edition of the complete psychological works of Sigmund Freud* (vol. 5). London: Hogarth Press and the Institute of Psychoanalysis.

Millon, T. (1981). *Disorders of personality: DSM-III, Axis II.* New York: Wiley.

Millon, T. (1990). *Toward a new personology: An evolutionary model.* New York: Wiley.

Shapiro, D. (1965). *Neurotic styles.* New York: Basic Books.

6

Object Relations Theory and the MCMI-III

ERIC J. VAN DENBURG

The average psychologist who seeks to understand object relations theory will discover a dizzying array of concepts. Not only is the language arcane and esoteric, but the concepts are often internally inconsistent. One will be even more confused without a background in psychodynamic theory. This chapter will discuss object relations concepts, integrate them with Millon's personality theory, offer psychotherapy suggestions, and provide case material, including MCMI-III indications.

It must be stressed that there is no *one* object relations theory. Many theorists fall under this umbrella, but their theories of development and psychopathology are quite divergent. There is controversy about whether certain psychodynamic theorists (e.g., Sullivan and Kohut) should be seen as object relations theorists or as independent and distinct. There are recent attempts to bridge object relations theory, Sullivan's work, and self-psychology (Bacal & Newman, 1990). This chapter will cover Kohut and Sullivan, following Greenberg and Mitchell (1983) and including these theorists within the object relations school.

The psychoanalytic meaning of the word *object* needs clarification. Hinsie and Campbell's standard psychiatric dictionary (1960) cites Freud's definition:

"From the instinctual point of view, the *object* of an instinct is that in or through which it can achieve its aim" (Freud, 1915). LaPlanche and Pointalis (1973), in their well-respected dictionary of psychoanalysis, note that

> "Object" is understood here in a sense comparable to the one it has in the literary or archaic "the object of my passion, of my hatred, etc'. It does not imply, as it does ordinarily, the idea of a "thing", of an inanimate and manipulable object as opposed to an animate being or person." (p. 273)

It is useful to review other commonly used psychoanalytic terms containing the term object: these include *object permanence, object constancy,* and *transitional object*. Object permanence is a Piagetian concept of cognition, referring to the retention of a mental representation of a physical object in its absence. Once object permanence is in place, in the 16th to 18th month of life, children can begin the process of achieving object constancy, which refers to the capacity to retain a benign, stable image of a primary caretaker in their absence. A transitional object (Winnicott, 1953) is a physical object that the child uses and treats as an extension of caretakers when they are absent. A favored blanket or teddy bear might serve such a function.

The term *object representation* is a hypothetical construct, conveying the concept that relationships with others (objects) in reality or fantasy produce a mental picture (representation), composed of memories, affects, and meanings. It is presumed that the earliest experiences with caretakers are salient and lay the foundation on which subsequent experiences with people are built. These representations become organized over time, possibly split into "good" (gratifying) or "bad" (punishing) representations, and form a person's enduring modes of perceiving others, fantasizing about them, and ultimately relating to them. An object relations theory must come to terms with the development of these representations, their interplay, influence on fantasy and behavior, and probable manifestations in psychotherapy.

Object Relations Theory

Historical Development

Object relations theory has a long history. Freud was conscious of the need for understanding the development and organization of people's relations with one another. As Greenberg and Mitchell (1983) point out, however, in classical Freudian theory, relations with others are secondary in importance to the development of pathways for discharge of sexual and aggressive drives. That is, the purpose of the object in early relationships is simply to serve as a conduit or container for the gratification of drives. Pushing the theory to its logical extreme, Freud views the human as a drive-discharging organism who seeks out others primarily for hedonic needs. At its most basic form, in the oral stage of development, the child already needs and wants the breast for more than simply nourishment: "Sucking at the mother's breast is the starting-point of the whole of sexual life, the unmatched prototype of every later sexual satisfaction, to which fantasy often enough recurs in times of need. This sucking involves making the mother's breast the first object of the sexual instinct" (Freud, 1917, p. 314).

Melanie Klein is viewed by several authors as a seminal figure in object relations theory (Greenberg & Mitchell, 1983; Guntrip, 1973; Hamilton, 1989). She took the position that people are object-related from birth. She states: "The analysis of very young children has taught me that there is no instinctual urge, no anxiety situation, no mental process which does not involve objects, external or internal; in other words, object relations are at the centre of emotional life" (Klein, 1951). In this author's opinion, however, the actual qualities of caretakers are less important in her view than the innate developmental unfolding of the child's instinct-driven fantasies. What Klein emphasizes is the inherent and early process of projection and reintrojection of impulses and fantasies "into" and "back from" the object.

Other more contemporary Kleinians, however, put more emphasis on the actual qualities of the social environment, including the mother (Bion, 1962; Grinberg, Sor, & Tabak de Bianchedi, 1977; Racker, 1968). These theorists posit that it is the parent's job to help the infant manage affective experience and persecutory anxiety. By the parent serving as a "container" of intense feelings, boundaries are established, the child feels loved, and the capacity for frustration tolerance and self-soothing is internalized. While the processes of projection, introjection, and projective identification remain as important as they did for Klein, *how* the projections are processed is more significant. Kleinian concepts have vast implications for psychotherapy. The way the therapist processes and feeds back projections and interactions with the patient is vital; countertransference examination is essential, so that interpretations to the patient are not too colored by the therapist's own neurosis or therapeutic "ambitions" (Racker, 1968).

It is often written (Guntrip, 1973; Greenberg & Mitchell, 1983) that Fairbairn is the first pure object relations theorist. Minimizing drive theory, he focused on the formation and structure of the ego through experiences with others in the child's world. He developed his theory outside of the British psychoanalytic orthodoxy. Being in Edinburgh, Scotland, he was isolated, able to develop his own model and free himself of the political battles between Melanie Klein and Anna Freud in England. Fairbairn focuses on the ego, energies of the ego, conscious and unconscious parts of the ego, and objects linked to the ego. First, he postulates the presence of what he calls the central ego, which is partly conscious and partly unconscious. Along with the split in the central ego, which occurs early in life, there is a splitting of unconscious ego parts into: (1) the libidinal ego, linked to what Fairbairn calls the "needed or exciting object" (Fairbairn, 1952, p. 111) and (2) the anti-libidinal ego (or internal saboteur), linked with the "frustrating or rejecting object" (p. 111). "Psychopathology and characterological phenomena of all kinds [can be seen] in terms of the patterns assumed by a complex of relationships [within a] variety of structures" (p. 129).

Highly influential, and suited to the pragmatism of the American spirit, Harry Stack Sullivan was a primary proponent of the relational, interpersonal model (Greenberg & Mitchell, 1983; Sullivan, 1953). Sullivan was hesitant to reify his concepts, suspicious of speculations about intrapsychic mechanisms, and thus never presented a systematized theory of the mind. Interested particularly in anxiety and its influence on the formation of the self-system, Sullivan had a developmental model that went beyond the Oedipal period into the "juvenile era," adolescence, and young adulthood. Sullivan urged the examination of gradients of anxiety and actual relations between people. His bluntness and style are revealed when he stated:

> I think that a grasp of the concept of anxiety—and seeing where it fits into the development of a person's living—will save a great deal of psychiatric effort if one is a therapist, and prevent a great many commonplace stupidities if one chooses to use psychiatry in other ways. (Sullivan, 1953, p. 12)

The work of D. W. Winnicott from Great Britain is clinically evocative, although not as systematized as other object relations theories. Originally a pediatrician, Winnicott was exquisitely sensitive to the way patients' issues affected and were affected by the therapist's manner and technique. His famous statement that "there is no such thing as an infant . . . whenever one finds an infant one finds maternal care, and without maternal care there would be no infant" (Winnicott, 1965) underscored his insistence on the importance of the environment in forming the child's early psyche. Another of his concepts that has been widely applied is the "holding environment." This refers to the verbal and nonverbal features of the caretaker and social context that help the child with containment and "holding" of affects and experience. A final influential concept is that of the "true" and "false" self (Winnicott, 1965). The false self is seen as a complex personality structure formed to meet the needs of the other self, thus gaining some measure of nurturance. Meanwhile, the true, actual needs of the person are split off, hidden from view, and felt to be shameful and flawed.

Current Thoughts

Contemporary object relations theory has built on early work by Freud, Klein, and Winnicott. The newer viewpoints are informed by child development work, infant observation, and the burgeoning concepts of splitting, borderline psychopathology, and narcissism.

Margaret Mahler (Mahler, Pine, & Bergman, 1975) has been very influential with her developmental model of infancy and early childhood. Originally from Vienna, and like Winnicott a pediatrician, she emigrated to the United States in the 1930s, began studying child development, and then extrapolated her findings to the treatment of adults (Mahler, 1971). Her by now well-known developmental stage model (Mahler, 1968) begins with "normal autism," or a brief objectless state, then moves to "symbiosis," where the object and self are fused. The next phase is known as "differentiation," where the child psychologically "hatches" and begins to search beyond the mother-child unit. The stage of "practicing" follows, a period after the first year associated with glee in extending the self outside the maternal orbit through increased locomotion. The final stage is called "rapprochement," a period of increased sense of vulnerability coupled with continued development of independence.

Through a series of books and articles, Otto Kernberg has synthesized ego psychology and object relations theory to form a comprehensive model (Kernberg, 1966, 1976, 1984). Central to his theory is the process of splitting, which was spoken of frequently by Klein, and briefly by Freud. Although controversial (Marmar & Horowitz, 1986; Pruyser, 1975), splitting is usually viewed both as a defense, relieving persecutory anxiety and protecting good internal objects, and as a method of ego development. Taking Kernberg's perspective, the ego develops through splitting and internalization of object relations. Experience with caretakers leads to the formation of the ego and how others are viewed. If experiences are primarily negative, there is a proliferation of "bad internal objects," composed of a fused negative self-experience and a negative experience of the other. The fusion is due to the lack of differentiation of the self and other. The obverse is true with positive experiences.

James Masterson and Donald Rinsley (Masterson, 1981; Masterson & Rinsley, 1975; Rinsley, 1977), much influenced by Kernberg, provide a schematic to understand splitting and object relations theory. They coined the acronyms *RORUs* and *WORUs*, *rewarding object relation units* and *withdrawing object relation units*, respectively, to help understand interpersonal internalizations, structural formation, and behavior. These theorists posit that many children are rewarded for clinging and dependency, leading to structural formation of a needy, dependent self who must comply and accommodate to gain the nurturance and protection of the stronger, dominant other. The WORU, in contrast, is composed of an independent but neglected self, linked with a disinterested or even punitive other. The self-object linkages are split off from one another, leading to mutually exclusive ego states. These intrapsychic "units" are presumed to oscillate back and forth as conflictual situations arise.

Stern (1985) and Christopher, Bickhard and Lambeth (1992) criticize the notion of splitting as Kernberg, Masterson, and Rinsley present it. Stern questions whether split ego experiences are truly as impenetrable and walled off as Kernberg claims. He cites experimental evidence pertaining to memory consolidation in varying affective (e.g., manic and depressive) states that contradicts Kernberg's assumptions. Christopher and his colleagues call Kernberg to task for the apparent illogic of his affective valence metaphors, internal contradictions, and "reification of clinical observation into explanatory concepts." (p. 485). They call, instead, for the simpler concept that an "extreme emotional state contains the seeds of its own change." (p. 485). The instability of the emotional extremes is inherent in the nature of the process; in short, a feedback mechanism ensures that there will be swings from extremes to balance the affective system. They give the example that marked idealization, with its built-in distorted extremes of hope, cannot but lead to eventual failure of expectations and disillusionment.

As the author of this chapter views splitting as central to the application of object relations theory, a clinical example will be offered to illuminate the phenomenon. Ms. R. was a 19-year-old woman hospitalized on an eating disorders unit for severe bulimia and seen by the author in individual treatment four times a week. The patients on this unit were on a "level" system in which they had to meet requirements pertaining to ward activity and eating behavior before moving to the next level. Ms. R., while polite and superficially cooperative, pushed for greater privileges at an increasing rate. While her personality diagnosis was in question initially, the following interchange helped elucidate her core dynamics and object representations.

After careful consideration by her treatment team, a decision was made to *not* honor the patient's request for greater privileges and, instead, to "hold her" to her prior week's level. It was the function of the primary therapist (the author) to convey this information to her. The session began with her sweetly and demurely inquiring about what the team had decided. Immediately after being told, she began raging at the therapist, swearing loudly and voicing feelings and concerns that she had never expressed prior to this intervention. "You never cared about me! I will never trust you or anybody again!" She sobbed fitfully, screamed ever louder, and left the interview room, slamming the door with a flourish. A maintenance worker on the unit vacuuming the carpet in the milieu area saw the patient run from the door and made some modest inquiry as to her well-being. With a vengeance the patient turned her wrath on this worker, screamed with an ever-greater ferocity, and ran into her room, slamming the door behind her.

How can we understand this clinical vignette? First, it is apparent that there was a part of Ms. R. that wanted distance from the treatment team, so that she could leave the protected confines of the unit. She sought to continue the long-standing self-object linkage of an independent, but ultimately false, self and a disinterested, neglecting other. When we refused to cooperate in this dynamic and insisted that she remain and be dependent on our aid, she grew enraged. The philosophy of the program was that she needed to be dependent in a new way, not in a clinging manner, but still protected from the dangers of premature flight into pseudo-independence. Our protection and concern were felt by her to be enslavement to a controlling other, who would expose her underlying dependencies and longings. Thus, she sought to break loose from this experience through destructive rage.

The final object relations theorist discussed will be Heinz Kohut, of Chicago, initially an orthodox, classical analyst. He had several experiences with patients, however, that led him to doubt the traditional analytic understanding of psychological problems being caused by Oedipal conflicts over sexuality and aggression. Kohut came to believe that many of his patients were expressing a new form of transference that had been misunderstood. He developed the concepts of mirror transference and idealizing transference, to capture the notions that many patients need either a nonintrusive acceptance of their needs for reflection and acceptance or the opportunity to view the therapist as flawless and heroic. Rather than prematurely interpreting these transferences as defenses against the emergence of Oedipal material, Kohut allowed such manifestations to develop. He felt this was necessary to allow self development to resume. A primary tool for the therapist in Kohut's model was the provision of nonjudgmental, experience-near empathy. His position was that therapeutic impasses and difficulties were often a function of disruptions in the empathic bond that developed between therapist and patient. An adequate empathic bond would lead to a "selfobject" tie, or new form of dependency on the therapist. We all need these selfobject connections throughout our life, said Kohut, questioning the notion of separation and autonomy from others. While his views are controversial, and some find him difficult to understand, his accumulated writings have been very important and widely cited (Kohut, 1971, 1977, 1984).

Theoretical Commonalities

The previous section reflects the multiplicity of viewpoints in object relations theory. However, certain common ideas in the theorists' works, seem to exist, although they may not be clearly articulated. All the theorists discussed postulate the importance of early experiences with caretakers in forming underlying views of others in the present. These experiences seem to form internal structures, or at least "dynamisms" (Sullivan, 1953). All seem to believe that many of these experiences are not consciously recalled, but instead influence fantasy or behavior via unconscious means. Finally, all assume that these experiences will no doubt influence psychotherapy. However, as a clinical psychologist steeped in the Boulder tradition, one becomes eager to see if such concepts can be researched and tested, rather than simply speculated about. It is unclear how readily this theory can be investigated empirically, although researchers have made attempts to quantify object representations through clinical interviews, scales, or projective assessment techniques (Azim et al., 1991; Bell, Billington, & Becker, 1986; Blatt et al., 1976). There have also been attempts to apply these concepts to objective personality testing, including the MCMI and MMPI (Hibbard, 1989; Trimboli & Kilgore, 1983). Due to the dearth of accurate data, attempts to combine object relations theory and Millon results into treatment planning remain at the exploratory level (Millon, 1990). Nonetheless, this chapter will make such an attempt, using what empirical research exists.

Object Relations and Millon's Personality Domains

In Millon's schema the object representations of a given patient fall within the phenomenological level of clinical analysis (Millon, 1990). He views the phenomenological level as one of four traditional methods of organizing clinical data, a simple definition of phenomenology being "the study of phenomena or events as they occur immediately in experience without interpretation" (Chaplin, 1975, p. 384).

To extrapolate from this definition and Millon's premises, people consciously and immediately experience others in consistent ways. The clinical understanding of object representations would rely on the reports of these experiences. We then make assumptions based on these reports of underlying object representations, formed by experiences with caretakers. Presumably, one could follow the same process in the use of objective psychological tests. For example, the patient consciously responds to a given item on the MCMI in a way consistent with others of a given personality style and symptomatic picture. We assume that there is lawfulness to how this style develops and becomes manifest in an adult. To take the example of a histrionic person, we assume that dramatic behavior and emotional responsiveness were attended to and underlined by early caretakers. To keep the love of the parent who enjoys such expressions, the emotionality and colorful mannerisms continue. When others are met later, the early expectations of what is responded to are brought to bear. For the histrionic person, people in the present are a potential audience that applaud the same lines and gestures as did the parents.

Object representations are presumed to possess structural, rather than simply functional attributes. By the term *structure* we imply an underlying consistency, organization, and stability across time. Salient memories of others ne's early life are encoded, then remain "solid" over the years, coloring life ces and relationships. Their apparent invariance, consistency, and resise to change leads to our legitimately calling them structural attributes of mind. In Millon's words, structural domains are "substrates and action ositions of a quasi-permanent nature" (Millon, 1990, p. 148). "Quasinanence," of course, leaves room for new experiences to alter underlying ctural attributes of object relationships. A course of psychotherapy would ach an experience. Differing personality styles are presumed by Millon to ess characteristic, distinct object representations (see Table 6-1).

The aggregation and coalescing of early experiences with others lead to a tant, lasting manner of taking in new experiences with people; others are ithin the original representational template. These structural representations, Millon adds, possess varying qualities and forms. For example, the object representations of the histrionic personality are described as "shallow," composed of "superficial and segregated affects, memories and conflicts" (Millon, 1990, p. 152), while the compulsive personality has "concealed" (p. 153) object representations, with limits to what such a person can tolerate consciously experiencing. It would be difficult, for example, for a proper, controlled accountant to allow himself to consciously experience his boss as a tyrant whom he would like to kill.

Intervention Techniques

In his 1990 book *Toward a New Personology,* Millon suggests that "methods of classical analysis or its more contemporary schools may be especially suited to the realm of 'object representations', as would the methods of Beck" (p. 170). This section will focus on dynamic approaches, although the interested reader is urged to peruse the cognitive-behavioral literature on treatment of personality disorders (Beck & Freeman, 1990), as well as refreshing attempts to integrate these seemingly disparate techniques (Westen, 1991).

While Millon provides no specific guidelines for altering structures within the object representation domain, he does mention that it is useful to focus one's therapeutic attempts on altering underlying polarities within a personality. These attempts would follow his overarching multipolar personality framework, consistent with Freud's (1915) construction of mental life. These personality polarities are activity-passivity, pleasure-pain, and self-other focus (Millon, 1986). Thus, those personality styles with an unbalanced polar structure would be helped by establishing a more adaptive, balanced equilibrium.

Extrapolating from multiple object relation models as presented in simplified form by Horner (1991), other therapy techniques are often used. Perhaps most important are transference interpretations. The theory follows classical Freudian assumptions of a continual reliving of past conflicts in the present. It is assumed that salient object representations will eventually appear

TABLE 6-1 Object Representations Domain

Schizoid Personality
Meager Objects (e.g., internalized representations are few in number and minimally articulated, largely devoid of the manifold percepts and memories of relationships with others, possessing little of the dynamic interplay among drives and conflicts that typify well-adjusted persons)

Avoidant Personality
Vexatious Objects (e.g., internalized representations are composed of readily reactivated, intense, and conflict-ridden memories of problematic early relations; limited avenues for experiencing or recalling gratification, and few mechanisms to channel needs, bind impulses, resolve conflicts, or deflect external stressors)

Depressive Personality
Forsaken Objects (e.g., internalized representations of the past appear jettisoned, as if life's early experiences have been depleted or devitalized, either drained of their richness and joyful elements, or withdrawn from memory, leaving one to feel abandoned, bereft, and discarded, cast off, and deserted).

Dependent Personality
Immature Objects (e.g., internalized representations are composed of infantile impressions of others, unsophisticated ideas, incomplete recollections, rudimentary drives, and childlike impulses, as well as minimal competencies to manage and resolve stressors).

Histrionic Personality
Shallow Objects (e.g., internalized representations are composed largely of superficial memories of past relations, random collections of transient and segregated affects and conflicts, as well as insubstantial drives and mechanisms)

Narcissistic Personality
Contrived Objects (e.g., internalized representations are composed far more than usual of illusory and changing memories of past relationships; unacceptable drives and conflicts are readily refashioned as the need arises, as are others often simulated and pretentious)

Antisocial Personality
Debased Objects (e.g., internalized representations comprise degraded and corrupt relationships that spur revengeful attitudes and restive impulses that are driven to subvert established cultural ideals and mores, as well as to devalue personal sentiments and to sully, but intensely covet, the material attainments of society denied them)

Sadistic (Aggressive) Personality
Pernicious Objects (e.g., internalized representations of the past are distinguished by early relationships that have generated strongly driven aggressive energies and malicious attitudes, as well as by a contrasting paucity of sentimental memories, tender affects, internal conflicts, shame, or guilt feelings)

Compulsive Personality
Concealed Objects (e.g., only those internalized representations, with their associated inner affects and attitudes that can be socially approved, are allowed conscious awareness or behavioral expression; as a result, actions and memories are highly regulated, forbidden impulses sequestered and tightly bound, and personal and social conflicts defensively denied, kept from awareness, maintained under stringent control)

Negativistic Personality
Vacillating Objects (e.g., internalized representations of the past comprise a complex of countervailing relationships, setting in motion contradictory feelings, conflicting inclinations, and incompatible memories that are driven by the desire to degrade the achievements and pleasures of others, without necesarily appearing so)

Self-Defeating Personality
Discredited Objects (e.g., object representations are composed of failed past relationships and disparaged personal achievements, of positive feelings and erotic drives transposed into their least attractive opposites, of internal conflicts intentionally aggravated, of mechanisms for reducing dysphoria being subverted by processes that intensify discomfort)

Schizotypal Personality
Chaotic Objects (e.g., internalized representations consist of a piecemeal jumble of early relationships and affects, random drives and impulses, and uncoordinated channels of regulation that are only fitfully competent for binding tensions, accommodating needs, and mediating conflicts)

Borderline Personality
Incompatible Objects (e.g., internalized representations comprise rudimentary and extemporaneously devised, but repetitively aborted learnings, resulting in conflicting memories, discordant attitudes, contradictory needs, antithetical emotions, erratic impulses, and clashing strategies for conflict reduction)

Paranoid Personality
Unalterable Objects (e.g., internalized representations of significant early relationships are a fixed and implacable configuration of deeply held beliefs and attitudes, as well as driven by unyielding convictions that, in turn, are aligned in an idiosyncratic manner with a fixed hierarchy of tenaciously held but unwarranted assumptions, fears, and conjectures)

---

in psychotherapy. The sensitive therapist will come to see how the patient places the therapist into these object "templates," seeking the same responsiveness that was elicited long ago. Horner (1991) also stresses the importance of "finding the metaphor" (p. 129) in a patient's material, dreams, or even in a compulsive ritual. If found, one can begin to understand core conflicts and central object representations.

Treatment methods, of course, need to follow from a synthesis of what meets Platonic ideals of good treatment and what is pragmatically probable.

It is necessary to take into account patient variables as well as economic and practical issues. Unfortunately, clinicians function in a less than perfect world. Many work in training settings, with bright and talented, but transient, inexperienced students. Third-party providers increasingly push for more speedy and efficient treatment. Many patients are deeply troubled but have little money or ego strength. Therefore, the leisurely examination to unfold object relationships within the transference all too often becomes either a fiction, a wish, or an unlikely event. It is thus suggested that often one must perform shorter-term, supportive treatment with theoretical sophistication, or add supportive elements into longer-term treatment to expedite progress. Choca, Shanley, and Van Denburg (1992) discuss their clinical experience in using results from the MCMI to provide a framework for organizing supportive psychotherapy. This framework will be followed, but integrated with ideas culled from the psychoanalytic literature that pertain to longer-term, insight-oriented approaches. I will separate "personality styles," which are milder variants and have some adaptive features, from what we call the "personality aberrations," where it is difficult to see how the type is anything other than destructive or maladaptive.

The Personality Styles

Schizoid

First discussed is the schizoid personality type, who is seen by Millon as possessing *meager* object representations. Others are seen without much definition or discrimination. When describing experiences of others, the schizoid patient is vague and without empathy. There is a lack of interest in others, a passive indifference to relationships.

Ideally, in psychotherapy the schizoid patient must move to a position of attachment and activity, rather than detachment and passivity. However, to establish rapport, the therapist at first will likely need to tolerate the interpersonal distance and reserve of the schizoid. Long discussions of inanimate objects or abstract concepts will likely characterize the sessions. It may only be after a long period of time (Guntrip, 1969) that the schizoid patient can come to more fully trust the therapist and expose underlying vulnerabilities or needs. Guntrip gives the evocative example of an infant, encased in a steel shell, crying out but incapable of expressing sound, to typify the schizoid's dilemma.

Avoidant

The avoidant personality prototype is seen by Millon as possessing *vexatious* object representations. The avoidant person actively detaches from others because of fears that others will reject, hurt, or shame him or her. There are underlying strong needs for others, but these needs and fantasies of relationships are so colored by uncomfortable affect that the avoidant person shies away from relatedness.

To assist the avoidant in treatment, one would first need to focus a great deal of attention on nonverbal parameters. Being accepting and relaxed will counter old object ties and help create the ambiance necessary to explore painful material. There is a human phobic quality that must be overcome in the transference, and gradually with others outside of the session. Interpretations should be couched carefully, lest the patient be injured and further traumatized.

Depressive

The depressive is viewed by Millon as an extension of the avoidant. The thought is that after years of negative affect associated with social interaction and the underlying objects, the object representations become minimized to avoid further hurt. Indeed, earlier objects are *forsaken* lest they continue the cycle of need and hurt. These individuals, therefore, appear to lack solid objects, and object relations are without life. The loss of the objects leaves the patient feeling lost and alone and resembles a grief reaction.

Therapeutically, the earlier objects must be revivified and brought back to life. Discussions of the past are indicated, with an emphasis on the positive aspects of the memories and people. The situations and objects must become real again to the patient through slow exploration to recover the richness that has been left behind. After this occurs, the therapist can focus on the object relation difficulties as they present themselves.

Dependent

Dependent personalities are frequently found in outpatient psychotherapy work, and the dependent high point is found in 37 percent of MCMIs (Donat et al., 1992). Underlying object representations are *immature,* characterized by fantasies of magical refueling and provision of endless supplies by omnipotent, benevolent others.

To change, the dependent personality must eventually become more active and independent. However, as anyone who has ever attempted this ambitious task can tell you, this is not easy! Instead, we often have to "go with the defenses" of the dependent person, and at least partially gratify the oral wishes through taking a more dominant, protective posture. Being the "wise Doctor" who will care for the patient come hell or high water is often the attitude one must convey in dealing with such a person in a supportive treatment. If one is more ambitious in one's treatment planning, one could use judicious silence and interpretive strategies to expose and work with the underlying fantastic wishes for passive feeding by an all-giving and all-good omnipotent object.

Histrionic

Histrionic personality types possess *shallow* object representations. Memories, affects, and feelings are fluid and ethereal, although they sometimes appear more substantive due to the dramatic setting in which they are placed. The person with histrionic personality disorder lives life as if in a melodrama, with ruthless enemies and saintlike allies.

Into this play walks the psychotherapist, who ordinarily must form a therapeutic alliance by allowing the patient to have the stage and be entertaining. It is also important, of course, to be a sincerely appreciative audience. This is sometimes difficult, as the plight of the histrionic person may seem not genuine or larger than life. As Storr (1979) points out, however, the therapist must see beyond the superficial facade presented by the patient to meet object needs. When this occurs, the therapist will find a sad and empty self whom the therapist can help as a new object. Ideally, the histrionic person requires more independence in functioning and an increased ability to be reflective and passive at times, rather than action-oriented and outer-directed.

Narcissistic

The narcissistic patient is viewed by Millon as being self-focused and passive in accommodation to reality. Underlying object representations are seen as *contrived*, while "inner representations are composed far more than usual of illusory ideas of memories" (Millon, 1990, p. 152). Following these assumptions, we would expect that the narcissist creates object representations that are exaggerated versions of actual life experiences to buoy the sense of superiority and independence. The narcissist defensively believes that all good objects are already inside, and thus he or she needs no one.

To help the narcissist, we would need to encourage empathy toward others and urge activity in meeting goals and ambitions. The reader interested in treatment planning from the somewhat divergent self-psychological perspective might examine Kohut and Wolf (1978).

Antisocial

Antisocial personalities, who possess an active-independent style, are difficult cases. The underlying object representations of the antisocial person are *debased*. The antisocial person is contemptuous of perceived weakness or sentimentality. To work with such people, one must empathize with their version of reality as highly competitive. Such an attitude is typified by ex-baseball manager Leo Durocher's quote that "Nice guys finish last." Thus, staying firm with bounds and limiting self-disclosures of feelings gives the therapist greater credibility. Others are to be challenged and even fought against. Envy of others, including the therapist, and subsequent "spoiling" to deal with such feelings are common phenomena with this type of patient.

Clinical lore suggests that these people are more treatable during crises or when aging mellows the rage and aggressiveness. At these times, object needs are greater, and defensive fantasies of an omnipotent self-representation crumble.

Sadistic

The sadistic personality likely is seen in certain settings more than others (e.g., forensic sites). Object representations are *pernicious,* likely brought on by a history of physical abuse by caretakers. There is an identification with persecuting objects with such patients; they master the experience of being abused by objects by becoming abusive. This turning of what was passively experienced into active behavior results in a splitting off and disavowal of the weak, vulnerable, abused self-representation. Sentiment and vulnerability in others are also then despised and taken advantage of.

Psychodynamic therapists who have experience working with such patients (Meloy, 1988; Vaillant, 1975) suggest that usual modes of outpatient treatment are unlikely to work. In addition, with more severe patients of this type the best decision may be to not treat them, or only treat if external controls (e.g., working with a parole officer) are available. Meloy suggests that the therapist completely assess the degree of psychopathy through specialized measures (e.g., Hare, 1985), while Vaillant underlines the importance of peer identifications in altering behavior (e.g., AA or Synanon).

Compulsive

In contrast to the sadistic personality, the compulsive personality type is usually passive, with ambivalence over whether to relate dependently or independently. The underlying object representations are often *concealed.* What is overtly seen are socially acceptable attitudes, impulses, and behavior. Fantasies of unbridled rage or lust toward others are tightly controlled and only begrudgingly admitted.

To reach the compulsive person in therapy, one has to meet them half way. An attitude of respect, organization, and timeliness helps, as does an initial acceptance of the world as composed of hierarchies and a clear pecking order. Once rapport is developed, the therapist can introduce "humanizing" interventions, such as encouragement of fantasy life, the use of dreams in decoding true object representations, or the value of a sense of humor. Clinical lore suggests that if they can be engaged in a psychoanalytic process, the way is long and tortuous. Nonetheless, such patients, if neurotically organized, are acceptable patients for dynamic treatment, although objects remain ambivalently viewed for a long time (Dewald, 1969).

Negativistic

The next ambivalent personality style, seen by Millon as an "active variant," relates in a way that is neither solely independent nor dependent. The negativistic personality type is deceptive and difficult. They appear on the surface to want help, are compliant and dependent, but covertly are hostile or undermining. Millon views such people as having *vacillating* objects, with highly conflictual memories of interactions with others. In Kleinian terms, such patients have struggles over taking in the "good breast", presumably because their hostility is disowned and projected into the other.

Supportive interpretations and empathic reflections are deflected, refused, or "spit out," although the patients may also appear grateful, submissive, or even obsequious. Working with such patients is frustrating and confusing. It has been this author's experience that one must avoid giving advice or being directive with such people, as the attempts are doomed to fail, for benign direction by a new object invariably comes to be felt as persecution and control. Unfortunately, such patients also request such directive interventions. When the request is denied or interpreted, anger will result, which should be processed. It is important for the therapist to be tolerant of moodiness and indirect contentiousness. For such patients to change at a deeper level, their use of projection and projective identification must be owned.

Self-Defeating

Self-defeating individuals are passive, unhappy people for whom things always turn out to be painful and difficult. Millon posits that such people have *discredited* objects. Relationships with others are repetitively unsatisfying and uniformly lead to humiliation and abuse. Memories of others involve feeling exploited and demeaned. Others are cruel and inflict pain and suffering.

In this author's experience, therapy with these individuals from an object relations point of view requires increased activity by the therapist, once a therapeutic alliance is formed. Exploration of fantasies of the therapist's dislike of the patient is useful, as is confrontation and interpretation of repetitive, self-destructive behavior. It is helpful to conceptualize the seemingly bizarre destructive repetition as an attempt to relive an early object attachment. For example, it may be that a patient was given attention only when abused, or that contrition and love would follow abusive interactions. It should also be remembered that for most people any object is better than no object.

Schizotypal

Another severe personality type, the schizotypal person, has *chaotic* object representations, composed of "part-objects" (Klein, 1951) or unintegrated bits and pieces of memories, affects, and thoughts. Rado (1962) and Meehl (1962) were among the first contributors to the understanding of this personality disorder.

A more recent paper by Stone (1985) helped to clarify the concept and offered suggestions as to the psychotherapeutic treatment of such people. He proposes that treatment is quite difficult but can be improved through certain therapeutic measures. He advocates firm boundaries in the treatment (e.g., being strictly punctual for sessions), providing reality testing and re-education at times, adopting an active approach, and being highly attentive to countertransference feelings of boredom and disconnectedness from the patient.

Like Stone, this author has found such patients to be quite difficult. In one case an increase in dependency on the therapist led to a psychotic decompensation and fleeing from treatment. With another the cessation of treatment due to a student leaving the institution led to the appearance of delusional material directed toward the patient's parents, who had been "safe" objects prior to termination. Other cases, however, make slow progress, provided a nonintrusive stance is taken. A current case this author is supervising adamantly requests no more frequent sessions than biweekly; it has seemed wise to honor his request and accept that progress will be slow and fitful.

Borderline

Borderline patients are increasingly seen in outpatient practice, possibly due to our increasingly fragmented society with subsequent poor child rearing and/or the enormous popularity of the diagnostic concept. Object representations in such people are *incompatible* and conflictual, swinging from extremes of idealization to devaluation. (See the previous discussion of splitting.) The interested reader will find that the borderline syndrome is a "booming confusion" (Blatt & Auerbach, 1983).

Experienced therapists will verify that the intensive treatment of such patients is a roller coaster ride. Many authors (e.g., Adler, 1975; Chessick, 1977) hold that the therapist must first become a stable, benign internal object before any personality change can be effected. This will likely involve much testing of the therapist's trustworthiness and caring, in ways that are perplexing and difficult. Only later can interpretations of underlying complex object representations occur. A useful schematic to keep in mind is the Masterson and

Rinsley's WORUs and RORUs model. Frantic, dependent clinging, fears of abandonment, and rage at disappointments can be understood as attempts to feel temporarily whole through devouring the "slippery" introject of a benign therapist.

Paranoid

Paranoid personality disorders are probably one of the most difficult people to see in psychotherapy. Beset by *unalterable* object representations, such people have deep convictions that others are malevolent. The rigidity of the paranoid's convictions is probably the most striking clinical feature. Typically, from an object relations perspective, the paranoid is viewed as someone who constantly and continually projects all internal "badness" onto the world. Any negative feelings about self, narcissistic injuries, or self-doubt are seen as the products of an evil other or environment.

It is extraordinarily difficult to help the paranoid to see the self-fulfilling nature of the projections or to own any feelings of vulnerability or depression. Such people rarely seek outpatient psychotherapy, unless some external agency or person requests it. At times such patients are seen as part of a dysfunctional couple, where, for example, the husband is pathologically jealous, possibly abusive, and extraordinarily controlling of the wife's behavior. While such people appear "strong" on the outside and initially provide protection and certainty for the insecure, frightened spouse, soon the costs of such protection grow wearing. The interested reader who may undertake to treat such people individually is referred to an excellent text by W. W. Meissner entitled *Psychotherapy and the Paranoid Process* (1986).

CASE STUDY

To bring life to the preceding material, a full case example is provided. An MCMI-II was given at the beginning of therapy 3 years ago, and an MCMI-III was recently given to assess therapy outcome. This patient exhibited a mixture of avoidant, schizoid, and narcissistic traits, along with an equivocal dysthymia on Axis I. As is often the case clinically, mixtures of traits are more common than pure personality prototypes.

Presenting Problems

Mr. X was a 32-year-old, white, never-married male. When he initiated treatment, he stated that his friends "suggested I get therapy, and I thought it was worth a try, to see what you had to say." He reported he "was sitting around the other day at home, alone, watching TV and realizing that I could be in the same spot at the age of 50, still alone. Something seems like it's missing." He related his relationship history of becoming involved with women to a point, then feeling disillusioned, then dating another simultaneously, thereby titrating the intensity of the first relationship. This "juggling" would continue until one or the other of the women would desire greater intimacy. The romantic relationship would then end, although he would often continue the relationships, either becoming a platonic friend or later having a brief "fling."

History

An only child, Mr. X was raised by two accountants, who worked together full time. He had two early memories: In one, he is gnawing on the stairs at his parents' home. In another, later in his childhood, he hears his parents speaking at the dinner table about mathematical equations. He states, "I want to talk about something else!" They ask, "What would you like to talk about?" He retorts, "I don't know, but something else." They look with confusion, then return to their conversation. He remembered driving with his parents to their office late in the evening, bringing along a sleeping bag for him, then being left in the car while they went in to work in the office. He also recalled that in the sixth grade they left him home alone while they were away for a week at a conference. As he related the latter two stories, he grew visibly anxious, as if he realized, but was afraid to experience, that his parents were somewhat neglectful.

He was a good student, especially in the sciences and mathematics, but didn't immediately go to college. He worked on rebuilding cars and raced cars for several years. He eventually completed a bachelor's degree and began a computer software firm. He lives alone and has a small circle of friends, most of whom he met through work. He dates one woman for the most part, but when she leaves town, he secretly goes out with others.

MCMI

According to the scores that Mr. X obtained on the MCMI-II 3years ago (see Table 6-2), his personality style largely was characterized by sensitive (avoidant) traits.

Typically, similar people are hypersensitive to rejections. They assume others will not value them and are worried about risks of interpersonal humiliation. They fear the reoccurrence of their early, anxiety-ridden, vexatious objects. This fear makes them ill at ease socially, since they feel that they have to put their best foot forward and be on guard. Even though they

TABLE 6-2 Case Study Initial MCMI-II

MCMI-II Inventory		Base Rate
	Validity	0
X	Disclosure	63
Y	Desirability	34
Z	Debasement	69
1	Schizoid	86**
2A	Avoidant	94**
3	Dependent	10
4	Histrionic	50
5	Narcissistic	80*
6A	Antisocial	69
6B	Aggressive (Sadistic)	67
7	Compulsive	39
8A	Negativistic	70
8B	Self-Defeating	66
S	Schizotypal	60
C	Borderline	56
P	Paranoid	54
A	Anxiety	59
H	Somatoform	52
N	Bipolar: Manic	41
D	Dysthymia	67
B	Alcohol Dependence	51
T	Drug Dependence	60
SS	Thought Disorder	40
CC	Major Depression	60
PP	Delusional Disorder	41

*BR 75–84
**BR 85–94

are often sensitive people who can show understanding and compassion for others, they tend to be nervous and uncomfortable. To avoid memories of early object anxieties, and the discomfort attached to current interpersonal contact, they shy away from social situations. This presented a problem for Mr. X, since he claimed he wanted friends and acceptance. However, the discomfort associated with social risks often made it easier to forfeit the support that he could get from others than to do otherwise. Similar people, as a result, tend to be isolated and function best with few objects and interpersonal interactions. A complicating feature of his MCMI-II protocol was the presence of narcissistic and schizoid features. Thus, one would expect to see him at times retreat into aloofness or adopt a posture of *not* needing others. This lack of need may express itself as contemptuousness; spoiling other's attributes; or grandiose, well-defended self-absorption.

The equivocal clinical evidence of a concurrent Axis I Dysthymia was also equivocally present on the MCMI-II, with a subclinical elevation on that scale. No other Axis I diagnoses were predicted by the MCMI-II results, as did the case clinically.

The MCMI-II would predict that given his personality style, Mr. X would have difficulties establishing a therapeutic alliance. Discomfort in the relationship and fears of rejection may prevent emotional attachment. Similar patients are occasionally forced to employ a maladaptive coping strategy to distance themselves from the therapist. Even after the relationship is established, the therapist should be careful not to offer interpretations that can be experienced as rejections. If the therapy is successful, however, Mr. X may derive much benefit from experiencing the closeness of the therapeutic relationship since he may have few other opportunities for such closeness. The lack of distress (anxiety and dysthymia), however, bodes poorly for the continuation of therapy. There may be little felt affect to keep this patient in treatment.

Treatment Course

There were many awkward and lengthy silences in treatment. The anxiety at times was palpable in the room, although behaviorally he might appear content and at ease. He had tremendous difficulty with fantasizing, using dreams, or accessing feelings. He was quite passive in therapy, waiting for the therapist to ask questions or suggest useful areas of exploration. At times when he was going through business and economic travails, he would become even more removed and silent. When more defended, he would be subtly contemptuous of the therapist's observations or interpretations, saying, "Well, we knew that," or, "That's a bit of an overgeneralization." Attempts at more directive interventions designed to access feelings or thoughts between sessions were never followed. His economic problems in the workplace led to him being chronically late with payments, which he was terribly embarrassed by, but hesitant to admit. Mr. X's object world seemed barren, undefined, and elusive. He never was certain about any feeling and could never tell if he loved the women he dated. His descriptions of his parents were limited, his feelings while a child could not be articulated, and the overall presentation was of a vague past and vacuous present.

Mr. X had a difficult time using transference interpretations. As predicted by the MCMI-II, he experienced such interventions as injurious. He defended himself by spoiling the intervention and remaining aloof. The author would then feel ineffectual and of no use to him. A central transference-countertransference dynamic was the identical one that his girlfriends experienced. I (like them) would initially bend over backward and tolerate his silence, distance, and tardy payments, only to eventually feel exasperated, angry, and bewildered. He would at times treat me as his parents must have treated him; when I attempted to be interested in what was on his mind, I would be rebuffed and regarded with confusion or bewilderment.

Not all was lost, however. Certain interventions helped, and it was possible to engage him in a long-term, weekly treatment, despite his initial presentation on the MCMI-II as lacking felt affect. First, long silences soon seemed contraindicated. I risked being an intrusive object and continued to ask questions and make small talk to put the patient at ease. Moodiness and subtle contempt were accepted and not confronted heavy-handedly. As Millon suggests, active understanding and empathy toward his girlfriends was supported. A responsive interest in his subjective world and sharing affects (e.g., spontaneous laughter) were salutary and seemed to counter his view of people as disinterested or wooden.

Treatment Outcome

At present, therapy is still ongoing, but possibly winding down. This remains unclear. Mr. X has been able to show more affect in the sessions, especially anger and sadness. For moments he has been in touch with the paucity of his object world and with his deep loneliness. For example, in a recent session he said, "I don't know if anybody has ever really been on my side." He is more honest and direct with his girlfriend and seems to be moving toward a bit more intimacy with her. An MCMI-III (see Table 6-3), given to Mr. X recently, revealed a diminution of his avoidant, schizoid, and narcissistic traits. His shyness and continued vexatious object representations continue to come through in the test results, but to a much lesser degree than at the beginning of treatment. There is a greater amount of reported anxiety; this may have been a situational artifact, tied to some financial problems at the time of the MCMI-III assessment.

Summary

This chapter provided a historical overview of object relations theory, integrated the theory with Millon's model of personality, suggested techniques of working with varying personality types, and gave an illustrative case example with MCMI data. Object relations theory uses a developmental perspective to explain how early experiences with caretakers lead to structural formation of representations of others. These representations become templates within which subsequent experiences are placed. While underresearched, the theory

TABLE 6-3 Case Study Followup MCMI-III

MCMI-III Inventory		Base Rate
	Validity	0
X	Disclosure	65
Y	Desirability	55
Z	Debasement	56
1	Schizoid	72
2A	Avoidant	74
2B	Depressive	0
3	Dependent	30
4	Histrionic	42
5	Narcissistic	49
6A	Antisocial	73
6B	Aggressive (Sadistic)	26
7	Compulsive	34
8A	Negativistic	38
8B	Self-Defeating	0
S	Schizotypal	0
C	Borderline	10
P	Paranoid	0
A	Anxiety	78*
H	Somatoform	69
N	Bipolar: Manic	24
D	Dysthymia	60
B	Alcohol Dependence	60
T	Drug Dependence	63
PT	PTSD	45
SS	Thought Disorder	0
CC	Major Depression	60
PP	Delusional Disorder	25

*BR 75–84

is a useful heuristic device that combined with MCMI results can effectively guide psychotherapy.

References

Adler, G. (1975). *Borderline psychopathology and its treatment.* Northvale, NJ: Aronson.
Azim, H., et al (1991). Quality of object relations scale. *Bulletin of the Menninger Clinic, 55,* 323–343.
Bacal, H., & Newman, K. (1990). *Theories of object relations: Bridges to self psychology.* New York: Columbia University Press.

Beck, A. (1976). *Cognitive therapy and the emotional disorders.* New York: International Universities Press.

Beck, A., & Freeman, A., et al. (1990). *Cognitive therapy of personality disorders.* New York: Guilford Press.

Bell, M., Billington, R., & Becker, B. (1986). A scale of the assessment of object relations: Reliability, validity and factorial invariance. *Journal of Clinical Psychology, 42,* 733–741.

Bion, W. R. (1962). *Learning from experience.* London: Heinemann.

Blatt, S., & Auerbach, J. (1983). Differential cognitive disturbances in three types of borderline patients. *Journal of Personality Disorders, 2,* 198–211.

Blatt, S., Brenneis, C., Schimek, J., & Glick, M. (1976). Normal development and psychological impairment of the concept of the object on the Rorschach. *Journal of Abnormal Psychology, 85,* 364–373.

Chaplin, J. P. (1975). *Dictionary of psychology.* New York: Dell.

Chessick, R. (1977). *Intensive psychotherapy of the borderline patient.* Northvale, NJ: Aronson.

Choca, J., Shanley, L., & Van Denburg, E. (1992). *Interpretative Guide to the Millon Clinical Multiaxial Inventory.* Washington, DC: American Psychological Association.

Christopher, J., Bickhard, M., & Lambeth, G. (1992). Splitting Kernberg: A critique of Otto Kernberg's notion of splitting. *Psychotherapy, 29,* 481–485.

DeWald, P. (1969). *Psychotherapy: A dynamic approach.* New York: Basic Books.

Donat, D., Geczy, B., Helmrich, J., & LeMay, M. (1992). Empirically derived personality subtypes of public psychiatric patients: Effect on self-reported symptoms, coping inclinations, and evaluation of expressed emotion in caregivers. *Journal of Personality Assessment, 58,* 36–50.

Fairbairn, W. R. (1952). *Psychoanalytic studies of the personality.* London: Routledge & Kegan.

Freud, S. (1915). Instincts and their vicissitudes. From S. Freud (1924), *Collected Papers* (vol. 4). London: Hogarth Press.

Freud, S. (1917/1977). *Introductory lectures on psychoanalysis.* New York: Liveright Paperbacks, Norton.

Greenberg, D., & Mitchell, S. (1983). *Object relations in psychoanalytic theory.* Cambridge, MA: Harvard University Press.

Grinberg, L., Sor, D., & Tabak de Bianchedi, E. (1977). *Introduction to the work of Bion.* Northvale, NJ: Aronson.

Guntrip, H. (1969). *Schizoid phenomena, object relations and the self.* New York: International Universities Press.

Guntrip, H. (1973). *Psychoanalytic theory, therapy, and the self.* New York: Basic Books.

Hamilton, N. G. (1989). A critical review of object relations theory. *American Journal of Psychiatry, 146,* 1552–1559.

Hare, R. (1985). *The psychopathy checklist.* Vancouver, Canada: University of British Columbia.

Hibbard, S. (1989). Personality and object relational pathology in young adult children of alcoholics. *Psychotherapy, 26,* 504–509.

Hinsie, L., & Campbell, R. (1960). *Psychiatric dictionary* (3d ed.). New York: Oxford University Press.

Horner, A. (1991). *Psychoanalytic object relations therapy*. Northvale, NJ: Aronson.
Kernberg, O. (1966). Structural derivatives of object relations. *International Journal of Psychoanalysis, 47*, 236–253.
Kernberg, O. (1976). *Object relations theory and clinical psychoanalysis*. Northvale, NJ: Aronson.
Kernberg, O. (1984). *Severe personality disorders: Psychotherapeutic strategies*. New Haven, CT: Yale University Press.
Klein, M. (1951/1981). Excerpts from *Envy & gratitude*. In R. Langs (Ed.), *Classics in psychoanalytic technique* (p. 12). Northvale, NJ: Aronson.
Kohut, H. (1971). *The analysis of the self*. New York: International Universities Press.
Kohut, H. (1977). *Restoration of the self*. New York: International Universities Press.
Kohut, H. (1984). *How does analysis cure?* Chicago: The University of Chicago Press.
Kohut, H., & Wolf, E. (1978). The disorders of the self and their treatment—an outline. *International Journal of Psychoanalysis, 59*, 413–425.
LaPlanche, J., & Pontalis, J. (1973). *The language of psychoanalysis*. New York: Norton.
Mahler, M. (1968). *On human symbiosis and the vicissitudes of individuation*. New York: International Universities Press.
Mahler, M. (1971). A study of the separation-individuation process and its possible application to borderline phenomena in the psychoanalytic situation. *Psychoanalytic Study of the Child, 26*, 403–424.
Mahler, M., Pine, F., & Bergman, A. (1975). *The psychological birth of the human infant: Symbiosis and individuation*. New York: Basic Books.
Marmar, C., & Horowitz, M. (1986). Phenomenological analysis of splitting. *Psychotherapy, 23*, 21–29.
Masterson, J. (1981). *The narcissistic and borderline disorders*. New York: Brunner/Mazel.
Masterson, J., & Rinsley, D. (1975). The borderline syndrome. The role of the mother in the genesis and psychic structure of the borderline personality. *International Journal of Psychoanalysis, 56*, 163–177.
Meehl, P. (1962). Schizotaxia, schizotypy, schizophrenia. *American Psychologist, 17*, 827–838.
Meissner, W. (1986). *Psychotherapy and the paranoid process*. Northvale, NJ: Aronson.
Meloy, J. R. (1988). *The psychopathic mind*. Northvale, NJ: Aronson.
Millon, T. (1986). A theoretical derivation of pathological personalities. In T. Millon & G. Klerman (Eds.), *Contemporary directions in psychopathology. Toward the DSM IV*. New York: Guilford Press.
Millon, T. (1990). *Toward a new personology*. New York: Wiley.
Pruyser, P. (1975). What splits in splitting? *Bulletin of the Menninger Clinic, 39*, 1–46.
Racker, H. (1968). *Transference and countertransference*. New York: International Universities Press.
Rado, S. (1962). Theory and therapy: The theory of schizotypal organization and its application to the treatment of decompensated schizotypal behavior. In S. Rado (Ed.), *Psychoanalysis and behavior, collected papers* (vol. 2, pp. 127–140). New York: Grune & Stratton.
Rinsley, D. (1977). An object relations view of borderline personality. In P. Hartocollis (Ed.), *Borderline personality disorders* (47–70). New York: International Universities Press.

Stern, D. (1985). *The interpersonal world of the infant: A view from psychoanalysis and developmental psychology.* New York: Basic Books.
Stone, M. (1985). Schizotypal personality: Psychotherapeutic aspects. *Schizophrenia Bulletin, 11,* 576–589.
Storr, A. (1979). *The art of psychotherapy.* New York: Methuen.
Sullivan, H. S. (1953). *The interpersonal theory of psychiatry.* New York: Norton.
Trimboli, F., & Kilgore, R. (1983). A psychodynamic approach to MMPI interpretation. *Journal of Personality Assessment, 47,* 614–626.
Vaillant, G. (1975). Sociopathy as a human process. *Archives of General Psychiatry, 32,* 178–183.
Westen, D. (1991). Cognitive-behavioral interventions in the psychoanalytic psychotherapy of borderline personality disorders. *Clinical Psychology Review, 11,* 211–230.
Winnicott, D. (1953). Transitional objects and transitional phenomena: A study of the first not-me possession. *International Journal of Psychoanalysis, 34,* 89–97.
Winnicott, D. (1965). *The maturational processes and the facilitating environment.* New York: International Universities Press.

7

The MCMI-III and Treatment of the Self

JOSEPH T. MCCANN

As a construct, the self has long held a place in most comprehensive theories of personality. Despite this lengthy history, much confusion remains as to how the self should be defined, what psychological processes are involved in self functions, and the relative degree of importance that is placed on the self in therapeutic interventions. Some theories view the self as just one of many psychic structures that make up the entire personality (Millon, 1981, 1986a, 1986b, 1990). Other theories place the self at the center of all psychological processes and structures making up the personality (Kohut, 1971, 1977).

Effective treatment of personality disorders requires accurate assessment and understanding of all aspects of the individual's functioning. Thus, psychometric instruments such as the MCMI-III can be helpful in revealing the person's self experiences. In the same way, therapeutic interventions are often applied in clinical settings that demand effective techniques in a relatively brief period of time. Often it is not feasible to await formal development of treatment techniques over long periods of time. Thus, theories of personality and the treatment techniques suggested by those theories often develop concurrently.

As a result, schools of psychotherapy develop out of various theoretical models of personality. Thus, while the theory of Millon (1981, 1990) provides a comprehensive model of personality that guides various treatment modalities, it is not surprising that other theoretical models have generated alternative treatment approaches. One of these theoretical models that has gained much prominence among clinicians in recent years is psychoanalytic self psychology as outlined by Heinz Kohut (1971, 1977).

The purpose of this chapter is to outline the specific role of the self in Millon's theory and to review how clinical assessments with the MCMI-III can be utilized to derive greater insights into disturbances in the self. In addition, the treatment techniques postulated by self psychology are very useful and can be implemented to alleviate psychological disturbances. Therefore, an attempt will be made to compare and contrast ways in which the self is defined by Millon and Kohut. Through this effort it may be possible to examine how these theories define pathology in self-image, self structure, and other self-regulatory mechanisms so that various psychotherapeutic treatment techniques can be derived from MCMI-III assessments to address self pathology more effectively.

Theory and Therapy of the Self

Millon's Formulation of the Self

Through the course of development the inner world of the person begins to show a degree of order and continuity in the way psychic structures are cohesively organized; the manner in which memories, attitudes, and feelings about important people are related; and the way in which an individual comes to view his or her self (Millon, 1990). The self takes on a distinct and stable set of ideas and beliefs. According to Millon (1990), "most persons have an implicit sense of who they are, but differ greatly in the clarity and accuracy of their self-introspections" (p. 148).

The self is a structural component of personality that is stable, organized, and deeply entrenched within the personality. It represents a template of embedded memories, attitudes, and beliefs about one's self that guide and direct experiences in a person's life. For example, a person who holds a strong self-image of being inept and ineffective will avoid situations and opportunities in life that may create an opportunity for growth and personal fulfillment. At the same time, personal compliments that are at odds with the self-image of inadequacy will be rejected or ignored, since they are at odds with how the person sees his or her self.

The nature of self experiences dictates how clinicians should conduct their assessment. According to Millon, self-image is derived largely from how an individual construes experiences and must therefore be approached primarily on a phenomenological level. Thus, self-image can best be understood through methods that allow the therapist access to the person's experiences of the self. Self-report instruments such as the MCMI-III provide indirect access to self experiences by providing a direct measure of what patients have to say about themselves.

Kohut's Self Psychology

Whereas Millon views the self as one component of the entire personality, self psychology views the self as the primary personality structure. As such, the self is that aspect of the psychic structure that lies at the center of all psychological experiences and provides the individual with a sense of "selfhood" (Wolf, 1988). In Kohut's theory the self is conceptualized as a stable structure that changes slowly over time and which has a bipolar structure. At one end of the self lies the person's need to have others mirror and recognize his or her experiences, harboring the need to be affirmed, acknowledged, and confirmed. The other pole of the self arises out of the person's need to be idealized and thus provides the motivation to seek out idealizing experiences. Each of these poles is connected to the other by a tension arc.

To further understand the self from a self psychology perspective requires an understanding of the selfobject experience. Wolf provides this description: "If a person is to feel well—to feel good about himself, with a secure sense of self, enjoying good self-esteem and functioning smoothly and harmoniously without undue anxiety and depression—he must experience himself consciously or unconsciously as surrounded by the responsiveness of others" (p. 39).

Thus, the person experiences self through selfobjects, which necessarily involve both relationships with other persons and involvement in activities that affirm feelings of competence. Such a conceptualization is somewhat different, but consistent nevertheless, with the self defined by Millon. In Millon's theory, selfobjects implicate the "other" dimension that is central to his theory.

In general, it can be concluded that the self as described by Millon and Kohut is a stable structure of the personality involving experiences at the phenomenological level of understanding. Moreover, a strong sense of self is necessary for adaptive functioning. Differences between the two theories and their approach to defining the self are also present, however. Whereas Millon places the self as one component within the personality, Kohut puts the self at the core of all personality processes. Additionally, Kohut places critical emphasis on the role of selfobjects in understanding the self, while Millon views interpersonal relationships as an equally important component to understanding personality. On the other hand, self psychology de-emphasizes the use of psychometric instrumentation in the assessment process in favor of empathic attunement for understanding the person's self experiences. Millon views psychometric instrumentation such as the MCMI-III as an important component of the assessment process.

Despite the differences in emphasis and focus between these two theoretical approaches, there are sufficient similarities to warrant further consideration. Both theories view changes in the self structure as necessary for successful long-term therapeutic change. Therefore, formulation of a treatment plan from MCMI-III profiles that addresses disturbances in the self can implement many of the techniques of clinical self psychology.

The Technique of Clinical Self Psychology

The focus of treatment in self analysis is to strengthen a weakened or defective self. If the patient is alienated, inept, or discontented, the goal is to make the self more connected to selfobjects, more competent, or restored to some level of equilibrium. Patients who experience the self as being sociable, admirable, or conscientious are prone to periods of fragmentation and overburdened affect when selfobject experiences fail to confirm or support how the patient views his or her self. Thus, the primary goal of treatment is to strengthen and stabilize the self. This also entails achieving experiences with others that complement and support, rather than attack or overwhelm, selfobject needs of the patient.

Specific techniques in psychotherapy are more difficult to define and classify with the more unstructured, analytic-oriented treatment approaches. In psychoanalytic self psychology, interventions are structured around two basic treatment goals or principles: (1) understanding and (2) explaining (Rowe & MacIssac, 1989; Wolf, 1988). The primary tenet of self psychology is that a therapist must first understand the patient's self experiences. This is achieved through empathy or empathic attunement with the patient's self experiences. True empathic understanding of the patient involves both an affective component, whereby the patient's self reports evoke similar preconscious and unconscious perceptions in the therapist, as well as a cognitive understanding of the patient's self experiences. More importantly, empathy takes place not based on the content of what the patient says, but rather on the experiential level.

Empathic attunement leads to the patient feeling understood, respected, and accepted by the therapist. This process is a continuous aspect of the treatment, and the therapist must constantly monitor the effectiveness of therapy through empathic examination of the patient's response to each intervention. Interventions that lead to improved therapeutic relations, a feeling by the patient of being understood, and more cohesive personality processes may be considered accurate empathic statements. Interventions that agitate, confuse, or otherwise disrupt the patient's functioning are generally not accurate, and the therapist must begin listening and tracking the patient's self-reports to re-establish an empathic therapeutic stance.

If the therapist is accurately attuned to the patient's experiences, then the next goal of explaining the observed phenomena can proceed. Through interpretation and explanation, specific meaning is given to the patient's difficulties within the context of a particular theoretical frame of reference. For example, once the patient feels that the therapist understands his or her experiences, explanation of the observed phenomena gives order and meaning to confusing and distressing experiences. There are two methods through which the therapist can explain the patient's conflicts and symptomatology. The first is through interpretation, in which the therapist brings out the meaning of the problems within the framework of a specific theory (e.g., psychoanalysis, personology, etc.). The second method of explanation is enactment, in which the patient's unconscious or preconscious conflicts or communications are expressed in a specific interpersonal context.

In psychotherapy, development of a selfobject transference is the primary method by which the treatment setting becomes a vehicle for enactment to take place. Understanding how Millon and Kohut each conceptualize specific forms of self pathology can assist in identifying how each of the disturbances will manifest itself in the transference setting. In this way, successful treatment of the self depends on accurate empathic attunement with the patient, a theoretical model upon which to base interpretation and explanation, and a framework for understanding ways in which transferences develop and how they can be resolved in the treatment setting.

Disturbances of the Self

A formal system of classification for specific disturbances in personality is useful for organizing information and designing appropriate interventions. To this end, the theory that underlies the MCMI-III (Millon, 1990) provides a nosology of self-image disturbances for each *DSM-IV* personality disorder (see Table 7-1). These specific self disturbances can be understood, in part, from results of psychometric assessment with the MCMI-III, and such an understanding, in turn, helps to position the therapist in treatment. In the same way, psychoanalytic self psychology works with a nosology of understanding psychopathology as disturbed self states (i.e., understimulated, fragmented, overstimulated, and overburdened self states) and characterologically disturbed patterns (i.e., mirror-hungry, ideal-hungry, alter-ego–hungry, merger-hungry, and contact-shunning personalities; Wolf, 1988). Each of the *DSM-IV* personality disorders in Table 7-1 will be analyzed from both a personological (Millon) and self psychology (Kohut) perspective.

The schizoid and avoidant personalities both represent the detached styles in Millon's theoretical model and are viewed as having *complacent* and *alienated* self-images, respectively. These styles are similar to what Kohut calls contact-shunning personalities, with isolated and withdrawn styles of interaction and minimal introspection. In terms of self pathology, the complacent schizoid

TABLE 7-1 Self-Image Domain

Schizoid Personality
Complacent Self-Image (e.g., reveals minimal introspection and awareness of self; seems impervious to the emotional and personal implications of everyday social life, appearing indifferent to the praise or criticism of others)

Avoidant Personality
Alienated Self-Image (e.g., sees self as socially inept, inadequate, and inferior, justifying thereby his or her isolation and rejection by others; feels personally unappealing, devalues self-achievements, and reports persistent sense of aloneness and emptiness)

Depressive Personality
Worthless Self-Image (e.g., judges oneself of no account, valueless to self or others, inadequate and unsuccessful in all aspirations; barren, sterile, impotent, sees self as inconsequential and reproachable, if not contemptible, a person who should be criticized and derogated, as well as feel guilty for possessing no praiseworthy traits or achievements)

Dependent Personality
Inept Self-Image (e.g., views self as weak, fragile, and inadequate; exhibits lack of self-confidence by belittling own attitudes and competencies, and hence not capable of doing things on one's own)

Histrionic Personality
Gregarious Self-Image (e.g., views self as sociable, stimulating and charming; enjoys the image of attracting acquaintances by physical appearance and by pursuing a busy and pleasure-oriented life)

Narcissistic Personality
Admirable Self-Image (e.g., believes self to be meritorious, special, if not unique, deserving of great admiration, and acting in a grandiose or self-assured manner, often without commensurate achievements; has a sense of high self-worth, despite being seen by others as egotistic, inconsiderate, and arrogant)

Antisocial Personality
Autonomous Self-Image (e.g., sees self as unfettered by the restrictions of social customs and the constraints of personal loyalties; values the image and enjoys the sense of being free, unencumbered, and unconfined by persons, places, obligations, or routines)

Sadistic (Aggressive) Personality
Combative Self-Image (e.g., is proud to characterize self as assertively competitive, as well as vigorously energetic and militantly hardeaded; values aspects of self that present pugnacious, domineering, and power-oriented image)

Compulsive Personality
Conscientious Self-Image (e.g., sees self as devoted to work, industrious, reliable, meticulous, and efficient, largely to the exclusion of leisure activities; fearful of error or misjudgment and, hence, overvalues aspects of self that exhibit discipline, perfection, prudence, and loyalty)

Negativistic Personality
Discontented Self-Image (e.g., sees self as misunderstood, luckless, unappreciated, jinxed, and demeaned by others; recognizes being characteristically embittered, disgruntled, and disillusioned with life)

Self-Defeating Personality
Undeserving Self-Image (e.g., is self-abasing, focusing on the very worst personal features, asserting thereby that one is worthy of being shamed, humbled, and debased; feels that one has failed to live up to the expectations of others and, hence, deserves to suffer painful consequences)

Schizotypal Personality
Estranged Self-Image (e.g., exhibits recurrent social perplexities and illusions as well as experiences of depersonalization, derealization, and dissociation; sees self as forlorn, with repetitive thoughts of life's emptiness and meaninglessness)

Borderline Personality
Uncertain Self-Image (e.g., experiences the confusions of an immature, nebulous, or wavering sense of identity, often with underlying feelings of emptiness; seeks to redeem precipitate actions and changing self-presentations with expressions of contrition and self-punitive behaviors)

Paranoid Personality
Inviolable Self-Image (e.g., has persistent ideas of self-importance and self-reference, perceiving attacks on one's character not apparent to others, asserting as personally derogatory and scurrilous, if not libelous, entirely innocuous actions and events; is pridefully independent, reluctant to confide in others, highly insular; experiences intense fears, however, of losing identity, status, and powers of self-determination)

---

reflects what Kohut calls an understimulated self, whereas the alienated avoidant has characteristics that reflect the overburdened self. The overburdened self is also the etiology of the depressive personality. Here the burdens become so overwhelming that the self is viewed as *worthless* and impotent.

The dependent and histrionic personality disorders hold disturbed self-image patterns that are characterized as *inept* and *sociable,* respectively, as described in Table 7-1. Each of the descriptions of the self for these personality disorders has a parallel classification in self psychology. That is, the inept self-image of the dependent most closely fits an overburdened self in an ideal-hungry personality; these individuals experience the world as threatening, they lack the self-soothing structures necessary to cope with stress, and they feel worthwhile only if there are other people in their life to idealize. Likewise, the sociable self of the histrionic is best represented by what Kohut refers to as an understimulated self in a mirror-hungry personality. Such personalities seek to attract attention and admiration from others in order to counteract underlying feelings of neediness and worthlessness when others ignore or reject them.

As Table 7-1 indicates, the narcissistic and antisocial personality disorders, representing Millon's independent personality styles, hold self-images that are pathologically *admirable* and *autonomous*, respectively. The behavioral characteristics of the narcissistic personality's admirable self-image closely reflect what Kohut has referred to as an overstimulated self in a mirror-hungry personality. These individuals are often flooded with fantasies of their own greatness and seek to evoke the attention of others by displaying achievements and other admirable qualities. In the same way, antisocial personalities, with an autonomous self-image, reflect what Kohut has described as an understimulated self in a merger-hungry personality. Such a style is found in persons who stir up excitement through the active manipulation of others and who need to control others in order to ward off feelings of boredom and emptiness. Thus, the autonomous self-image emerges, leaving the individual unrestrained by social norms or personal loyalties.

The ambivalent personality disorders are represented in Table 7-1 by the compulsive and negativistic styles, which are characterized by *conscientious* and *discontented* self-images, respectively. In self psychological terms, the conscientiousness of the compulsive is represented by an understimulated self within an alter-ego–hungry personality. These individuals engage in excessively ritualistic and self-stimulating behavior and they seek out relationships with others who will share similar opinions, values, and ideals. On the other hand, the discontented self-image of the negativistic personality is represented within self psychology as an overburdened self state in a merger-hungry personality. These individuals have difficulty soothing themselves and managing intense affect; they view the world as hostile and they often need to control others because of fears of independence and separation.

Millon's discordant personality styles are represented by the self-defeating and sadistic disorders, which hold *undeserving* and *combative* self-images, respectively. Accordingly, an overburdened self state within an alter-ego–hungry personality represents the self psychology equivalent of the undeserving self-defeating personality. These individuals seek to be around others who will share the same negative and hostile opinion they hold of themselves, and they have difficulty managing traumatic experiences. The competitive sadistic personality, on the other hand, seeks out relationships that will reinforce the tough, domineering, and power-oriented image they hold of themselves and are best represented in self psychological terms as an overstimulated self in a merger-hungry personality; such personality types seek to control and oppress others to cope with internal tension.

Finally, each of the severe personality disorders in Table 7-1, namely, the schizotypal, borderline, and paranoid styles, represent variations of what psychoanalytic self psychology has referred to as fragmented self states. Such individuals lack the integrating and internal regulatory mechanisms to effectively manage affect and disruptive thoughts. Schizotypal personalities represent a fragmented self state in the contact- shunning personality *(estranged)*, borderlines represent fragmentation in the merger-hungry personality *(uncertain)*, while paranoid personalities reflect a fragmented self state in the alter-ego–hungry personality *(inviolable)*.

As Table 7-1 and the preceding discussion reflect, a classification of various forms of psychopathology is important to any comprehensive theory of psychopathology (Millon, 1990). To this end, a comparison of the various approaches to describing disturbed self states is relevant to understanding the ways in which psychoanalytic self psychology can be integrated into the treatment plan that can be derived from MCMI-III data.

Treating the Personality Disorders

Because the self is a stable, structural element of personality, it follows that treatment aimed at modifying self structure can be lengthy. The use of psychoanalytic self psychology technique to bring about such change can be hampered by transference and countertransference processes that make therapeutic change in the self difficult. While each personality disorder brings unique challenges to the treatment setting, it must be remembered that treatment from a self psychology perspective hinges on appropriate understanding and explanation of the patient's experience through appropriate attention to the transference (i.e., enactment) process and through reparative selfobject experiences (i.e., empathic attunement) in the relationship with the therapist.

Schizoid

The *complacent* image of the schizoid personality renders the self prone to deeply embedded feelings of boredom. Major difficulties in treatment will arise when attempts are made to empathize or join the schizoid in his or her experiences. The therapist may be acknowledged while the session is ongoing, but the schizoid tends to have much difficulty maintaining a connection to the therapist between sessions.

Countertransference with the schizoid is likely to take the form of "forgetting" about the patient between sessions. Schizoids are often viewed as good patients, once they agree to continue in treatment, only because they tend to make few demands outside sessions. The complacency of the schizoid's self experiences may manifest itself in the therapist's failure to think about or even discuss the patient with colleagues between sessions because the schizoid evokes few feelings or concerns in the therapist. During sessions, however, schizoids can be quite demanding. Establishing a therapeutic bond will take longer, and sometimes heroic patience is required to maintain an empathic stance toward understanding the patient's experiences. Respect for needs to maintain interpersonal and emotional distance will help to maintain a working alliance. In later stages of treatment, schizoid patients may respond well to the therapist's disclosures about how the therapeutic relationship is seen as a mutual sharing, since this may permit the schizoid greater access to emotional material. It also models the appropriate use of affect and may stimulate for the patient a sense within the self that others are caring and responsive.

Avoidant

Fears of rejection characterize the *alienated* self-image of the avoidant personality. This creates extreme hypersensitivity in treatment that can make the avoidant patient very prone to feeling injured by the therapist. Interventions such as interpretation and confrontation aimed at increasing awareness are often viewed as criticism and harsh judgment. Transference reactions may take the form of anxious fearfulness toward the therapist, who, in turn, is apt to feel defensive and frustrated at having to explain and clarify interventions. Clarification and empathic understanding of experiences work well with these patients. Once they begin to feel accepted and safe in the relationship, alienation in the self begins to subside, at least within the therapeutic relationship, but it is often replaced by isolation of the therapeutic setting from the rest of the world. The avoidant begins to experience the self as alienated and rejected by the rest of the world, while therapy is somehow viewed as different or special. Thus, avoidant patients feel that gains made over the course of therapy will never occur outside of treatment. In these circumstances, maintaining a self-enhancing individual therapy, while encouraging other adjunctive measures such as group or other interpersonal therapy, will help address the impediments of alienation and isolation.

Depressive

The self-image of the depressive personality is *worthless*. There is little of value seen by the patient, and both the actions toward and the final products of accomplishments are devalued. There is an increasing sense of impotence and sterility of the self. This has the effect of being self-fulfilling, with little internal reward system or change in the view of the self. In therapy the depressive patient has little motivation to improve, and therapists find interacting with such patients demanding and unrewarding. The self-image of these patients is so limited and negative that there appears initially little with which to work. As therapy begins to develop, initial reaction from the patient will be resistant due to the sense that the self is undeserving of a more positive self-image and interpersonal interactions. The patient may seek out criticism from the therapist in order to confirm worthlessness. Therapeutic interpretation, therefore, should be carefully crafted so as to avoid reinforcing the patient's distorted self-image while maintaining a consistent and reliable connection. The aim is to develop at least one positive interpersonal relationship on which to build.

Dependent

A dependent personality experiences the self as *inept,* overburdened, and inadequate to handle the demands of life. In the therapeutic setting the patient's lack of self-confidence creates difficulties for the clinician who attempts to move him or her toward greater self-efficacy and independent functioning. Strong dependence upon the therapist is a common transference that develops; however, this is frequently accompanied by the patient devaluing his or her ability to utilize treatment. That is, the dependent patient will comment on how important the therapist is and will develop strong ties to the relationship. However, progress is often hampered by the patient's inability to feel competent to utilize treatment efficiently. Any progress made will be attributed by the patient to the therapist and not to any self gains. As a result, countertransference feelings of omnipotence or control are frequently evoked; however, these feelings reflect what is lacking in the self-image of the dependent individual. Evocation of this selfobject transference and therapeutic efforts to help the patient understand can be quite helpful in altering the dependent individual's self-perceptions. While empathizing with feelings of inadequacy, the therapist can also point out other behaviors that demonstrate the patient's self-efficacy, autonomy, and competence, thus contradicting the inept self-image. Given the importance the therapist often has in the patient's life, such gentle but direct intervention can carry considerable weight.

Histrionic

Therapy is often viewed by the *gregarious* histrionic personality as an opportunity to socialize. Rather than engage in serious and in-depth exploration of feelings and conflict, the histrionic personality views the therapist as a selfobject whose admiration, attention, and support are highly valued. Thus, the histrionic individual will try to seek favorable attention to affirm the self-image of a sociable, attractive, and interesting person. This detracts from the more important task of exploring problem areas. At times the therapist may be drawn into a countertransference reaction of being entertained and enjoying the excitement a histrionic individual generates. Likewise, the patient tends to elicit feelings within the therapist of being an idealized, all-knowing person and that large and significant strides in treatment are being made in short periods of time. The management of more severe acting out, such as demands for social contact outside the treatment setting, sexually provocative statements, and continuous avoidance of relevant issues, needs to be done directly. Thus, clear treatment goals, an explicit treatment contract, refocusing treatment on the need for addressing goals, and limit setting are useful in addressing problems arising in treatment of the histrionic personality.

Narcissistic

Because the narcissistic personality exhibits extreme self-confidence focusing mostly on *admirable* personal attributes and achievements, the patient expects the same focus from the therapist, not direct interpretation or other attempts at understanding. Any interventions that are inconsistent with the patient's experience of the self as admirable and worthy of support will be met with anger and rage. Direct attacks on the therapist's competence, sensitivity, and credentials result when there is a lack of empathic attunement or other self-enhancing experiences in psychotherapy. When the treatment is threatened by such disruption of the selfobject functions a therapist provides for the patient, there is a risk of succumbing to anger, irritation, or resentment at such attacks on one's professional skills. The primary method for re-establishing the alliance is to avoid interpretation or other attempts at explaining the patient's anger and to revert to the goal of understanding through empathic attunement. Giving recognition to the therapist's failure to understand the patient's experience properly will help to re-establish a therapeutic alliance, even if the therapist's interventions are the "cause" of the patient's disruptive experiences.

Antisocial

Much of the psychotherapy literature is replete with clinical and anecdotal accounts of how difficult it is to treat the antisocial personality. Because patients with this style see themselves as *autonomous* and unrestrained by social rules and formalities, they have very little investment in the therapeutic relationship. The therapist is viewed as just another selfobject that is to be manipulated for personal gain or to be discounted and devalued. Within the therapeutic context such social formalities as honesty, personal trust, and mutual respect are viewed with distain or they are casually discarded by the antisocial as unnecessary. Therefore, a working therapeutic alliance is most difficult to achieve. If the antisocial individual is to maintain much of the control and personal autonomy, therapy can best proceed by rationally examining choices and decisions the patient is making in his or her life outside of treatment. Modification of the autonomous self-image, however, is quite difficult and is unlikely to occur in even long-term treatment. The best measure of therapeutic success is the degree to which the patient can adaptively examine and reflect on the decisions he or she is making.

Sadistic

Since the sadistic personality experiences the self as dominant and *combative*, the therapist frequently comes to be viewed as an opponent to be conquered, rather than an ally or helping professional. In each session the patient looks for personal weaknesses that can be utilized to intimidate and overpower the therapist. For example, one patient who was mandated for treatment by a parole officer candidly admitted that he knew treatment was required and his attendance would be monitored. However, he had no intention of discussing specific issues other than marital problems. He challenged the therapist to formulate a specific treatment plan involving marital therapy, but he would not address any other issues that needed attention. Psychotherapy became a competition as to whose treatment plan was to be followed. By following the patient's lead, some productive marital work was carried out. Thus, allowing the sadistic patient to take the lead may permit the therapist to avoid competitive struggles and to achieve some form of working alliance that can be utilized later on for more important issues. The main caution here is that a therapist must be careful not to be led into a situation that challenges professional ethics or which makes the therapist uncomfortable.

Compulsive

Perhaps in direct contrast to the antisocial and sadistic personalities, the patient with compulsive personality disorder experiences the self as conscientious, reliable, hard-working, and efficient. The patient will quickly adapt to and follow the therapeutic ground rules of honest and open discourse. The patient tends to be punctual and does not present many problems that impede treatment at first. However, careful clinical observation may reveal how the compulsive personality becomes the *conscientious* patient. Therapy becomes a job or task that must be carefully attended. Such a posture inhibits affective expression and leads to self-disclosures that are guided more by expectations (i.e., "What does a good therapy patient say?") rather than personal experience (i.e., "What is it that I'm feeling?"). When the patient is observed to be conscientiously playing out the role of a hard-working therapy patient and not being more genuine, direct interpretation may help to show the patient that therapy is a process that naturally unfolds; it is not a job that has a particular outline or set of duties that must be followed without deviation.

Negativistic

Therapy with the *discontented*, negativistic personality disorder is often difficult for many reasons. These individuals come into treatment feeling that the world completely misunderstands them, and they have little hope that therapy will be any different. They are quick to let the therapist know that he or she does not understand the major issues. Even when empathic tracking is felt to be proceeding well, negativistic patients easily generate countertransference feelings of frustration and exasperation by making it known that even if the therapist does understand, it changes nothing. Strongly pessimistic and disgruntled attitudes toward therapy itself are prominent. These attitudes are difficult to confront, and perhaps the best approach is to maintain an empathic focus, taking effort to understand the patients' discontent with themselves, as well as all others. In the face of these feelings, the patients may remain in treatment, in which case the next question to be understood is what they are getting from the treatment despite perceiving the self as misunderstood and unappreciated. Once the therapist has understood the patients' needs (e.g., the therapist is the first person to maintain interest despite the patients' negativity), a therapeutic alliance can be fostered further.

Self-Defeating

Under normal circumstances, successful therapy will alleviate psychic distress and bring about more adaptive functioning. The self-defeating personality experiences the self as *undeserving* and unworthy of such relief. Therefore, therapeutic gains will be minimized and opportunities for relief avoided through the patient's focus on the worst or most troubling aspects of life. One of the most immediate threats to treatment is the self-defeating patient's conviction that he or she does not deserve relief or help and that psychotherapy is something for more deserving individuals. This threat can often be addressed by specific contracting around the length and frequency of sessions at the very beginning of treatment. Sometimes familial support for treatment can help maintain the patient's involvement in therapy. In the later stages of treatment the self-defeating personality will generate strong negative countertransference, and their frequent frustration of therapeutic gains and feelings of unworthiness may render the therapy ineffective. Angry and sadistic fantasies may result as part of this countertransference in the form of wishes to abruptly terminate treatment or otherwise act out against the patient. It is important to recognize that such negative empathic reactions by the therapist frequently represent projective identification of the patient's own angry and hostile feelings that are unconscious and have resulted from years of being treated as unworthy and undeserving by significant persons in the patient's life.

Schizotypal

Long-term psychoanalytic self analysis with the schizotypal personality is not likely to be effective, unless some of the more fragmented, disorganized, and *estranged* symptoms are treated first. The illusions, periods of depersonalization, and self-alienation that characterize the schizotypal personality make psychotherapy a difficult, if not fruitless, venture at the outset. These individuals usually are brought into treatment by family members or some other third party and the patient is generally not a willing participant. Medication can be useful in treating thought disturbances (antipsychotics) or depressive states (antidepressants) that interfere with effective interpersonal communication (cf. Wolf, 1988). Forming a therapeutic alliance with the schizotypal patient is difficult because of the fairly intractable distance and alienation these individuals exhibit in all their relationships. Rather than utilizing empathic interventions and other attempts at understanding and explaining, therapy is best served by clarification of confused or vague verbalizations and by maintaining a firm and stable presence in the patient's life through regular appointments, long-term case management, and support. If the patient commits to the treatment, then he or she may begin to feel less fragmented and less estranged.

Borderline

The pervasive instability and repetitive periods of regression that characterize the borderline personality disorder create numerous therapeutic impasses, crises, and setbacks. Because there is much *uncertain* in borderline individuals' self-perceptions and their identity diffusion results in chaotic choices and directions, there are several threats to successful treatment. These threats include uncontrolled rage reactions directed at others (including the therapist), self-injurious acting out, brief psychotic episodes, and obsessive preoccupations (e.g., following a therapist home). Specific methods for managing regressions of the borderline include seeking outside consultation for psychotropic medication, changing the frequency of sessions, setting limits around acting out (e.g., hospitalization, referral to another therapist, etc.), actively confronting acting out, reminding the patient of the need to work on stated goals, and seeking supervision and consultation from colleagues. Consistency in how the transference acting out is handled can help model stability that may later be processed, understood, and internalized by the patient, thus leading to less uncertainty and fragmentation in the self.

Paranoid

In therapy the paranoid personality sees his or her self as *inviolable*. Self-determination and control over one's own life are valued above all else, and any threat to these values by the therapist can lead to early termination, at the least, and to fragmentation and acting out at the more severe end. Thus, direct interpretation, benign reframing, or other attempts to understand and explain can be perceived as attempts to control the patient. As a result, agitated behavior, paranoid and grandiose ideation, and periods of psychosis can completely disrupt therapy. Any hope of maintaining a working alliance hinges on providing the patient with an ongoing sense of self-determination. Keeping empathic interventions on the level of understanding other people in the patient's life and the therapist's own cognitive understanding of the patient's story, and away from the patient's experiences, will work best. The paranoid individual's responses to situations, whether adaptive or maladaptive, can be acknowledged as understandable choices. However, the therapist can then offer other, more adaptive ways of viewing or responding to a situation. The consequences of each maladaptive strategy can be explored, with the patient left to his or her own devices to decide on an appropriate strategy. If therapy is successful in providing the patient with good choices, the therapist may come to be viewed as someone who respects the patient's autonomy and self-determination, and a better working alliance may result.

CASE STUDY

To illustrate how self psychology techniques can be utilized in treatment planning with the MCMI-III, the following discussion will outline a course of treatment for a clinical case from the author's files.

History

Ms. C. is a 32-year-old, single, white female. At the time treatment began, she was working three different jobs as a waitress, while also attending nursing school full-time. Though Ms. C. had a bachelor's degree in education, she never had any success in finding a teaching job, so she planned a career change to nursing.

The treatment occurred over the course of a 2-month hospitalization, which was precipitated by a suicide attempt in which Ms. C. took an overdose of 30 meprobamate tablets (250 mg each). Over a period of several weeks prior to admission, she experienced an increase of anxiety and depression. She was sleeping very poorly (only 3 to 4 hours per night) and complained of confusion, hopelessness, and dizziness. Additionally, she found her mother and sisters to be very controlling.

Ms. C.'s family history revealed psychiatric disturbance in both parents. As the second youngest of four sisters, she was responsible for taking care of her mother, who was hospitalized for depression when Ms. C. was 13. The mother's depression was in response to the suicide of Ms. C.'s father, who had been in and out of hospitals for several years for treatment of a bipolar illness. Ms. C. also had been hospitalized on one prior occasion, approximately 2 years before this most recent admission, for panic attacks and depression. That admission had also been precipitated by a suicide attempt.

Ms. C. maintained regular contact with her family, even though they were very controlling in her life. They would constantly assume control of her finances and tell her that she was incapable of functioning independently. For example, Ms. C.'s mother took over responsibility for Ms. C.'s car payments when she went into the hospital and then allowed the vehicle to be repossessed, since she felt that Ms. C. was incapable of maintaining such an expense. Moreover, Ms. C.'s family felt she should be placed in residential, long-term care because of her lengthy history of maladaptive behavior. This behavior consisted of repeatedly exhausting her financial resources, getting involved with abusive men, and changing jobs. In particular, Ms. C. had carried on a 10-year relationship with an older man who was described as both physically and emotionally abusive.

There was no history of childhood sexual abuse, and Ms. C. denied any history of drug or alcohol abuse. She was in good physical health, generally, though she had complained of irregular menses and "skin problems" for several years.

On initial interview, Ms. C. presented with very tearful and anxious affect, with an underlying depressed mood. Over the first several days of admission she stayed in bed, and the unit staff had much difficulty getting her to attend milieu activities. While her thoughts were generally goal-directed and relevant, their content was dominated by fears that she would never be fully capable of functioning independently. She had recurrent suicidal ideation, with no clear plans and with varying intent. There were noticeable problems with concentration and short-term memory. Moreover, Ms. C. felt very guilty for being such a "burden" to her family. There were recurrent feelings of self-doubt and occasional panic attacks precipitated by thoughts of falling behind in school and fears of being unable to pay her bills while in the hospital. According to *DSM-IV* criteria, Ms. C. was diagnosed as follows:

Axis I: Major Depressive Disorder, recurrent Panic Disorder without Agoraphobia
Axis II: Dependent Personality Disorder, with self-defeating and borderline traits
Axis III: Irregular menses
Axis IV: Psychosocial Stressors: conflict with family; school and financial problems
Axis V: Current GAF: 50; Highest GAF past year: 70

MCMI-III

The MCMI-III for Ms. C. is provided in Table 7-2. From a clinical standpoint, the most noticeable aspect of the profile is a marked elevation on scales measuring anxiety and depression. In addition, there is strong evidence of somatic symptoms associated with these clinical problems. The personality disorder profile reveals strong dependent and self-defeating features. The MCMI-III provides some insight into how Ms. C. views herself; she sees herself as a very inept and undeserving individual. This self-image is consistent with her history and presenting clinical picture. She is overbur-

TABLE 7-2 Case Example MCMI-III

MCMI-III Inventory		Base Rate
	Validity	0
X	Disclosure	70
Y	Desirability	51
Z	Debasement	76*
1	Schizoid	60
2A	Avoidant	70
2B	Depressive	69
3	Dependent	97***
4	Histrionic	51
5	Narcissistic	27
6A	Antisocial	64
6B	Aggressive (Sadistic)	48
7	Compulsive	69
8A	Negativistic	40
8B	Self-Defeating	83*
S	Schizotypal	45
C	Borderline	75*
P	Paranoid	0
A	Anxiety	104***
H	Somatoform	115***
N	Bipolar: Manic	60
D	Dysthymia	81*
B	Alcohol Dependence	62
T	Drug Dependence	62
PT	PTSD	71
SS	Thought Disorder	68
CC	Major Depression	95***
PP	Delusional Disorder	0

*BR 75–84
**BR 85–94
***BR 95 and above

dened by the demands of life, and she is in need of selfobject experiences that will provide her with all that she sees as lacking in herself.

Treatment Course and Outcome

As is common in disturbances of the self that are associated with anxiety and depression, treatment of Ms. C.'s clinical symptomatology was necessary to make her more amenable to self-oriented psychotherapy. Thus, she was initially placed on a combination of fluoxetine and doxepin for her depressed mood, insomnia, mental confusion, and lack of energy. She was also seen daily for individual psychotherapy. In addition, empathic attunement with her extremely burdened self experiences and gentle encouragement to partake in milieu activities were useful in forming a good working relationship.

Over the next 2 weeks, Ms. C.'s depression began to lift, leaving a general dysphoria and highly anxious mood. She began to express doubts that she would ever again be able to function independently. Much of the impetus for these fears came from her mother and sisters, who began to make plans (against the advice of hospital treatment staff) for Ms. C. to go into a highly structured residential living facility after discharge.

Despite her frequent self-doubts and self-deprecating comments, Ms. C. also expressed that she did not want to live a completely disabled existence. When these individual aspirations and goals were empathically affirmed by the therapist and reflected back to her as very worthwhile goals, she began to formulate realistic plans for leaving the hospital and easing her way back into school gradually over the course of several months.

The next several weeks of therapy were punctuated with numerous advances and setbacks. Each time Ms. C. made gains toward more autonomy and confidence through the therapist's empathic response to her goals, she had contact with her family and would revert to presenting as an inept, helpless, and powerless individual. A meeting was arranged in which Ms. C. attempted to "stand up" to her family with the therapist's support and encouragement (satisfying her ideal-hungry needs), but Ms. C. found her family totally lacking in ability to hear what she wanted. She left the meeting feeling devalued and defeated.

During the last few weeks of treatment, Ms. C. had finally begun to develop strong defenses against her family. These changes came about when the therapist sought to explain her inability to be more assertive and powerful with her family as being due to her lifelong attempts to behave in any way that would gain the approval and love of family members, regardless of what her own personal needs were. However, each time Ms. C. was ready for discharge, she became fearful that she could not be strong outside the hospital—her mother and sisters were seen as too powerful. Ms. C. was able to transfer her ability to utilize the positive selfobject experiences with the therapist onto a supportive aunt who was able to recognize and support her wishes for greater autonomy and independence. To this end, Ms. C. decided to move across the country to live with her uncle, in order to gain distance from her mother and sisters and to continue her treatment in a setting that would afford her greater independence.

Upon discharge, Ms. C. went to live with the uncle and his family. On a followup contact 4 months later, Ms. C. was found to be doing well. She had returned to part-time employment, she was functioning well in her uncle's home, and she had remained in intensive, individual psychotherapy; this was the longest she had ever remained in therapy outside of a hospital setting. Ms. C. was planning to continue her nursing studies at a university near her uncle's home.

Summary

This chapter compared and contrasted the theoretical approaches to understanding the self from both a psychoanalytic self psychology (Kohut) and a personological (Millon) perspective. While some differences exist between the two models, there are sufficient similarities to permit self psychological techniques to be integrated into the MCMI-III–based treatment planning process. It is recognized that successful treatment of disturbances in the self may take longer than other forms of treatment. The major goals of treatment are understanding the patient's experiences through empathic attunement and explaining behavioral patterns through interpretation and re-enactment of disruptive selfobject transferences within the therapeutic setting. Specific methods were discussed for treating particular personality disorders. A case example outlined treatment planning with the MCMI-III and intervention within the framework of psychoanalytic self psychology.

References

Kohut, H. (1971). *The analysis of the self*. New York: International Universities Press.
Kohut, H. (1977). *The restoration of the self*. New York: International Universities Press.
Millon, T. (1981). *Disorders of personality: DSM-III, Axis II*. New York: Wiley.
Millon, T. (1986a). Personality prototypes and their diagnostic criteria. In T. Millon & G. L. Klerman (Eds.), *Contemporary directions in psychopathology: Toward the* DSM-IV (pp. 671–712). New York: Guilford Press.
Millon, T. (1986b). A theoretical derivation of pathological personalities. In T. Millon

& G. L. Klerman (Eds.), *Contemporary directions in psychopathology: Toward the DSM-IV* (pp. 629–669). New York: Guilford Press.

Millon, T. (1990). *Toward a new personology: An evolutionary model.* New York: Wiley.

Rowe, C. E., & MacIssac, D. S. (1989). *Empathic attunement: The "technique" of psychoanalytic self psychology.* Northvale, NJ: Aronson.

Wolf, E. S. (1988). *Treating the self: Elements of clinical self psychology.* New York: Guilford Press.

8

An Intersubjective Approach to Assessing and Treating Ego Defenses Using the MCMI-III

STEVEN R. KUBACKI and PAULA R. SMITH

Psychoanalytic approaches to assessment have traditionally favored projectives because paper-and-pencil tests have generally been regarded as simplistic and inadequate in the determination of complex defenses and characterlogical dynamics (e.g., Jaffe, 1990; Sugarman, 1991; cf. Gergen, Hepburn, & Fischer, 1986). Although the MMPI and all paper-and-pencil tests were argued by one of the fathers of objective assessment to be projective (Meehl, 1945), little attention has been paid to this with few exceptions, for example, Trimboli and Kilgore (1983), who addressed how the MMPI could be interpreted in terms of psychodynamic theory. In this regard, Millon's MCMI can be welcomed as a "projective" paper-and-pencil test that can be applied to determine characterlogical dynamics and ego defenses. A major drawback to projectives in psychoanalytic assessment is adequate time and training. Projectives can be time-consuming, and individuals assessing with projectives have at times received little or poor training. In this regard, the MCMI-III with its focus on characterlogical dynamics and diagnosis can be an excellent instrument of choice when time, money, and especially interpretive competency are in question.

Although Millon's more recent theoretical conceptualizations (1990) are different from psychoanalytic formulations of character types and ego defenses, especially in terms of development, there is nonetheless considerable overlap in terms of how personality disorders are described in terms of ego defenses. This chapter will examine the application of the MCMI to modern psychoanalytical therapy and assessment, especially in regard to characterlogical defenses or regulatory mechanisms. Modern psychoanalytic assessment can be viewed as an integration of object relations and self psychology in the explication of assessment data and studies using projective and paper-and-pencil tests. An intersubjective approach (Stolorow & Atwood, 1992; cf. Kohut, 1982; Stolorow, Atwood, & Brandchaft, 1987) to the treatment and assessment of ego defenses will be discussed and applied to a clinical case based on the MCMI-III results of the client.

An Intersubjective Model of Assessment and Therapy

An intersubjective model of assessment is an extension of the intersubjective approach to psychoanalysis that was delineated by Stolorow and Atwood (1992; Stolorow, Atwood, & Brandchaft, 1987). This approach to psychoanalysis has its roots in Kohut's self psychology (1971, 1982) and British object relations theorists, particularly Winnicott (Winnicott, Shepard, & Davis 1989) and Fairbairn (1954). It is similar to self psychology in its emphasis on viewing the therapeutic process from the client's subjective world. Kohut (1982) argues that understanding and validation of the client's subjective experiences must precede explanation; otherwise, the client will experience the therapist's interpretation as a form of re-traumatization. The client's experience of re-traumatization, in turn, can be regarded by the therapist as resistance, which when thus interpreted can lead to further resistance and invalidation of the client's self-experiences. Not surprisingly, cycles of increasing resistance and re-traumatization can escalate, ultimately resulting in therapeutic failure.

In self psychology the developmental roots of the client's invalidation can be found in the child's subjective experience of neglectful, unpredictable, and traumatizing selfobjects. Selfobjects can be defined as representing the child's perceptions and understanding of significant others (see McCann, chapter 7). According to Kohut and Wolf (1978), a developing child needs: (1) mirroring selfobject relationships, in which the caretaker functions as a mirror in which the child recognizes himself or herself as important and efficacious; (2) idealizing selfobject relations, in which the child looks to others to provide safety, guidance, and meaningfulness; and alter-ego selfobject relations, in which the child feels a sense of familiarity, connectedness, and equality with others. Negative experiences and invalidation centered around these needs lead to various maladaptive attempts by the self to defend against suffering and to create a false sense of importance, continuity, and relatedness. For example, narcissistic grandiosity could develop to compensate for feelings of emptiness and sadness that result from a lack of mirroring. These maladaptive ego defenses can be changed through an intersubjective approach by validating the client's traumatic perceptions, supporting the client's attempts to make sense of those traumas, and generating through the transference new experiences that promote growth and adaptability.

The intersubjective model departs from self psychology in its explicit emphasis not only on the client's subjective states and experiences but also on the therapist's, which in turn can impede or facilitate treatment. The subjective worlds of the client and therapist are co-determined through shared verbal and nonverbal meanings. These meanings are based in the relational experiences of the therapist and client that are formed by culture and social history. Subjective experiences are consequently interpreted through these shared meanings, that is, through an intersubjective knowledge. Subjective states and experiences are viewed as embedded in an intersubjective or relational matrix, in contrast to the Cartesian myth of the isolated individual (Habermas, 1984, 1987; Kubacki, in press). The exploration of this intersubjective knowledge and how it affects and interacts with the client's and therapist's subjective experiences is the work of analysis. This work occurs in three domains: the pre-reflexive unconscious, the dynamic unconscious, and the unvalidated unconscious.

The pre-reflexive unconscious contains the basic assumptions, intersubjective processes, and metaphors that enable us to interpret our experiences and define reality. Psychoanalysis constitutes an education and discovery of those assumptions and processes that are co-determined by client and therapist. The dynamic unconscious represent the familiar conflictual model in psychoanalysis, wherein the client has defended maladaptively against psychic trauma. When the client's ego defenses are aroused in interaction with the therapist's subjective states, that is, as resistance, the client experiences the therapist as threatening and potentially traumatizing. The therapist then needs to validate the client's perception of threat, determine what action by the therapist has evoked this perception, and understand and explore how this is a repetition of previous trauma or neglect. The unvalidated unconscious represents deficits in the client's organization of subjective experience, that is, experiences that have not been integrated into the self or that have been developmentally neglected or arrested. In this case, treatment focuses on providing a holding environment so that the self can mature, expand, and differentiate, for example, by mirroring the client's narcissistic needs. Therapy is viewed as a symphony between these three domains of the unconscious, each receding and advancing in prominence depending on the client's and therapist's level of personality development, therapist's skills, and the context and phase of treatment.

The empathic exploration and working through of these three realms reveals: (1) the invariant principles upon which the client and therapist have learned to maladaptively define their subjective experiences and self and (2) a discovery and development of alternative ways of defining and structuring subjective experience. Invariant principles represent broad conceptualizations of the self based on early infantile experiences that then structure and filter later experiences. For example, the client's perception of self-assertiveness and spontaneity as destructive early in life can serve as an invariant principle to misinterpret all subsequent experiences of assertiveness and anger as destructive.

In conclusion, the application of the intersubjective model to psychological assessment and therapy involves not only the assessment of the client but the therapist as well, since their interaction co-determines the transference, counter-transference, and the progression of therapy. Testing with the MCMI can provide valuable information on the client's ego defenses and how these will interact in therapy with the therapist's defenses. Indeed, ego defenses can be viewed as an interaction between the client's and the therapist's projective identifications. Whereas Kernberg's (1984) model of projective identification in therapy views the client as drawing out of the therapist feelings and behaviors that the client has projected upon the therapist, an intersubjective model includes the therapist as also drawing out feelings and behaviors from the client that the therapist has projected, and which can then impact on therapeutic progress.

A General Psychoanalytic Approach to Assessment

Symptoms and behavior in psychoanalytic assessment can be viewed as representing a complex interaction between several dimensions (Table 8-1): (1) overall personality organization and dynamics (Kernberg, 1975, 1984; Acklin, 1992, 1993), (2) character types or clusters of related personality features (e.g., Kernberg, 1984; Lerner, 1991; Schafer, 1954), (3) self/other development (Blatt & Schichman, 1983), (4) the individual's history of adaptation and maladaptation as reflected in defenses (e.g., Lerner, 1991; Shapiro, 1965; Vaillant, 1977, 1992), and (5) current stressors and personal history. While there is some overlap and redundancy between these dimensions, each dimension in an analytically informed assessment adds to a complete and thorough description of the client and therapist. Moreover, such an assessment is critical to optimizing therapeutic treatment, that is, in understanding how client and therapist co-determine the therapeutic process. The MCMI can be readily applied to each dimension.

Dimension 1, general personality organization, delineates the overall structural development of an individual without reference to specific personality features or behaviors (Acklin, 1992, 1993). Personality organization has three basic levels: (1) psychotic, (2) personality-disordered (borderline and prepsychotic), and (3) neurotic (Table 7-1). The designation of personality-disordered is often synonymous with borderline and/or prepsychotic levels of severity in assessment literature (Acklin, 1992, 1993). Level of personality organization is critical in determining how to proceed therapeutically; for example, the interpretation of the transference for a neurotic may be more direct, while for a borderline client more supportive and displaced (Kohut, 1982).

In a psychoanalytic assessment using the MCMI, an individual could be organized at a borderline level across a range of personality scales or character types, such as histrionic, antisocial, paranoid, narcissistic, dependent, etcetera. Likewise, character types on the MCMI personality scales can be viewed as cutting across all levels of personality organization. For example, indications of narcissism on the MCMI could suggest a range of personality organization: (1) at neurotic and preborderline level (i.e., as phallic narcissism), (2) at the borderline level (i.e., as borderline narcissism), and (3) at the psychotic level (i.e., as paranoid schizophrenia with grandiose delusions).

Consequently, in addition to defining overt symptomatology, psychoanalytic assessment focuses on distinguishing between overt and covert personality organization and development (Sugarman, 1991). For example, a suicidal and hospitalized histrionic personality-disordered individual and a "successful" but ruthless, antisocial executive (moving up the corporate ladder) may both be organized at the borderline level. In the latter case, an executive's highly competitive and ruthless work behavior may be socially sanctioned by a particular work culture, and so not appear borderline. However, in other contexts, such as in interpersonal relationships, this executive may display primitive defenses, such as splitting, low-level devaluation, and grandiosity, that indeed are borderline and unacceptable to others.

Because character types or clusters of related personality features are expressed across levels of personality organization, how they are manifested in behavior and symptoms can be quite complex. For example, though two clients may meet the criteria for a borderline personality disorder according to *DSM-III-R,* these two clients could differ substantially in terms of degree of pathology or whether, for example, histrionic or antisocial features predominate. Hence, therapeutic interventions in these two cases may be quite different. For this reason, modern psychoanalytic assessment regards each of the personality disorders in *DSM-III-R* as representing a cluster of related personality behaviors or character types. Character types constitute Dimension 2, which is similar to Millon's (1981, 1990) descriptions of personality disorders and the MCMI personality scales. Character types can differ in terms of severity, that is, level of personality organization, or they can be combined with other character types.

Dimension 3, developmental focus, divides personality organization into

TABLE 8-1 Five Dimensions in a Psychoanalytic Assessment

I. **Personality Organization***
   1. Psychotic
   2. Personality-Disordered
      A. Prepsychotic
      B. Borderline
   3. Neurotic
II. **Character Types****
   1. Schizoid
   2. Avoidant
   3. Depressive
   4. Dependent (Infantile)
   5. Histrionic (Hysterical)
   6. Narcissistic
   7. Antisocial
   8. Aggressive (Sadistic)
   9. Compulsive
   10. Negativistic (Passive-Aggressive)
   11. Self-Defeating (Masochistic)
   12. Schizotypal
   13. Borderline
   14. Paranoid
III. **Self/Other Development*****
   1. Deviant
      A. Anaclitic (relational or other-focused)
      B. Introjective (identity- or self-focused)
   2. Healthy
   3. Integrated self/other development
IV. **Psychoanalytic Defenses******
   1. *Psychotic*
      A. Delusional Projection
      B. Psychotic Denial
      C. Psychotic Distortion
   2. *Personality-Disordered (Borderline)*
      A. Projection, Projective Identification
      B. Schizoid Fantasy
      C. Hypochondriasis
      D. Passive Aggression
      E. Acting Out
      F. Dissociation, Splitting
   3. *Neurotic*
      A. Displacement
      B. Intellectualization
      C. Repression
      D. Reaction formation
      E. Minimization
   4. *All Levels of Personality Organization*
      A. Denial
      B. Idealization
      C. Devaluation
V. **Current Stressors and Personal History**

*Adapted from Kernberg (1975, 1976; cf. Acklin 1992, 1993).
**According to Millon's personality scales (1994), with corresponding psychoanalytic types in parentheses.
***Adapted from Blatt & Schichman (1983).
****Adapted from Vaillant (1992) and Lerner (1991).

two deviant types: anaclitic (relational) and introjective (self); and a normal type, in which anaclitic and introjective are integrated (Blatt & Schichman, 1983). This dimension can be related to Millon's (1990) conceptualization of personalities as emphasizing either an orientation to the self or toward others.

Anaclitic types define themselves and their problems in terms of others or relationships, while introjective types define themselves and their problems in terms of self. As a result of their desire to be loved, anaclitics overidealize others, avoid aggression, identify with intimacy, and show exaggerated attempts to preserve unsatisfying relationships. Introjectives, in contrast, overidealize self, identify with aggression and the desire for mastery, and define self as separate from others. For example, histrionic borderlines are melodramatically immersed in tumultuous relationships, while paranoid borderlines are fully absorbed in defending the self from the perceived threats of others. Both types, nonetheless, exhibit defenses typical of borderline organization (splitting, projective identification, low-level idealization and devaluation). This dimension appears useful in matching anaclitics and introjectives respectively with either supportive psychotherapy (i.e., therapy that is face to face and more interactive) or expressive psychotherapy (i.e., therapy that is analytically more traditional) (Blatt, 1992; Blatt et al., 1988).

Ego Defenses

In psychoanalytic literature, ego defenses have been described and categorized in numerous taxonomies (e.g., Cramer, 1991; Vaillant, 1992, 1993) and have become accepted constructs across diverse therapeutic orientations (e.g., Cramer, 1991; Vaillant, 1993). As Dimension 4, ego defenses represent broadly how individuals adapt or maladapt to internal and external stimuli and demands. Ego defenses in psychoanalytic assessment are related to the level of personality organization, predominant character types, current levels of stress, and self/other development (Table 8-1). In modern psychoanalytic assessment (e.g., Cramer, 1991; Kernberg, 1975), defenses do not have a one-to-one correspondence with personality disorders, though they are differentiated in terms of severity or in terms of primitive versus more mature development (Stolorow & Lachmann, 1978; Vaillant, 1992, 1993; Willick, 1985).

In contrast to psychoanalytic taxonomies, each of the scales on the MCMI is associated with a prototypic defense (Table 8-2; Millon, 1990), that is, a regulatory mechanism that represents the characteristic or distinctive manner in which persons with each type of personality disorder protect themselves, gratify needs, or resolve conflict. Regulatory mechanisms "show how the patient denies or distorts painful feelings or incompatible thoughts, often setting into motion a sequence of events that intensify the very problems he/she may have sought to circumvent" (Millon, 1990). The MCMI differentiates level of severity among the characteristic ego defenses of the personality scales in terms of score; that is, above 75 but below 85 may be suggestive of a neurotic to borderline level of personality organization, and above 85, borderline to psychotic.

Clients at the borderline to prepsychotic levels of personality organization will in psychotherapy exhibit diffuse boundaries and archaic needs, with ego defenses marked by splitting, or an inability to integrate positive and negative identifications and introjects (Cooper, Perry, & Arnow, 1988), as well as projective identification, denial, primitive idealization, devaluation, and omnipotence. Not surprisingly, these clients are difficult to treat because of the intense transference and countertransference experiences that are generated. In the defense splitting, for example, both client and therapist may experience alternating identifications with negative and positive projections. In this instance a major goal in treatment would be to create a safe setting so that the client could begin to integrate split affects and cognitions. The therapist's countertransference difficulties could, however, lie in not being able to tolerate the affective turmoil and projections of the client.

In contrast, psychotherapy with clients at the neurotic level of personality organization is generally characterized by more stable boundaries between client and therapist and greater toleration of affect. Repression at this level is the major defense, bolstered by intellectualization, rationalization, undoing, isolation, and higher-level forms of denial and projection (Lerner, 1991). At the preborderline level, repression remains the major defense, but reaction formation, projection, and denial are more common.

Psychotherapy at the neurotic level is directed more at the dynamic unconscious than at the unvalidated unconscious, which is more problematic for clients at the borderline level of personality organization. Although both dynamic and unvalidated unconscious alternate in terms of pre-eminence throughout the process of therapy regardless of the client's personality organization, borderline clients exhibit comparatively greater deficits in self development, hence a greater unvalidated unconscious than do neurotic clients. Consequently, an intersubjective approach with borderline clients tends to focus on the unvalidated unconscious with minimal interpretations around the dynamic unconscious, that is, minimal interpretations of the borderline client's ego defenses and resistances—since these interpretations will be experienced by the borderline as additional invalidation. In contrast, with neurotic clients there is greater tolerance for interpretations of defenses and resistances, that is, in terms of the dynamic unconscious, because neurotics have had more sustained and stable early experiences of self-validation.

At the psychotic level of personality organization borderline defenses are even more primitive, without boundaries, and archaic. While borderline defenses serve to maintain and protect a fragmented self, psychotic defenses help to avert total disintegration and loss of self (Kernberg, 1984). Psychotherapy at this level should focus almost entirely on the lack of a validated self.

Psychotics will not be able to tolerate interpretations of their defenses, but instead decompensate further if those defenses are weakened.

Last, the level of current stress and personal history, Dimension 5, determines the effectiveness of defenses on all the preceding assessment dimensions (Cramer, 1991; Schafer, 1968). For example, a narcissistic character type organized at the borderline level, effectively defended, and under little stress might exhibit the defenses of devaluation of others and grandiose self-inflation. However, when such a narcissist decompensates, defenses more characteristic of the borderline level of organization begin to emerge. Thus, the person might regress to more primitive splitting and to devaluation of self, becoming depressed, suicidal, and affectively labile (Kernberg, 1984).

It is thus important therapeutically to realize that clients who appear highly functional at first may decompensate to very low levels of functioning later in treatment because their personalities were organized at more primitive levels. Knowing this through an assessment would be advantageous to the therapist, so that the therapist does not act unempathically toward such clients when they begin to decompensate.

An Intersubjective Approach to Personality Disorders

Similar to Millon's approach to regulatory mechanisms, character types in analytic assessment are viewed in terms of their typical defenses. However, in addition to determining what defenses are typical of character types, analytic assessment and therapy also differentiate defenses developmentally and in terms of severity, that is, according to the level of personality organization and self/other development.

The following section will briefly describe the prototypic defense identified by Millon as characteristic of each of the MCMI scales and compare it with similar psychoanalytic defenses. In addition, typical transference and countertransference issues will be delineated with each prototypic defense. While ego defenses that are most typical of the personality scale will be discussed, the reader should keep in mind related defenses as previously described in terms of personality organization.

Schizoid

In Millon's (1981) schema, the hallmark of the passive-detached personality is a fundamental incapacity to experience emotional life. Consequently, such individuals are unable to discern the thoughts and feelings of others. Because they do not experience reward through interactions with others, they instead become interested in things, objects, or abstractions. Hence, in Millon's view (see Table 8-2), the defense mechanism of choice for this scale is *intellectualization*. Because of a failure to grasp affective implications, this type views emotional issues from an impersonal, intellectual perspective, while others perceive them as bland and unresponsive.

In psychodynamic theory the term *intellectualization* is often reserved for neurotic ego defenses, while more primitive manifestations of intellectualization are seen as denial (Lerner, 1991) or schizoid fantasy (Vaillant, 1992). At the neurotic level, denial is represented by intellectualization, negation, minimization, and repudiation. The schizoid scale in the MCMI can be viewed as capturing these developmental differentiations.

From a psychoanalytic perspective, schizoid individuals are unsociable because of an extreme fear of intimacy (Seinfeld, 1991). Detachment and intellectualization are viewed as defenses to protect the self from its own intimate needs. Schizoids are lonely, eccentric, and frightened and can benefit from psychotherapy (Fairbairn, 1954; Seinfeld, 1991). Such individuals need to feel in total control of their therapy. The therapist must therefore take care not to be too personable but accept this type's need for interpersonal distance. Diminished interpersonal contact compared to that with other clients may affect the therapist so that he or she becomes impatient, brusque, or withdrawn. A therapist who tends to be detached or withdrawn from clients because of an exaggerated need to be neutral would share and so collude with the schizoid's defense of intellectualization.

Avoidant

Although both avoidant and schizoid personality types avoid interpersonal contact, the schizoid group is chronically underreactive, that is, underaroused and interpersonally indifferent, while the avoidant group is chronically overreactive and hyperalert to interpersonal nuances (Millon, 1981). Rather than being emotionally detached, this type seeks social isolation out of fear of humiliation or rejection. Because of this desire for, yet fear of interpersonal relationships, Millon identifies *fantasy* as the primary defense for this scale. He postulates that fantasy can be used to gratify needs and wishes, such as aggression and affection, that the avoidant personality finds too threatening to pursue in reality.

Psychoanalytically, the defense of fantasy can be viewed as a variant of the general defense of denial across all levels of personality organization (Lerner, 1991), though for the avoidant the focus is on others rather than self.

The therapist must be aware that because of their interpersonal sensitivity these individuals will be prone to misinterpret the therapist's actions or words as trying to dictate how the client should think and feel. They are consequently prone to feeling shamed by the therapist while remaining superficially compliant. They will test the therapist continuously for signs that demonstrate the

TABLE 8-2 Regulatory Mechanisms Domain

Schizoid Personality
Intellectualization Mechanism (e.g., describes interpersonal and affective experiences in a matter-of-fact, abstract, impersonal, or mechanical manner; pays primary attention to formal and objective aspects of social and emotional events)

Avoidant Personality
Fantasy Mechanism (e.g., depends excessively on imagination to achieve need gratification, confidence building, and conflict resolution; withdraws into reveries as a means of safely discharging frustrated affectionate, as well as angry, impulses)

Depressive Personality
Asceticism Mechanism (e.g., engages in acts of self-denial, self-punishment, and self-tormenting, believing that one should exhibit penance and be deprived of life's bounties; not only is there a repudiation of pleasures, but there are harsh self-judgments, as well as self-destructive acts)

Dependent Personality
Introjection Mechanism (e.g., is firmly devoted to another to strengthen the belief that an inseparable bond exists between them; jettisons independent views in favor of those of others to preclude conflicts and threats to relationship)

Histrionic Personality
Dissociation Mechanism (e.g., regularly alters and recomposes self-presentations to create a succession of socially attractive but changing facades; engages in self-distracting activities to avoid reflecting on and integrating unpleasant thoughts and emotions)

Narcissistic Personality
Rationalization Mechanism (e.g., is self-deceptive and facile in devising plausible reasons to justify self-centered and socially inconsiderate behaviors; offers alibis to place onself in the best possible light, despite evident shortcomings or failures)

Antisocial Personality
Acting Out Mechanism (e.g., inner tensions that might accrue by postponing the expression of offensive thoughts and malevolent actions are rarely constrained; socially repugnant impulses are not refashioned in sublimated forms, but are discharged directly in precipitous ways, usually without guilt or remorse)

Sadistic (Aggressive) Personality
Isolation Mechanism (e.g., can be cold-blooded and remarkably detached from an awareness of the impact of own destructive acts; views objects of violation impersonally, as symbols of devalued groups devoid of human sensibilities)

Compulsive Personality
Reaction Formation Mechanism (e.g., repeatedly presents positive thoughts and socially commendable behaviors that are diametrically opposite one's deeper contrary and forbidden feelings; displays reasonableness and maturity when faced with circumstances that evoke anger or dismay in others)

Negativistic Personality
Displacement Mechanism (e.g., discharges anger and other troublesome emotions either precipitously or by employing unconscious maneuvers to shift them from their instigator to settings or persons of lesser significance; vents disapproval by substitute or passive means, such as acting inept or perplexed or behaving in a forgetful or indolent manner)

Self-Defeating Personality
Exaggeration Mechanism (e.g., repetitively recalls past injustices and anticipates future disappointments as a means of raising distress to homeostatic levels; undermines personal objectives and sabotages good fortunes so as to enhance or maintain accustomed level of suffering and pain)

Schizotypal Personality
Undoing Mechanism (e.g., bizarre mannerisms and idiosyncratic thoughts appear to reflect a retraction or reversal of previous acts or ideas that have stirred feelings of anxiety, conflict, or guilt; ritualistic or magical behaviors serve to repent for or nullify assumed misdeeds or "evil" thoughts)

Borderline Personality
Regression Mechanism (e.g., retreats under stress to developmentally earlier levels of anxiety tolerance, impulse control, and social adaptation; among adolescents, is unable to cope with adult demands and conflicts, as evident in immature if not increasingly infantile behaviors)

Paranoid Personality
Projection Mechanism (e.g., actively disowns undesirable personal traits, and motives and attributes them to others; remains blind to own unattractive behaviors and characteristics, yet is overalert to, and hypercritical of, similar features in others)

---

therapist's lack of responsiveness. Ultimately, these clients are afraid that they will merge with the therapist if they openly express their relational needs, and so develop a transference relationship with the therapist through secret fantasies. The therapist may countertransferentially choose to ignore these fantasies because of fears of merging and loss of professional identity. The therapist may thus collude with the client to avoid addressing both client and therapist fantasies, while at the same time maladaptively meeting each other's secret relational needs.

Depressive

The depressive is seen by Millon as an avoidant who can no longer deal with the overt pain and discomfort of social interactions. The extreme self-denial of all pleasure is termed *asceticism*. This self-denial may further take the form of active punishment as penance for past sins.

Psychoanalytically, this is a form of devaluation and self-punishment. At the neurotic level this may appear as a dysthymia or depressive neurosis. At the borderline level it may take on more elements of self and social destructiveness. Finally, at the psychotic level the lack of social contact and reality testing inherent in the depressive personality may result in delusional material.

Unlike the case of a patient with a major depression, here the depression *is* the defense mechanism. The depressive is invested in asceticism as a means of avoiding rage toward others, especially early love relationships. Ultimately, the depressive fears loss of those relationships and the resulting loneliness if the rage were acted upon. These clients are often quite facile at emoting depressive affect and so can mislead the therapist into believing that such emotion is productive. To the contrary, their depressive defenses are only strengthened and self-agency lessened to avoid issues of rage. Empathic neutrality toward the client's investment in depressive affect can reduce collusion with that affect. Exploring the client's avoidance of self-agency may be difficult for the therapist who fears the rage that may be projected as a consequence of the client owning that rage.

Dependent

Because of their marked need for approval, attention, and support from others, dependent personalities will often subordinate their desires and needs to those from whom they obtain support. Their low self-esteem leads them to devalue themselves. Millon identifies their primary defense mechanism as *introjection*. They go beyond identification to seek internalization of a more powerful other "with the hopes of creating an inseparable interpersonal bond" (Millon & Everly, 1985, p. 114). Introjection protects against threats and conflicts in relationships by obscuring the dependent individual's own autonomy and identity. Denial may be used as a secondary defense as it allows dependent personalities to smooth over uncomfortable interpersonal events or threatening hostile impulses (Millon, 1981).

In psychodynamic terms, the defense of introjection is regarded in terms of devaluation of the self and over-idealization of others across all levels of personality organization and may also include hypochondriasis and passive-aggression (Vaillant, 1993).

These patients are often extremely compliant and self-deprecating in therapy. They will agree with everything the therapist says and express discomfort or disagreement indirectly, by missing appointments "accidentally" or psychosomatically through illness. The therapist is openly idealized or introjected but is also secretly devalued. This type of client will try to manipulate the therapist to provide advice and guidance, while at the same time not carrying out even the most undemanding suggestion. Therapists who have not worked through their own needs for idealization may be gratified by such superficial attentiveness, and so try to avoid the client's repressed rage for having been dominated by others. As the therapist unwittingly dominates the client, this rage will build. Rage also festers in the therapist because the client only superficially meets the therapist's need to be idealized. Because the client will resist any suggestion of autonomy, the therapist may succumb to more direction of the client's life, thereby increasing the client's defense of introjection or need to be dependent on the therapist.

Histrionic

In contrast to dependent personalities, histrionic personalities actively seek the protection and approval of others through captivation or seduction. As a consequence, their lifelong orientation to other's thoughts and feelings leads them to neglect and avoid their own. Thus, they regulate threatening unconscious emotions by *dissociation*. Secondarily, what remains of their inner world is repressed. This splitting off from conscious awareness results in intrapsychic impoverishment. Psychological growth is precluded, resulting in immature and childish behaviors.

Psychodynamically, dissociation often corresponds to splitting at the borderline level. At the neurotic level, disassociation can be regarded as repression. Treatment of histrionic individuals involves the gradual reintegration of dissociated or repressed feelings or ideas. Through repression, affect is expressed while the individual remains unaware of the associated idea (Vaillant, 1993). Thus, the histrionic type can claim innocence *(la belle indifférence)* when his or her conduct results in interpersonal conflict, a claim that can be frustrating for the therapist. The blocking of the idea can also result in the psychosomatic complaints that are so common to this disorder. Treatment would need to integrate idea with affect.

For therapists who are emotionally staid and undramatic, this type of personality can be emotionally and sexually seductive. Such therapists may find themselves fantasizing along with such clients, while outwardly focusing on cognitive aspects of their conflicts. Transferentially, therapy can then come to mirror the disassociation of affect from cognition and repressed fantasies. An exploration of the client's secret feelings toward the therapist is necessary as well as the client's subjective experiences that led to such a split.

Narcissistic

Because narcissistic individuals overvalue their personal worth and have unrealistically high notions of their abilities, Millon postulates that they resort to rationalization as their main defense. Through the use of *rationalization*, they are able to provide excuses and justifications for incongruities that might challenge their own sense of self-worth. Secondarily, narcissistic personalities may also use fantasy, repression, and projection as defenses (Millon, 1981). Fantasy can allow them to reassert their pride and status; with repression they can simply keep the uncomfortable from awareness; or they can accuse others of deception and selfishness through projection.

In psychodynamic terms, rationalization is closest to over-idealization of the self, with self-devaluation occurring covertly. The narcissistic character type is conceptualized at the neurotic level as phallic narcissism, the borderline level as borderline narcissism, and the psychotic level as paranoid schizophrenia with grandiose delusions. Phallic narcissists, unlike those organized at a borderline level, are able to recognize that others exist independently of their thoughts. Their issues are more competitive than the internal emptiness against which borderline narcissists defend. In addition, narcissists may present with marked antisocial and aggressive features at the borderline level. This variant was described by Kernberg (1975) as cold, arrogant, ruthless, and exploitative. The defenses of omnipotence and grandiose self-image compensate for a seriously impaired sense of self and profound disturbances of self-esteem (Blatt & Schichman, 1983).

Rationalization and grandiosity protect narcissists from deeper, depressive feelings and internal emptiness (Kohut, 1971), that is, their covert self-devaluation. Therapists who have not explored their own issues of emptiness and ego deflation may countertransferentially try to protect the narcissistic clients from experiencing feeling of barrenness and so collude with narcissists ego inflation or rationalizations. Therapists who generally feel threatened by devaluations will react nonempathically to narcissists who openly devalue their abilities. Such therapists may either punish narcissists with anger or withdrawal, further increasing their need to defend with rationalization, self-inflation, and devaluation of the therapist. Narcissistic defenses need to be acknowledged and explored rather than interpreted and challenged. The latter approach leads to increased resistance and re-traumatization; whereas the former leads to authentic self-validation, so that maladaptive grandiosity is no longer necessary for self-protection.

Antisocial

Antisocial personalities actively seek to prove their superiority, even if it means usurping the rights of others. They are motivated to cultivate their own power through aggression because of a general distrust of others. The primary defense mechanism of *acting out* allows them to discharge tensions directly, with little or no concern for interpersonal consequences. Thus, when possible, they impulsively blurt out feelings or vent urges directly rather than suffer the inner tension that would allow them to refashion the behavior into more socially acceptable forms. However, when necessary, these individuals will use rationalization, sublimation, and projection to soften and redirect urges

(Millon, 1981). Thus, they employ socially acceptable excuses, sublimate their aggression in professions that are highly competitive, and justify their aggression as protection against malevolent others.

Acting out would be regarded psychodynamically as a type of splitting in which affect and cognition are divorced from action. Acting out at the neurotic level may be socially constructive as opposed to the more destructive actions found at more primitive levels of development. An example of constructive acting out is political activism, in which authority is challenged, but within the context of changing the status quo for the benefit of others.

Psychodynamic theory identifies other defenses, in addition to acting out, that would be important to address in therapy. Grandiosity can protect against experiences that would otherwise arouse feelings of anxiety and helplessness. Close relationships arouse anxiety because antisocials are terrified of their own dependency; hence, there is a need to devalue others. Therapy would need to address these underlying dynamics through the recognition of underlying anxiety and pain as well as the fear of dependency and its accompanying vulnerability. Therapists might respond to the antisocial patient by being angered or frustrated at the slow progress in treatment or by the client's attempts to manipulate them or simulate improvement. With severe antisocial personalities, gaining their trust so that therapeutic work can begin may not be possible even over many years. Consequently, structured and directive therapies may be of more benefit to society than insight or experiential therapies.

Sadistic

Sadistic personalities may cloak their need for power over others in publicly approved roles and vocations, yet their competitive ambition and social brutality can be discovered in their dominating, antagonistic, and frequent persecutory actions. While antisocials act out by breaking social laws and norms, sadistic types also act out, but impersonally detached and through *isolation.*

Psychodynamically, isolation at the neurotic level is seen as splitting affects from relationships so they are impersonal. At the borderline level, relationships would be even more detached as defenses would include identification with the aggressor, intense devaluation of others, and self-idealization through aggression and power.

In psychoanalytic literature, aggressive personalities are divided into psychopathic and nonpsychopathic groups (Gacono, Meloy, & Berg, 1992; Meloy & Gacono, 1992). Nonpsychopathic aggressives act out in relationship to someone or some institution they know, for example, in killing a spouse or a gang-related crime. These aggressives are viewed as less primitive in their defenses because of a more developed capacity for object relations. Hence, they are better candidates for psychotherapy. In contrast, psychopathic antisocials dehumanize themselves and others. They often kill in crimes where the victim is not known, or they take pleasure in killing. Psychotherapy with psychopaths has a poor prognosis poor.

Treatment with nonpsychopathic aggressors centers on developing the capacity to relate to and empathize with others. Although these individuals are not likely to seek out psychotherapy, mandated therapy would involve the use of the therapeutic relationship as a template for other relationships as well as a means of recovering early feelings of victimization. These individuals have often been victimized as children in abusive or dysfunctional families. Therapy seeks to uncover buried and disavowed feelings in response to these early childhood experiences that resulted in isolation of affect. As with antisocials, the therapist must get in touch with the sadistic's humanity rather than focusing on outward defenses, if treatment is to have a lasting value.

Compulsive

Compulsive individuals appear to turn to others for approval and reinforcement, but they are actually struggling with impulses towards autonomy and self-assertion (Millon, 1981). They control such impulses through extreme rigidity and conformity. *Reaction formation* allows these individuals to repress their undesirable impulses by consciously having an attitude that is diametrically opposed to the repressed impulses. These reaction formations also allow such individuals to maintain conformity and social acceptability. However, the more they espouse and defend social rules, the more angry and resentful they feel. Compulsive personalities will identify with an authority figure so that they can vent hostile impulses in a socially acceptable way, for example, by "tattling" on another child to the adult caretaker (Millon, 1981). Compulsive personalities also isolate or compartmentalize unacceptable feelings and undo any supposed transgressions through ritualistic acts.

Psychodynamically, reaction formation is placed at the neurotic level. At the borderline level, this type could manifest as a compulsive paranoid, while at the psychotic level, paranoid schizophrenia might involve ritualistic, ruminative delusions.

Treatment of compulsive individuals would need to address the rigidity so characteristic of this disorder (Blatt & Schichman, 1983). Psychodynamic therapy, therefore, would seek to counter the narrow, fixed attention by providing experiences about what is outside the compulsive personality's focus. This cannot be accomplished by directly interpreting the compulsives defenses, which will become more exaggerated when threatened; to the contrary, the therapist must try to empathize with the client's need to use such defenses. Therapists who have an inordinant need to feel emotionally connected to their clients may focus on and become irritated by the compulsive's defenses, and so not recognize the wealth of emotional pain underlying those defenses. Such therapists may then try to conceal their anger and irritation by transforming those feelings into positive concern for the client, that is, by the defense of reaction formation. Transferentially, the compulsive's rigid and intellectualized defenses may be complemented by a therapist's compulsive need to be a "good" therapist. The therapist must therefore be careful not to join these defenses but empathically explore the client's affect. Likewise, therapy would call attention to the driven quality of the compulsive individual's activity, introducing in a nonthreatening way alternatives like spontaneity and playfulness to the "I shoulds."

Negativistic

Negativistic personalities vacillate between dependency/conformity and negativism/autonomy according to Millon (1990). They are negativistic in the sense that they tend to be contrary, unaccommodating, sulky, pessimistic, and complaining. Such individuals actively obstruct others. The most commonly employed defense mechanism is *displacement.* Instead of expressing negative impulses directly, they are displaced onto people of lesser importance, reducing the chance of retaliation or rejection from the true source of the hostile feelings. These individuals may turn destructive impulses against themselves through introjection, while at other times they will ascribe such impulses to others through projection (Millon, 1981).

In psychodynamic literature, negativistic is referred to as passive-aggressive and is itself a defense and not a personality disorder. Passive aggression and displacement involve overidealization of the self as well as devaluation of others.

Psychotherapy would involve openly exploring the ways in which the negativistic individual indirectly and unassertively expresses aggression and neediness towards the therapist by being contrary (Vaillant, 1992). The therapist should actively support the free expression of this aggression and neediness toward the therapist, while uncovering the depressive and invalidating experiences that lead the client to fear loss of autonomy, when others want to be close, and loss of connectedness, when others want to be alone. Treatment would thus focus on helping the client attain a sense of autonomy and connectedness that others cannot destroy. Therapists should monitor their own dynamics around intimacy and autonomy, examining how reactive and contrary they are when the client is expressing those needs.

Self-Defeating

Self-defeating personalities in Millon's (1990) schema prefer pain in interpersonal relationships, which may be intensified through self-denial and the acceptance of blame. Self-defeating individuals often relate to others in an obsequious and self-sacrificing manner. They will place themselves in an inferior light or abject position to compound their pain and anguish. The primary defense for these individuals is identified as *exaggeration*.

Psychoanalytically, exaggeration is similar to devaluation. At the neurotic level this defense could be expressed as someone who presents with self-esteem issues and who is self-effacing, at the borderline level as self-mutilation and involvement in sadomasochistic relationships, and at the psychotic level as denial with delusional self-mutilatory behavior.

Exaggeration can be viewed as turning against the self and a fear of autonomy. Thus, anger against others and the suppression of autonomy are expressed through self-destructive behavior. Therapy would seek to uncover these feelings and explore the clients' fantasies about what would happen if they were to become independent. At the borderline level of personality organization these fantasies involve an infantile conviction that the world and loved ones would all be destroyed and lost if autonomy were in any way encouraged. Complementing this masochistic behavior are also hidden feelings of grandiosity, which result from having survived intense victimization and self-deprecation (Chancer, 1992). In a perverted way, this surviving is equated with being autonomous. In most primitive level, masochists say, "I exist because I survived." Treatment would try to modify this invariant principle to "I exist because I am or because I am important." Countertransferentially, the therapist should be wary of becoming voyeuristic about their experiences, thereby further debilitating these clients, instead of assisting them to become more autonomous. This is especially true of therapists who are ignorant of or have not worked through sadistic aspects of their personality.

Schizotypal

To others, schizotypal individuals appear eccentric, aberrant, or bizarre in their actions, often showing odd speech patterns typical of autistic cognitions. Consequently, they are socially and affectively isolated. The most common defense, according to Millon, is *undoing*. Undoing is a means of repenting for some undesirable act or thought through complex or bizarre rituals or "magical" acts. These rituals are meant to cleanse or purify the individual.

Psychodynamically, this severe disorder is at the prepsychotic to borderline level of personality organization, with an emphasis on cognitive defenses of distortion and schizoid fantasy along with typical borderline defenses.

Therapy would focus on the meaning of the complex or bizarre rituals for the schizotypal individual. Because of the primitive nature of these individuals, self/other boundaries will be at best tenuous. Transferentially, this is dangerous because either (1) therapists will feel as if they do not exist while the schizotypal is holding forth, and so feel abandoned or unconnected; or, (2) that they have merged with the schizotypal in an idiosyncratic insight or joining of minds, so that they are seduced into feeling that they are truly empathizing when in fact they are colluding with the schizotypal's undoing. The transference can thus come to reflect the schizotypal's alternating experiences of barrenness or omniscience. Therapists should, in contrast, provide a "holding environment," in which split feelings and perception can be juxtaposed and ultimately integrated without the need of such desperate defenses.

Borderline

Borderline personalities are characterized by capricious, impulsive behavior and marked lability of mood. This affective instability is particularly vulnerable to environmental stress. Therefore, borderline personalities use *regression* to retreat, under stress, to an earlier developmental stage. Unable to cope with anxiety, these individuals revert to less mature functioning when life was less complex and stressful.

Borderline is used as a designation of personality organization in modern psychoanalytic assessment. Psychoanalytically, the Borderline MCMI scale comes closest to measuring histrionic borderlines or infantile borderline personalities (Blatt & Schichman, 1983). Hence, this scale will not always be elevated with a client who is at the borderline level of personality organization. For example, a well-defended antisocial with a borderline personality organization will generally have little elevation on this scale but will commonly have high scores on antisocial, aggressive-sadistic, and narcissistic scales.

Most texts on the treatment of borderlines often focus on histrionic or infantile borderlines because of their dramatic flavor and because, unlike other character types organized at a borderline level, such as paranoids, antisocials, aggressives, and narcissists, they are more often referred or self-referred for treatment. The regressive quality of their ego defenses, the seductiveness of their emotional dramatizations, and their intense neediness are, as previously stated (see Histrionic scale) a voyeuristic land mine for contemplative or underemotional therapists. Therapists may inadvertently maintain the client's pathology and so extend treatment for their own emotional needs. Conversely, such therapists may defend against such needs and become hostile and withdrawn to these clients. Hence, the disparaging comments one often hears about histrionic borderlines when they demand special treatment, act out suicidally, or call at all hours may indicate countertransference issues.

Paranoid

Paranoid individuals are characteristically suspicious, hostile, and resentful. They are constantly on guard and vigilant for any perceived threat. Because they detest being dependent, they resist any external influence or control.

Through *projection*, paranoid individuals attribute their own shortcomings and hostile motives to others. By this means, Millon (1981) postulates, they are able to see themselves as the innocent and unfortunate victim of others. Projection may also serve as justification for aggression or retaliation toward others.

Like the schizotypal type, this severe disorder in the MCMI is found only at the borderline to psychotic levels of personality organization. The borderline paranoid is often found in conjunction with antisocial traits. At the psychotic level, thought disorder and delusional scales on the MCMI would also be elevated.

In therapy, one of the first goals of treatment would be establishing trust in the therapeutic relationship. This type's hypervigilance will cause them to scrutinize the therapeutic situation for perceived threats and anomalies. Paranoid thinking itself should not be directly challenged. Rather, this thinking should be explored and empathized with. The therapist must be extremely patient and exhibit no other agenda other than to explore their issues. Empathic neutrality is thus very critical because paranoids will try to get the therapist to take a side and so confirm their projections. These projections will only be disconfirmed by providing an alternative experience of acceptance, in which there are no threats to a highly fragile but extremely defended self. A therapist who is overly invested in gaining the clients' trust may feel drained and defeated by paranoids in these attempts to gain these trust. Such feelings may indicate that the therapist is not allowing the paranoid to develop that trust in terms of the paranoids' own subjective understanding. By not "trusting" the paranoids, and hence the therapeutic process, the therapist increases the paranoids' need to project.

CASE STUDY

History

P. is a 39-year-old, white, married woman. She has been married for 17 years. She and her husband have one child, 15 years old, who has been diagnosed with attention deficit disorder. She has worked full-time for the past 10 years at an administrative department for a state government.
In the initial session, P. reported difficulties with obsessive thinking centering on two co-workers. She would drive past these people's homes in order to figure out where they were and what they were doing and would call them several times a day, breathing into the phone without saying anything. She used a pay telephone so that the calls could not be traced. She also shredded the personnel file of one of these individuals when she found it in an unlocked file drawer. She indicated that voices in her head told her

to harass these people. The voices were, however, temporal and context-specific, appearing to represent transient psychotic experiences. P. never developed a homicidal plan and denied any intention to follow through on these thoughts, instead indicating that she would kill herself before she would kill anyone else. In general, she reported feeling suspicious of others who seemed to be "doing things to her" even though, when asked, she freely admitted that their actions were part of their normal, everyday routine. She admitted that she tends to misinterpret what people say, becoming upset as a result. She also complained of feelings of depression. There was no significant medical or legal history.

MCMI-III

P.'s MCMI-III profile (Table 8-3) in conjunction with her history suggests a negativistic personality disorder at the borderline to prepsychotic level of personality organization (Borderline scale). Millon's prototypic defense is displacement, which is similar to passive-aggression (Vaillant, 1992). These defenses are organized at a very primitive level, that is, occurring within the context of intense devaluation of others, devaluation of self as a victim who is wronged by others, splitting, primitive denial, and projective identification. Splitting of others and self into all good or bad occurs when P. vacillates between fantasies to merge with others, while fearing engulfment and loss of self, with fantasies of independence, while fearing emptiness and profound loneliness. P. devalues others and externalizes blame for her inadequacies while exaggerating feelings of victimization (Paranoid scale) and dependency (introjection—Dependent scale). Often others are not aware of the intensity of this blame and devaluation until there is a major incident of acting out. Although P. defines herself in terms of others (anaclitic orientation) and desperately wants to be intimate with others, she is fearful of the consequences (e.g., loss of self), and so uses fantasy (Avoidant scale) to maintain distance from others. As anxiety and depression escalate (Anxiety, Dysthymia, and Major Depression scales), P. decompensates further into transient psychotic states defended by hyperactivity (Bipolar: Manic and Thought Disorder scales) and obsessive, ritualistic thoughts, which serve to structure unmodulated and chaotic fears, depression, and unmet needs. Manic defenses are indicated rather than a bipolar disorder by the presence of dysthymic feelings at the time of being "hyper." Last, P. has a marked tendency to somaticize her psychological difficulties (Somatoform scale), thereby disavowing responsibility for her psychological needs.

Therapist's History

The therapist has no psychiatric history, though he recalls emotional neglect and verbal abuse while with his family. In his mid- to late 20s, he experi-

TABLE 8-3 Case Example MCMI-III

MCMI-III Inventory		Base Rate
	Validity	0
X	Disclosure	76*
Y	Desirability	47
Z	Debasement	83*
1	Schizoid	50
2A	Avoidant	76*
2B	Depressive	77*
3	Dependent	77*
4	Histrionic	55
5	Narcissistic	68
6A	Antisocial	70
6B	Aggressive (Sadistic)	76*
7	Compulsive	32
8A	Negativistic	81*
8B	Self-Defeating	48
S	Schizotypal	72
C	Borderline	79*
P	Paranoid	77*
A	Anxiety	96***
H	Somatoform	85**
N	Bipolar: Manic	115***
D	Dysthymia	75*
B	Alcohol Dependence	63
T	Drug Dependence	64
PT	PTSD	65
SS	Thought Disorder	75*
CC	Major Depression	80*
PP	Delusional Disorder	70

*BR 75–84
**BR 85–94
***BR 95 and above

enced some emotionally traumatic events that eventually led to his decision to become a therapist. He has been in psychotherapy since working on his doctorate in clinical psychology. Testing and therapy indicate narcissistic defenses at the preborderline to neurotic level, involving higher-level idealization of self, higher-level devaluation of others, and rationalization. These defenses appear to be ameliorated by insight and openness to painful affective experiences as revealed through therapy.

Intersubjective Analysis of MCMI Results

Unresolved Co-Dynamics of Client and Therapist

A major weakness for the therapist would be his need for P. to trust and idealize him and P.'s need to devalue others and idealize self. The interaction between the therapist's and client's needs could result in alternating idealization and devaluation of the other. Unconsciously the therapist may try to promote in P. an idealization of himself as someone who is empathic and responsive to P.'s needs. Because P. feels victimized and desperately wants someone to believe in her, she may be susceptible to the therapist's need to be idealized as a special person. At the same time, the therapist's desire to be trusted may make it difficult for him to be comfortable with the client's negative feelings and rage toward him, engendered by fear of engulfment and emotional vulnerability, that is, a fear of being retraumatized. P. may then displace her rage from the therapist onto others and/or internalize it in terms of psychotic fantasy. In this manner, P. could deteriorate while the therapist works ardently to be empathic.

Because of her fear of engulfment by the therapist, P. will also try to devalue the therapy and the therapist. She will shift between the two extremes of devaluation and idealization. The therapist, in his need to be empathic, may collude with the client's devaluation of him. The therapist's belief that he can handle anything (rationalization) based on his own personal insight into trauma may become a form of masochistic grandiosity as a reversal of roles occurs: therapist becoming victim and client becoming aggressor or sadist.

From P.'s perspective, the therapist's other role as an insightful and empathic person can now, however, be reinterpreted as partially deceptive: The therapist is partly empathic in order to inflate his sense of importance. The therapist's desire to be important thus competes with P.'s desire to feel important. Unconsciously P. will realize that the therapist's empathy is conditional upon his self-inflation. This conditional empathy will then be experienced by P. as injurious and domineering. Though the therapist's intention is to do what is best for P., his own narcissistic issues may render him an aggressor and P. a victim.

Unless countertransference reactions are understood by the therapist and empathically interpreted, there is a danger the boundaries between client and therapist could deteriorate. This would make it unclear whose psychotherapy this was. The therapist's covert self-devaluation and P's dependency needs could engender countertransference feelings of anger toward P., so that the therapist is emotionally unavailable to P. when she most needs him to be empathic. Conversely, the therapist could be intrusive when P. needs to feel supported in her independence.

Projective identification can thus be said to have occurred with both client and therapist, with each evoking feelings and actions from the other that have been projected on the other. P. will develop a dependent, depressed, and regressed relationship with the therapist (victim role), while indirectly defending against this relationship through passive-aggression, flight into extreme fantasy and denial (psychotic delusions and hallucinations), and hyperactivity. The therapist will experience himself as highly valued and devalued in accordance with the effectiveness of his narcissistic defenses. The results will be unconscious collusion with the client's changing defenses and possible further retraumatization of the client.

Resolving Client and Therapist Co-Dynamics

These cycling roles of victim and aggressor for both P. and therapist need to be interpreted by the therapist in terms of two complementary processes: the dynamic unconscious and unvalidated unconscious (Stolorow & Atwood, 1992). When P. reveals that she experiences the therapist as retraumatizing because he is weakening her defenses (dynamic unconscious), the therapist needs to mirror her concerns and fears. In this way, the defenses that were developed to contain her conflicts can be lessened in severity as a result of the validation of P.'s subjective experience of the therapist. This lowering of defenses will then enable P. to reveal deficits in her early emotional and interpersonal experiences, that is, in terms of the unvalidated unconscious. The therapist's task here will be to assist the client in developing alternative experiences in the therapeutic relationship, or transference, through the reformulation of more adaptive interpersonal experiences and definitions of self. Successful therapeutic work can be viewed as continuous shifts between these two forms of the unconscious. The therapist must be able to tolerate and empathize with shifts in overt idealization to covert devaluation. The therapist's capacity to work through these shifts can be measured by the degree to which P.s pathology can be contained in the therapy session.

Treatment is obviously long-term. P. should be seen minimally twice a week with contingencies for other contact times, including hospitalization, when the experience of treatment cannot contain her maladaptive feelings and behaviors or when she acts out outside of treatment. In this regard, progress can be said to have occurred when transient delusions and hallucinations are experienced in terms of the transference rather than in other interpersonal settings. It would not be surprising for this client to develop delusions or hallucinations about the therapist, which would then need to be explored and validated through an interpretation of their meaning.

The therapist will need to monitor his negative feelings around P.'s lack of boundaries and dependency needs. An exploration of the therapist's negative feelings at an appropriate time may validate P. by acknowledging her perceptions of an unresponsive therapist, so that eventually both positive and negative aspects of any relationship (therapy included) can be accepted without defensive splitting, schizoid fantasy, and displacement. In short, treatment can be an arduous but rewarding experience for both P. and the therapist, if the therapist is willing to work through his co-dynamics with the client.

Summary

From a psychoanalytic perspective, personality assessment for practicing clinicians is regarded as useful if it can confirm and, more importantly, augment what is known about the client from a diagnostic interview, careful history, and/or a few therapy sessions. In this vein, Burish (1984) questions the usefulness of instruments that do not provide much more information than one could get from simply asking, especially, when the reason for assessment is simply clinical and not forensic or for research purposes. In this regard, the MCMI can confirm and provide additional information about hidden or covert personality dynamics. The MCMI can alert the therapist to the dominant defenses that the client will use in the transference and how these will manifest themselves through the course of treatment.

Because the reactions of the therapist co-determine the client's behavior and progress in an intersubjective model, the therapist is strongly encouraged to better understand his or her own defenses. This can elucidate how the therapist will react to the client's defenses and thereby enable the therapist to anticipate, understand, and reduce empathic disattunement, nontherapeutic reactions, and collusion in treatment.

References

Acklin, M. W. (1992). Psychodiagnosis of personality structure: Psychotic personality organization. *Journal of Personality Assessment, 58*, 454–463.

Acklin, M. W. (1993). Psychodiagnosis of personality structure II: Borderline personality organization. *Journal of Personality Assessment, 61*, 329–341.

Blatt, S. J. (1992). The differential effects of psychotherapy and psychoanalysis with anaclitic and introjective patients: The Menninger Psychotherapy Research Project revisited. *Journal of the American Psychoanalytic Association, 40*, 691–724.

Blatt, S. J., & Schichman, S. (1983). Two primary configurations of psychopathology. *Psychoanalysis and Contemporary Thought, 6*, 187–254.

Burish, M. (1984). Approaches to personality inventory construction. *American Psychologist, 39*, 214–227.

Chancer. L. S. (1992). *Sadomasochism in everyday life: The dynamics of power and powerlessness.* New Brunswick, NJ: Rutgers University Press.

Cooper, S. H., Perry, J. C., & Arnow, D. (1988). An empirical approach to the study of defense mechanisms: I. Reliability and preliminary validity of the Rorschach Defense scales. *Journal of Personality Assessment, 52,* 187–203.

Cramer, P. (1991). *The development of defense mechanisms: Theory, research, and assessment.* New York: Springer-Verlag.

Fairbairn, W. R. D. (1954). *An object relations theory of the personality.* New York: Basic Books.

Gacono, C. B., Meloy, J. R., & Berg, J. L. (1992). Object relations, defensive operations, and affective states in narcissistic, borderline, and antisocial personality disorder. *Journal of personality assessment, 59,* 32–49.

Gergen, K. J., Hepburn, A., & Fischer, D. C. (1986). Hermeneutics of personality description. *Journal of Personality and Social Psychology, 50,* 1261–1270.

Habermas, J. (1984). *The theory of communicative action* (vol. 1). Boston: Beacon Hill Press.

Habermas, J. (1987). *The theory of communicative action* (vol. 2). Boston: Beacon Hill Press.

Jaffe, L. S. (1990). The empirical foundations of psychoanalytic approaches to psychological testing. *Journal of Personality Assessment, 55,* 746–755.

Kernberg, O. F. (1975). *Borderline conditions and pathological narcissisms.* Northvale, NJ: Aronson.

Kernberg, O. F. (1984). *Severe personality disorders: Psychotherapeutic strategies.* New Haven, CT: Yale University Press.

Kohut, H. (1971). *The analysis of the self.* New York: International Universities Press.

Kohut, H. (1982). *How does analysis cure?* Chicago: University of Chicago Press.

Kohut, H., & Wolf, E. S. (1978). The disorders of the self and their treatment: An outline. *International Journal of Psycho-analysis, 59,* 413–425.

Kubacki, S. R. (In press). Applying Habermas's theory of communicative action to values in psychotherapy. *Psychotherapy.*

Lerner, P. M. (1991). *Psychoanalytic theory and the Rorschach.* Hillsdale, NJ: The Analytic Press.

Meehl, P. E. (1945). The dynamics of "structured" personality tests. *Journal of Clinical Psychology,* 296–303.

Meloy, J. R., & Gacono, C. B. (1992). A psychotic (sexual) psychopath: "I just had a violent thought. . . ." *Journal of Personality Assessment, 58,* 480–493.

Millon, T. (1981). *Disorders of personality: DSM-III: Axis II.* New York: Wiley.

Millon, T. (1990). *Toward a new personology: An evolutional model.* New York: Wiley.

Millon, T., & Everly, G. S. (1985). *Personality and its disorders: A biosocial learning approach.* New York: John Wiley.

Schafer, R. (1954). *Psychoanalytic interpretation in Rorschach testing.* New York: Grune & Stratton.

Schafer, R. (1968). The mechanisms of defense. *International Journal of Psychoanalysis, 48,* 49–61.

Seinfeld, J. (1991). *The empty core: An object relations approach to psychotherapy of the schizoid personality.* Northvale, NJ: Aronson.

Shapiro, D. (1965). *Neurotic styles.* New York: Basic Books.
Stolorow, R. D., & Atwood, G. E. (1992). *Contexts of being: The intersubjective foundations of psychological life.* Hillsdale, NJ: The Analytic Press.
Stolorow, R. D., Brandchaft, B., & Atwood, G. E. (1987). *Psychoanalytic treatment: An intersubjective approach.* Hillsdale, NJ: The Analytic Press.
Stolorow, R. D., & Lachman, F. M. (1978). The developmental prestages of defenses: Diagnostic and therapeutic implications. *Psychoanalytic Quarterly, 47,* 73–102.
Sugarman, A. (1991). Where's the beef? Putting personality back into personality assessment. *Journal of Personality Assessment, 56,* 130–144.
Thomson, P. (1991). Countertransference in an intersubjective perspective: An experiment. In A. Goldberg (Ed.), *The evolution of self psychology: Progress in self psychology* (vol. 7). Hillsdale, NJ: The Analytic Press.
Trimboli, F., & Kilgore, R. B. (1983). A psychodynamic approach to MMPI interpretation. *Journal of Personality Assessment, 47,* 614–626.
Vaillant, G. E. (1977). *Adaptation to life.* Boston.
Vaillant, G. E. (1992). *Ego mechanisms of defense: A guide for clinicians and researchers.* Washington, DC: American Psychiatric Press.
Vaillant, G. E. (1993). *The wisdom of the ego.* Cambridge, MA: Harvard University Press.
Willick, M. S. (1985). On the concept of primitive defenses. In H. P. Blum (Ed.), *Defense and resistance* (pp. 175–200). New York: International Universities Press.
Winnicott, C., Shepard, R., & Davis, M. (1989). *Psychoanalytic explorations.* Cambridge, MA: Harvard University Press.

9

Psychoanalytic Psychotherapy of the Personality Disorders toward Morphologic Change

DARWIN DORR

Morphology is the study of form or structure. In biology, morphology involves the study of the form and structure of animals and plants. In the study of personality, morphology refers to the study of the structural strength, interior harmony, and functional effectiveness of the personality system. In the Millon system of personality, morphologic organization is one of eight clinical domains of personality. Because the MCMI-III was developed to be isomorphic with Millon's personality theory, the test results can be used to help the clinician pinpoint deficiencies in each domain and, thus, rapidly identify targets for therapy and remediation. The purpose of this chapter, then, is to describe how the clinician practicing psychoanalytic psychotherapy might employ MCMI-III test results to address deficiencies in the morphological organization of patients presenting with personality disorder. To this end, I shall first summarize the basics of psychoanalytic psychotherapy, then describe how traditional psychoanalytic psychotherapy must be modified in the treatment of personality disorders. I shall then expand the discussion of the concept of morphologic organization of the personality. Following this, I shall outline ways in which MCMI-III results may assist the clinician to develop treatment plans that address morphologic deficits in each of the 14 personalities measured by the instrument.

Psychoanalytic Psychotherapy

Derived from classical psychoanalysis, psychoanalytic psychotherapy utilizes many, but not necessarily all, of the principles of Freud's personality theory. Like all other variants of psychoanalysis, psychoanalytic psychotherapy seeks to facilitate the growth of the ego, thus strengthening the person so that he or she can transcend the status quo and progress toward personal growth. The therapist focuses on matters of transference, resistance, countertransference, and, sometimes, dream analysis. There is an emphasis on establishing basic trust and the therapeutic alliance.

The therapist generally attends to thinking and emotions in the present and avoids visiting the past unless a specific event in the past is relevant to the patient's current conflicts. There is an emphasis on ego-building techniques. The therapist tends to follow the emotional level of the patient and becomes, within the constraints of the professional role, a "real person" as well as an object of transference.

The therapist seeks to facilitate growth through the analysis of resistance and transference, which allows the ego to resolve unconscious conflicts. The primary therapeutic tool is interpretation, which is intended to link the present with the past and the conscious (and preconscious) material with the unconscious. The aim of interpretation is to help the unconscious become conscious. The better patients understand the unconscious underpinnings of their behavior, the more self-awareness they have. With greater self-awareness, underlying needs, wishes, and fantasies can be more easily controlled. Further, previous contradictions become understandable.

Psychoanalytic psychotherapy is not a creed that Freud handed down to his disciples never to be changed; rather, it is a dynamic, growing, evolving method of helping people solve psychological problems. It is based on the optimistic premise that the human ego, when freed of overburdensome conflict, is generally capable of dealing with most of life's challenges. Psychoanalytic psychotherapy focuses primarily on problems of "neurosis."

Although psychoanalytic psychotherapy has been applied successfully to a broad population of individuals, it must be modified when used with patients presenting with personality disorder. This became apparent as early as the 1930s, when Stern (1938) described 10 criteria for identifying borderline (personality-disorder) patients. These patients initially appeared to have a neurotic personality structure and thus were presumed to be responsive to traditional psychoanalytic treatment. That is, it was assumed they had adequate capacity for repression, that they had achieved object constancy, and that their major difficulty was unresolved unconscious conflict. However, in the unstructured conditions of psychoanalysis, they were inclined to exhibit very primitive defenses. Further, they even occasionally succumbed to psychotic episodes during sessions, although they generally recompensated rapidly when the session was over. Initially clinicians believed that they had merely made a diagnostic error, assuming that these patients were presenting with a neurotic structure when, indeed, they manifested a psychotic structure. Please note that these investigators were speaking of the structure of the personality, not of active "psychosis" or "neurosis." With further study, however, investigators began to realize that the personality organization of these patients fell between the neurotic and psychotic levels of organization. That is, they fell in the "borderline" range of organization. Thus, the clinical concept of borderline personality organization became clarified. What also became clarified was that traditional psychoanalytic treatment had to be modified to meet the needs of these patients.

Contemporary investigators generally agree that all patients manifesting the current personality disorders (Axis-II disorders) present with a borderline personality organization. Patients with the diagnosis of borderline personality disorder represent but one type of personality disorder. Psychoanalytic psychotherapy can be used in treating personality disorders, but the approach must be modified somewhat to meet the needs of the patients.

Psychoanalytic Etiology of the Personality Disorders

We may say that patients with personality disorder differ from neurotic patients in four major ways. First, unlike the neurotic, whose emotional conflicts are presumed to derive from developmental arrest at the Oedipal stage (around 5 to 6 years of age), the personality-disordered patient's arrest is believed to occur much earlier, at the rapprochement subphase of separation-individuation. According to the theory emanating from the research of Margaret Mahler (1968), the separation-individuation subphase of development, spanning from about 5 months to 3 years, is a crucial period in which the child is psychologically born as a separate being quasi-independent from the parent. During the rapprochement subphase of separation-individuation (about 16 to 25 months) the aim of development is consolidation of autonomy and acceptance of separateness from the parent, in most but not all cases the mother. According to Mahler, if the negotiation of the rapprochement subphase goes smoothly for parent and child, the child develops a reasonably enduring, clear sense of self as a separate person with an accompanying sense of being connected with and loved by the parent. If things do not go well during this period, we may observe an inhibition of self-assertion because of abandonment fears, heightened anxiety, clinging to primitive defenses, excessive aggression, proclivity of depression, and a belief in magical solutions. The resulting clinical picture in adolescence and adulthood is not dissimilar to the stormy, overly needy, ambivalent, frightened, magical, and grandiose behavior of the 2-year-old child. Thus, as neurosis is a disorder primarily of anxiety, it can be said that personality disorder is a disorder of self.

Second, unlike the neurotic, whose conflicts lie safely buried in the unconscious sealed by repressive defenses, the personality-disordered patient enjoys little repression. The reason for this is that a more primitive defense, splitting, is employed to keep contradictory, primitive affect states separated from each other. The conflicts remain conscious, but they do not influence each other. The splitting mechanism also keeps apart internalized self and other representations mutually linked with these affect states. The result is a severe deficit in personal integration because the inevitable contradictions inherent in the personality are never dealt with and resolved. Further, interpersonal relations are predictably stormy. Their conflicts, instead of remaining safely in the unconscious, are acted out either in parasuicidal acts or stormy, conflict-ridden interpersonal relationships.

Third, because the developmental arrest theoretically appears to occur in the rapprochement subphase of separation-individuation, there is a failure in object constancy, meaning that the patient is incapable of retaining in his or her mind a consistent internalization of significant (loving) others when they are not present or when they are frustrating. That is, they lack the capacity to relate to others as complex, whole persons, both good and bad.

Fourth, because of the developmental-dynamic factors summarized above, personality-disordered patients have difficulty sustaining an adequate sense of self across interpersonal situations and along dimensions of time. Because there is little or no consistency in their internal representations of others, the self-representation is split, nonintegrated, and inconsistent internally and over time. As one clinician observed, their personalities present themselves as though illuminated by "strobe light" still lifes, in various situations, in various time periods, that have little continuity or cohesion.

The goal of psychoanalytic therapy with personality-disordered patients is not to free conflicts locked in the unconscious but rather to stop the self-destructive behavior, whatever form it might take, and to foster healthy repression and sublimation. Ideally, the goals of psychotherapy with personality-disordered patients is structural change. That is:

- To help these patients overcome the developmental arrest (in the rapprochement subphase)
- to integrate part (split) internalized representations of others into whole, integrated person representations
- to promote object constancy
- to achieve an integrated self-concept across interpersonal situations and along a dimension of time

Psychoanalytic Therapy Techniques with Personality Disorders

To begin, it should be obvious that the therapist should not embark on a therapy with a patient with a diagnosis of personality disorder unless he or she has at least some knowledge of the basic structural differences between the neurotic patient and the patient with a diagnosis of personality disorder. Properly armed, the therapist will not, for example, make the mistake of assuming that the therapeutic alliance, once established, will continue on a relatively stable plain. Because the personality-disordered patient has little, if any, basic trust, the therapist must expect that the patient will fall in and out of the therapeutic alliance in unexpected ways. Progress and emotional closeness may be followed more or less randomly by regression and distancing maneuvers. The therapist must be ever more steady and stable in his or her role in establishing and maintaining the therapeutic alliance.

Second, there is relatively little focus on the unconscious because a robust unconscious has not yet been developed. Thus, there is little emphasis on uncovering unconscious conflicts. Instead, the focus is on conflicted behavior and conflicted relations. Interpretation is rarely used, not because it is likely to hurt the patient, but because the patient is generally not sufficiently psychologically developed to make much use of the interpretation. Further, there is little focus on analysis of resistance. Instead, there is a persistent focus on the primitive defense of splitting, which keeps disparate conflictual material from being worked through and thus integrated in the personality.

Instead of interpretation, the primary technical tools that are used are clarification and, especially, confrontation.

Clarification

Clarification can be viewed as a first step toward helping the patient achieve some cognitive order. It is a nonchallenging exploration with the patients of any data that they present that the therapist feels is vague or contradictory. Clarification functions both to further elucidate specific data for the therapist and to discover the extent to which the patients understands the material they have presented. Clarification may address various areas such as the transference, external reality, patients' defenses, and internal reality. One example of clarification might be: "I notice that you have been looking at your watch with an anxious expression every time I move my chair. Do you have any thoughts about this?" Clarification seeks to "stop action" and help patients become more aware of their own behavior and thinking. Some other examples of clarification are:

- "What made you immediately stop the sexual play with your boyfriend when he smiled? . . . What do you mean when you say you become inhibited?"

- "And you are saying that all those fights with your father occur when the two of you are alone . . . is that the pattern you have noticed?"
- "And you have always played the role of 'champion' of the women in your life?"

Confrontation

Confrontation aims to make patients aware of conflictual and incongruous aspects of the material they present. Confrontation is employed when the therapist perceives that certain observed facts are dynamically and therapeutically significant and that the defense of splitting is being actively employed. Put another way, confrontation is employed by the therapist when patients are using splitting to keep internal contradictions apart, thus avoiding dealing with the conflicts and working them through. Confrontation challenges the patients' primitive defense system by helping them become aware of the conflict. This makes it difficult for the patients to persist in keeping the contradictory ego states separate and therefore encourages work toward resolution. Some examples of confrontation are:

- "Are you aware that you have been rejecting immediately, almost without giving yourself time to think, all of my observations in this hour, and at the same time you have repeatedly stated that I am not offering you anything to work with?"
- "You tell me that you felt enraged at your mother precisely at times when she would let you in on family secrets, indicating her preference for you. Are you aware of that? What do you make of that?"
- "The need to search for a new man seems to emerge in you every time your current boyfriend surprises you with unexpected nice qualities in him. What comes to mind as you think about that?"
- "Whenever you start to get control over yourself and your life, you get scared that if you continue to assert yourself, you will be left all alone. To fight off that feeling, you do impulsive things to make yourself feel better. But, in the long run, it's always against your best interests. Are you aware of this? What do you make of this?"

Transference and Countertransference

When working with patients with personality disorder, there is a much greater emphasis on object relatedness. Because the patients do not have a healthy internalized sense of self, nor rich, enduring internalized representations of significant others, their interpersonal relations are usually tumultuous, destructive, caricatures of mature relatedness. For these reasons, their transference reactions to the therapist are likely to be highly pathological, which tends to severely strain the therapist's capacity to manage the countertransference. Indeed, it may be argued that the single most important factor in treating personality disorder is the management of the transference and its inevitable countertransference in a sensitive, steady, predictable manner. This is by far the most difficult aspect of the treatment of patients with personality disorder and the most crucial. Managed well, patients will begin to experience stability and predictability in the relationship, which fosters the development of basic trust, an essential ingredient in healthy relatedness. The establishment of clear, proper boundaries provides cognitive clarity and security. Within these boundaries the patients can experience the acceptance and compassion of the therapist without fear that the therapist will attack, hurt, or otherwise annihilate them. Conversely, because the patients experience the therapist as sufficiently stable and secure, they will be comforted by the knowledge that they cannot attack, seduce, or otherwise abuse the therapist. If these matters are not managed well, the patients will merely experience yet another failure in a significant, close relationship and thus remain locked into repeating pathological behavioral patterns.

In addition to these "technical" psychotherapeutic matters, it is important to consider the developmental history of patients presenting with a personality disorder. We must remember that psychic structure is built slowly early in the developmental cycle and is maintained and modified throughout life. The developing child's temperament interacts with the environment provided by parents, family, and the broader socio-cultural forces in determining the relative health or weakness of the structural elements. External events influencing the child's development include what is "done to" the child (holding, petting, feeding) and the emotional ambiance of the persons who are "being with" the child (Wolff, 1971). Because of these developmental factors we must be very mindful of another essential factor in effective psychotherapy with personality, "treatment ambiance." The treatment ambiance recreates the "being with" developmental experience of the patients. Many theorists consider the treatment ambiance to be what determines the success or failure of the therapy. Chessick (1977) observed that the patients must continually experience the presence of the therapist. He writes that every session should represent "an encounter between the psychic field of the therapist—which in its maturity extends trust, confidence and hope—and the need-fear dilemma of the patient, who has fallen away from authentic living and being with another person" (p.160). Chessick goes on to describe how in this calm the patient experiences a subtle though powerful soothing. In this predictable, consistent, ambient, subliminal soothing environment the patient develops basic trust that allows the inner resources of the patient to be devoted to growth rather than to defense and also makes the patient more open and responsive to the interventions of the therapist. In this atmosphere, which recreates "good enough mothering" (Winnicott, 1963), old conflicts can be resolved, trauma can be converted to strength, cognitions can be clarified and tied to reality, new behaviors and habits can be learned, and mechanisms for managing emotion can be strengthened. From these changes, which will largely be behaviorally observable, we may infer that a change in structure has been achieved.

Although psychoanalytic psychotherapy is generally modified when employed with patients presenting with personality disorder, the approach remains psychoanalytic in spirit and method, and many of the basic tenets of the therapy remain constant. As in all psychoanalytic approaches, the therapist attempts to be sensitive to the meaning that patients ascribe to their life situation. There will be attention to symbolic meaning and to the emotions that are aroused as the patients attempt to make meaning of the world. The therapy remains feeling-oriented, and every attempt is made to listen for the patients' affects. The therapist will be interested in fears, fantasies, daydreams, memories, et cetera.

Morphologic Organization of the Personality Disorders

Addressing the concept of the domain of morphologic organization, Millon (1990) has written:

> The overall architecture that serves as a framework for an individual's psychic interior may display weaknesses in its structural cohesion, exhibit deficient coordination among its components, and possess few mechanisms to maintain balance and harmony, regulate internal conflicts, or mediate external pressures. The concept of morphologic organization refers to the structural strength, interior congruity, and functional efficacy of the personality system. "Organization" of the mind is almost exclusively derived from inferences at the "intrapsychic level" of analysis. (p. 149)

Millon acknowledges that his conceptualization is akin to current psychoanalytic concepts such as the levels of intrapsychic organization (neurotic, borderline, psychotic), but he tends to apply the concept of psychological morphology to describe stylistic variants in structure that characterize the morphologies of the fourteen personality types articulated in his system.

Although it is difficult to define structure operationally, it can be argued that structure can be studied through the examination of function. One does not act directly on structural deficiencies the way a behavior therapist pinpoints behaviors and manages contingencies. Structural changes necessarily are not directly observable. However, overt behavioral changes can provide us with data from which we can reasonably infer the existence of structural change.

TABLE 9-1 Morphologic Organization Domain

Schizoid Personality
Undifferentiated Organization (e.g., given an inner barrenness, a feeble drive to fulfill needs, and minimal pressures either to defend against or resolve internal conflicts or cope with external demands, internal morphologic structures may best be characterized by their limited framework and sterile pattern)

Avoidant Personality
Fragile Organization (e.g., a precarious complex of tortuous emotions depends almost exclusively on a single modality for its resolution and discharge, that of avoidance, escape, and fantasy and, hence, when faced with personal risks, new opportunities, or unanticipated stress, few morphologic structures are available to deploy and few back-up positions can be reverted to, short of regressive decompensation)

Depressive Personality
Depleted Organization (e.g., the scaffold for morphologic structures is markedly weakened, with coping methods enervated and defensive strategies impoverished, emptied, and devoid of their vigor and focus, resulting in a diminished if not exhausted capacity to initiate action and regulate affect, impulse, and conflict)

Dependent Personality
Inchoate Organization (e.g., owing to entrusting others with the responsibility to fulfill needs and to cope with adult tasks, there is both a deficient morphologic structure and a lack of diversity in internal regulatory controls, leaving a miscellany of relatively undeveloped and undifferentiated adaptive abilities, as well as an elementary system for functioning independently)

Histrionic Personality
Disjointed Organization (e.g., there exists a loosely knit and carelessly united morphologic structure in which processes of internal regulation and control are scattered and unintegrated, with *ad hoc* methods for restraining impulses, coordinating defenses, and resolving conflicts, leading to mechanisms that must, of necessity, be broad and sweeping to maintain psychic cohesion and stability and, when successful, only further isolate and disconnect thoughts, feelings, and actions)

Narcissistic Personality
Spurious Organization (e.g., morphologic structures underlying coping and defensive strategies tend to be flimsy and transparent and appear more substantial and dynamically orchestrated than they are in fact, regulating impulses only marginally, channeling needs with minimal restraint, and creating an inner world in which conflicts are dismissed, failures are quickly redeemed, and self-pride is effortlessly reasserted)

Antisocial Personality
Unruly Organization (e.g., inner morphologic structures to contain drive and impulse are noted by their paucity, as are efforts to curb refractory energies and attitudes, leading to easily transgressed controls, low thresholds for hostile or erotic discharge, few subliminatory channels, unfettered self-expression, and a marked intolerance of delay or frustration)

Sadistic (Aggressive) Personality
Eruptive Organization (e.g., despite a generally cohesive morphologic structure composed of routinely adequate modulating controls, defenses, and expressive channels, surging powerful and explosive energies of an aggressive and sexual nature threaten to produce precipitous outbursts that periodically overwhelm and overrun otherwise competent restraints)

Compulsive Personality
Compartmentalized Organization (e.g., morphologic structures are rigidly organized in a tightly consolidated system that is clearly partitioned into numerous, distinct, and segregated constellations of drive, memory, and cognition, with few open channels to permit interplay among these components)

Negativistic Personality
Divergent Organization (e.g., there is a clear division in the pattern of morphologic structures such that coping and defensive maneuvers are often directed toward incompatible goals, leaving major conflicts unresolved and full psychic cohesion often impossible by virtue of the fact that fulfillment of one drive or need inevitably nullifies or reverses another)

Self-Defeating Personality
Inverted Organization (e.g., owing to a significant reversal of the pain pleasure polarity, morphologic structures have contrasting and dual qualities, one more or less conventional, the other its obverse, resulting in a repetitive undoing of affect and intention, of a transposing of channels of need gratification with those leading to frustration, and of engaging in actions that produce antithetical, if not self-sabotaging, consequences)

Schizotypal Personality
Fragmented Organization (e.g., possesses permeable ego boundaries; coping and defensive operations are haphazardly ordered in a loose assemblage of morphologic structures, leading to desultory actions in which primitive thoughts and affects are discharged directly, with few reality-based sublimations, and significant further disintegrations into a psychotic structural level, likely under even modest stress)

Borderline Personality
Split Organization (e.g., inner structures exist in a sharply segmented and conflictful configuration in which a marked lack of consistency and congruency is seen among elements and levels of consciousness often shift and result in rapid movements across boundaries that usually separate contrasting percepts, memories, and affects, all of which leads to periodic schisms in what limited psychic order and cohesion may otherwise be present, often resulting in transient, stress-related psychotic episodes)

Paranoid Personality
Inelastic Organization (e.g., systemic constriction and inflexibility of undergirding morphologic structures, as well as rigidly fixed channels of defensive coping, conflict mediation, and need gratification, create an overstrung and taut frame that is so uncompromising in its accommodation to changing circumstances that unanticipated stressors are likely to precipitate either explosive outbursts or inner shatterings)

For each of the 14 personality types and disorders measured by the MCMI-III, Millon provides an adjective descriptive of the morphologic structure of that personality along with an expanded description. Table 9-1 summarizes these descriptors.

Schizoid

Millon describes the structure of the schizoid personality as *undifferentiated*. There is a feeble drive to fulfill needs and minimal pressure to defend against or resolve inner conflicts. There is an intrapsychic barrenness, and the inner structural pattern is noted best for its sterile order and limited coordination. A passive style is characterized by little sense of self and a deficiency in the capacity to experience pleasure or pain. Potential strengths of this patient are a steady, calm personality and a disinclination to become embroiled in conflict or enmeshed in pathological relations with others.

Morphologic therapeutic goals might include enhancing the sense of reality of the world and the self, clarifying and enriching the internal representations of self and others, enhancing intimacy, and transforming negative identity to positive identity.

Intervention may include exploring the patient's self-concept and sense of where he or she belongs in the world. A "being with" therapeutic strategy is as important as "doing to." The therapist "loans ego" to the patient. Self-esteem may be enhanced by emphasizing the virtue of the patient's steady, calm style. Confrontation should be minimal to nonexistent, but it may be useful to clarify the relation of emotions to thinking. Encourage the patient to be "present" with reality. Foster development of defenses to increase tolerance of social contact. However, do not set expectancies too high, overwhelm with affect, or collude with the patient's passivity by working harder than the patient.

Avoidant

Avoidant personalities are described as *fragile*. The structure is delicate, tenuous, and easily broken and destroyed. The personality is characterized as unsubstantial and frail. Internally there is a precarious complex of tortuous emotions that are singularly dealt with by the mechanisms of avoidance, escape, and fantasy. Hence, when faced with unanticipated stress, such individuals have few resources available to deploy and few positions to revert to except decompensation. They do not accept reality in the present. Unfortunately, energy is actively misdirected to avoid rather than adapt. Potential strengths include a general cautiousness and an unwillingness to impose on others.

Therapy should aim to reinforce the concept of self as a competent person.

The therapist had best focus on present realities. Discourage the substitution of reality with fantasy. Explore fears and fantasies regarding the consequences of becoming more assertive or effective (i.e., are these abandonment fears?). Supportively confront avoidance and assist the patient in ordering complex emotions. Encourage the patient to counterbalance caution with action. To this end, help the patient develop tolerance for the occasional failure. Finally, avoid taking on the patient's own responsibilities.

Depressive

Millon describes the mophology of the depressive personality as *depleted*. The structure of the personality has a drained, exhausted, impoverished, or bankrupt quality in which there is a supposition of a loss in effective functioning. The scaffolding for morphologic structure is markedly weakened. Coping methods are enervated, and defensive strategies are impoverished, emptied, and devoid of vigor and function. The result is a diminished if not exhausted capacity to initiate actions and regulate affect impulse.

These patients are generally more responsive to treatment and easier to treat than those exhibiting externalizing disorders. Attempt to bolster defensive functioning by fostering adaptive regression to help the ego rest. Facilitate healthy grieving and discourage unhealthy grieving. Help the patients substitute new object representations for lost ones. Highlight the potential growth-enhancing effects of honest self-criticism. Explore the patients' perceptions and experiences of loss. Review thoroughly losses in the patients' life and their past styles of coping with loss. Identify pathological patterns of diminishing, distorting, or deflecting sources of support. Encourage patients to remain in the present and avoid dwelling in the past. Examine internalized representations of significant others and the patients' capacity to retain object constancy.

Dependent

The dependent personality is described as *inchoate*, which means imperfectly formed—being partly but not fully in existence. This personality is incipient, expectant, potential, or contingent. There is both a deficit and a lack of diversity in internal mechanisms and regulatory controls in the dependent personality because of a marked tendency to expect others to take the responsibility for fulfilling needs and managing adult tasks. The result of this life strategy is a relatively undeveloped and undifferentiated capacity to adapt adequately, and the patient has difficulty functioning independently. Potential strengths include a devotion to others and the willingness to be a loyal follower.

The therapist may encourage autonomous functioning by reinforcing the separation-individuation process. A major goal will be to replace primary-process thinking with reality-based thinking. Explore fantasies and fears regarding the consequences of being more independent. Emphasize the positive aspects of this personality style, which include the loyalty and support of others. Address both the "weak" and the "strong" self-image and challenge the weak one. Work to strengthen object constancy in order to reduce the fear of abandonment while the patient strives to become more independent. Take pains to ensure that gains made by the patient do not merely represent temporary compliance with a strong, demanding therapist.

Histrionic

The morphologic organization of the histrionic personality is described as *disjointed*. The personality structure is characterized as disconnected, incoherent, or disordered—a loosely knit, carelessly united conglomerate in which functions of internal regulation and control are scattered and unintegrated. There are few methods of restraining impulses, coordinating defenses, and resolving conflicts. This leads to coping mechanisms that must, of necessity, be broad and sweeping to maintain psychic cohesion and stability. Unfortunately, these primitive defenses serve the purpose of isolating and disconnecting thoughts, feelings, and actions. Sublimation is poorly developed. Regulation of drives and emotions is weak, and energy is scattered and squandered. The extraverted style, however, can be effective and adaptive. These patients are likable, socially skilled, and expressive.

Therapy goals may be to increase orderly thinking and cognitive clarity by linking feelings and thinking as well as increasing sublimation. The therapist may attempt to help the patients integrate previously isolated and split-off aspects of the personality and to reinforce regulatory mechanisms. A major aim will be to decrease the predominant use of primitive defenses such as splitting and primitive idealization. Support the extraverted social style as an asset. Directly confront the diffuse cognitive style and primitive defenses, articulating how they make the patients feel better in the short run but impede mature growth and enduring happiness. Emphasize the need to curtail acting out and the need to develop alternative subliminal channels of expression. It may be advisable to make heavy use of clarification to help order and focus scattered cognition. Emphasize integration of thoughts and feelings.

Narcissistic

The morphologic organization of the narcissist is described as *spurious*. There is a quality of outwardly corresponding to something without having its genuine properties. There is a false, forged, and unauthentic character about these persons. The pathological narcissism of this personality style or disorder should not be confused with healthy narcissism, or self-esteem that must be possessed to some degree by any healthy person. The defenses of narcissistic patients are flimsy and transparent. Capacity to sublimate and control drives and emotions is marginally developed, and defenses and strengths are less substantial than they are in reality. It is an inner world in which conflicts are dismissed, failures are quickly rationalized, and self-esteem is attained by disingenuous, circuitous deception of self and others. Reality is bent or ignored to preserve or "manufacture" the grandiose self. Internalized representations of others are diminished to preserve precious self-image. Defenses consist mostly of devaluation of others and primitive denial. Fortunately, they generally function well in society in comparison to persons with other personality disorders.

With these patients, try to understand and be empathetic to the narcissistic wound. Work toward modification of the internalized representation of self and others. Encourage patients to perceive the self as acceptable, though less than precious. Help them perceive others as separate persons who cannot be expected to gratify infantile, narcissistic needs. Confrontation should be clear but gentle. Confront any omnipotent tendency to devaluate or idealize the therapist. Use clarification to highlight and perpetuate the need for unique identity or preciousness.

Antisocial

Millon's adjective for describing the psychic structure of antisocial patients is *unruly*. It is unlimited in extent, degree, or quantity. Structure is unchecked, lacking in restraint or control. The inner defensive operations are notable for their paucity, as are efforts to curb refractory drives and attitudes, leading to easily transgressed controls. These patients have low thresholds for impulse discharge, few subliminal channels, unfettered self-expression, and a marked intolerance of delay of frustration. Although there clearly is a deficit in super ego functioning, many writers assert that the main deficits lie in the ego itself (Blatt & Shichman,1981). In short, the morphologic deficits of the antisocial personality are severe.

Major aims will be to enhance reality testing, judgment, regulation and control, and adaptive regression. The therapist should work toward increasing the thresholds for impulse discharge by developing and enhancing subliminal channels and increasing the tolerance for frustration. Explore the patients' fantasies about their place in the world. Do not, however, allow uncontrolled expression of anger. The therapist should vigorously (yet calmly and politely) confront thinking patterns that represent failures in decentration and secondary-process thinking. The sense of entitlement should be persistently questioned. Also question the patients' self-image as tough, "number one," and superior to others. Highlight the potential benefits of replacing antisocial behavior with more adaptive, sensation-seeking behavior. Finally, the therapist should avoid any tendency toward sadistic, counteraggressive countertransference.

Sadistic

The sadistic personality is described as *eruptive*. That is, the morphologic structure is inadequate to contain and control drives and emotions. Although the structure is generally cohesive, being composed of routinely adequate modulation controls, defenses, and expressive channels, there are powerful aggressive and sexual energies that overwhelm the forces that generally regulate affect. The apparatus underlying delay of gratification is inadequately developed. The bursting forth of aggression may be sporadic. There is an inadequate balance between emotion and secondary-process activity. Inhibitory apparatus that employ thinking to postpone discharge are inadequate. On the positive side, the sadistic personality may be fearless and courageous. As well, the aggressive qualities may be useful in certain settings.

Therapy should attempt to strengthen regulation and control of drives and affect as well as secondary-process thinking. Use confrontation to help the patients gain a sense of the effect of the explosiveness on other people. Help patients redirect aggressive tendencies to socially appropriate targets. Work toward increasing awareness of the destructiveness of aggressive tendencies on self and others. Explore with patients their phenomenological view of the world that justifies or promotes aggressive-sadistic behavior. When confronting, do not withdraw or reject the patients. Communicate an attitude of accepting the patients but not the sadistic-aggressive behavior. Work toward empathy and decentration using modeling, educative techniques, and confrontation. Confront patients' belief that aggressive-sadistic behavior is "normal" and reasonable. Help the patients use thinking to postpone discharge. Emphasize cognition over emotion. Do not encourage catharsis and other emotional displays. Emphasize that cognition is the mental apparatus that assists the personality to tolerate additional tension. Help the patients realize that the modification of the aggressive-sadistic behavior is in their best interest.

Compulsive

The compulsive personality is characterized as *compartmentalized*. The structure of the personality is divided up or sectioned off. Various elements of the personality are separated into mutually isolated units. There is a marked tendency to divide or separate issues or contents into independent compartments or categories in a way that precludes interrelationships. This division into mutually isolated units results in a psychic structure lacking in normal interactions or cooperation. Because of the extreme compartmentalization, psychic structures are rigidly organized in a tightly consolidated system that is clearly partitioned into numerous, distinct, and segregated constellations of drive, memory, and cognition, with few open channels to permit interplay among these components. Compulsive personalities are not content to impose some minimally sufficient order on their apperceptive world to make it understandable and reasonably predictable. Compulsives mount efforts to organize in such a way as to preclude all or virtually all ambiguity. Interestingly, compulsives may be inconsistent in their thoroughness, being fastidious with some endeavors and remarkably irresponsible or untidy in others. Because of the compartmentalization, the patient may be totally oblivious to the inconsistencies. Further, because of the rigid compartmentalization, true integration, and thus wholeness or completion, is difficult to attain. Generally these patients are orderly, predictable, conscientious, and thorough.

The goal of therapy is to foster communication across the various elements or aspects of the personality. Explore with the patients what their fears and fantasies are about a more relaxed, flexible approach to life. Explore for possible thoughts and feelings that shame the patients, thus contributing to the rigid compartmentalization. Exploration of early traumatic memories that may have contributed to or reinforced the psychic rigidity may be especially useful.

The establishment of basic trust in the therapeutic relationship may be essential in contributing to a greater sense of confidence, which may in turn foster greater confidence in reducing rigidity. Support beneficial aspects of compulsivity while pointing our how it may limit creativity and effectiveness. The focus will be on affect and integrating affect and feelings. The therapist may encourage adaptive regression to provide an opportunity for psychic structures to reorder themselves into new configurations. Confrontation will be used primarily in attempts to link affect and thinking. Compulsive structures are generally highly resistant to treatment. Avoid responding in kind to intellectualized defenses.

Negativistic

Millon describes the negativistic personality disorder as *divergent*. By this he means that the personality is deviant or differing. A lack of convergence characterizes this personality disorder. There is a clear division in the pattern of internal structural elements such that coping and defensive maneuvers are often directed toward incompatible goals, leaving major conflicts unresolved and psychic cohesion impossible because fulfillment of one drive or need inevitably nullifies or reverses another. These patients, like the compulsives, are unwilling to give up anything, thus gaining little or nothing. Yet, unlike the compulsives, they exhibit no vigorous suppression of conflicts. There is a lack of commitment to singular selected goals; the patients may be described as inconsistent, and conflicts remain unresolved. Developmentally it may be speculated that there is a fixation at the separation-individuation stage of development in which there is considerable ambivalence and hostility.

The structural aim is convergence. The therapist may attempt to help patients break self-destructive repetition compulsion in which the individual recreates disillusioning experiences that parallel those of the past. The passive-aggressive personality usually evolves when a child internalizes extreme inconsistencies and vacillations in parental attitudes and behaviors. For this reason the "being with" aspects of the therapy coupled with the therapist's special care to be consistent and predictable will be especially important. Early childhood experiences of parental inconsistencies that were confusing and frustrating may be explored The therapist may point out that although the patients' use of repetition compulsion is reasonably intended to overcome conflict, in fact it serves the function of unnecessarily recreating disillusionment, which is destructive. There may be an attempt to help patients become aware of their tendency to recreate disillusioning experiences and to set up self-fulfilling prophecies of rejection and betrayal. The destructive effects of the practice of endlessly testing the sincerity of others may be pointed out. The patients will be helped to become aware of how they may contribute to disillusionment and how they can become more accepting of the frailties of others.

Negativistic patients can be expected to recreate the feared and anticipated rejection by the therapist. The therapist must be especially careful to "keep the therapeutic ball in the patients' court." At the same time, the patients' sense of vulnerability and disappointment is so great that such testing is inevitable, and only by repeated experiences with a consistent, nonwithdrawing therapist will the patients attain the confidence and security necessary for growth.

Self-Defeating

Millon describes the morphologic organization of the self-defeating personality as *inverted*. What is inverted is the normal tendency of the organism to pursue pleasure and avoid pain. The normal, expected tendency toward life tropism is turned inside out or upside down. Instead of pursuing life or pleasure in the expected way, the self-defeating patient reverses the pain-pleasure polarity . There is a dual quality about these persons, one more or less conventional and the other its obverse. This results in a masochistic, repetitive undoing of positive affect and adaptive behavior. Channels of need gratification are transposed, leading away from satisfaction and toward frustration. The result is that patients engage in actions that produce antithetical or even self-sabotaging consequences.

A major therapeutic goal will be to re-establish the basic aim and function of ego, which is adaptation. Explore the patients' fantasies and fears of the consequences of leading an adaptive, self-promoting life in which basic needs will be gratified. Identify and explore factors that encourage the self-defeating style. Explore the possibility of overidentification with sadistic life models (identification with aggressor.) Confront self-destructiveness in a treatment ambiance that fosters security and self-acceptance. Emphasize working relationships with adaptive, healthy aspects of the personality, drawing on the reasonably healthy structure. Help the patients identify and understand the role of the sadistic superego and the gratification of experiencing pain. Explore weaknesses in the mechanism of guilt expiation and help the patients develop more constructive methods of extinguishing guilt.

Be aware that such patients may develop a projective identification in which sadomasochistic tendencies are projected onto the therapist and then reacted to accordingly. The patients may invite sadistic treatment by the therapist. Avoid succumbing to this sadistic countertransference.

Schizotypal

Millon describes the schizotypal personality as *fragmented*. By this he means that the personality is broken or divided into disorganized or ununified pieces. The structure lacks focus, unity, purpose, or cohesiveness. Millon describes a structure in which coping and defensive operations are haphazardly ordered in a disorganized, loose assemblage. The structural deficit is very severe, making the patient prone to engage in spasmodic and desultory actions in which primitive thoughts and affects are discharged directly. The patient will be highly disorganized and generally incapable of mounting reality-based, adaptive behavioral plans. Even modest stress is likely to result in serious disintegration of structural integrity. Such a patient is generally receptive to benevolent interventions.

In therapy, assist the development of basic ego functions such as reality testing, judgment, regulation and control, and thought processes. The therapist should explore the patient's perception of the inner and outer world. Focus on reinforcing fragmented defenses and provide guidance in reality testing and judgment functions. Support existing mechanisms for regulation and control by setting limits on aberrant behavior. Help the patient order thoughts by clarification and educative techniques. The morphologic structure of the schizotypal is similar to that of the schizophrenic. Hence, the therapist should avoid placing too many demands on the fragmented structure. Finally, outcome expectations should be modest.

Borderline

Millon describes the structure of the borderline personality as *split*. The personality has a scattered, spread-out, confused, and difficult character that is hard to understand. There is a tendency to move in many directions. The personality lacks concentration and restraint. Inner structures exist in an undifferentiated configuration in which there is a marked lack of clarity and distinctness among the various elements of the personality. There is a blurring across levels of consciousness and an unrestrained flow across boundaries that usually separate unrelated percepts, memories, and affects. The result is a periodic, unpredictable dissolution of what limited psychic order and cohesion is normally present. Images of self and others are split and blurred. Potential strengths are a tendency to form attachments to the therapist and a rich complexity.

The primary goal of therapy is to establish the identity as a separate person. To do this, explore the patient's experience of separation from significant others and sense of self as an independent but socially interacting individual. Utilize the patient's intense emotional energy as fuel for the therapy. Confront splitting and other primitive defenses such as projective identification. Confront the deleterious results of acting out, pointing out how it and other regressive behaviors make the patient feel good in the present while perpetuating pathology and stifling growth. Relate to the patient's strengths as well as weaknesses. Although the therapist should anticipate periodic, cyclical regression, the expectation of continued growth should be clearly communicated.

As with no other personality disorder, vigorously control countertransference. Finally, avoid the overuse of confrontation, especially when the patient is not employing primitive defenses.

Paranoid

Millon's descriptor for the paranoid personality is *inelastic,* as they are slow to react or respond to changing conditions. There exists an inflexible, rigid, unyielding quality and a brittleness in which there is a lack of capability to recover from stress or react to change. When describing the structural deficits of the paranoid personality, Millon draws attention to the systemic constriction and inflexibility of the coping and defensive mechanisms. He focuses on paranoid individuals' rigidly fixed channels of conflict mediation and need gratification, characteristics that create an overstrung and taut frame that is so uncompromising in its accommodation to changing circumstances that unanticipated stressors are likely to precipitate either explosive outbursts or shattering of the inner structure.

The primary goals of therapy with this type of patient are to establish some degree of basic trust, relax defenses, and reduce hypervigilance. Hence, confrontation will probably be inadvisable. Slowly and progressively work toward building trust. Establish a quiet, formal, and genuine respect for the patient as a human being. Allow the patient to explore thoughts and feelings at a pace that can be tolerated. Establish an atmosphere in which the patient can share anxieties without the humiliation and rejection that he or she has come to expect. Support attempts to find satisfaction in the self and to nurture the self. Reveal neither personal weakness nor show undo compassion. Resist being intimidated.

CASE STUDY

Background

I have worked in psychotherapy with this woman for a number of years. She is in her early 50s and has been in treatment since college. Her mother, still living, has been diagnosed as schizophrenic and presents with a more or less hysterical or even "hebephrenic" quality marked by confusion, unpredictability, silliness, and contentiousness. The mother has been briefly hospitalized several times for psychoticlike symptoms but blandly (blithely) insists that the admissions were only for physical illness.

As few demands could be placed on the mother's scanty reserve of ego strength, her two daughters were raised primarily by their father with domestic help. A large financial trust provided the mother with economic security so that she had to manage few responsibilities, which has generally allowed her to cope at home and avoid hospitalization. Mother is usually confused, antagonistic, and unreliable.

My patient remembers many incidents from her childhood in which her mother "forgot" to pick her up after various youth activities such as attending a movie or going shopping. Her father was a stable and prosperous businessman. He provided her with warmth, love, and predictability and she was very close to him. He was steady, predictable, and rational, and she recalls that he provided her with warmth, love, and emotional support. Sadly, her father had been diagnosed with a slow-developing form of cancer and the family knew that he would die an early death. He did die when my patient was in college. His death precipitated her only psychiatric hospitalization for depression.

Thus, she grew up in an atmosphere of confusion, chaos, instability, and irrationality marked by a fear of loss and a sense of dread. Her mother was physically healthy but emotionally distant, unpredictable, undependable, and highly irrational. Father provided security, rationality, and predictability, but his disease constantly threatened to take him away from her while she was still in her formative years.

After her hospitalization she entered outpatient psychotherapy. With the help of diligent therapeutic work she managed to earn a college degree and develop technical skills that led to a career lasting about 15 years before she had to retire because of emotional as well as health reasons. However, she is at this time undergoing a series of surgical operations that may make it physically possible for her to work again. She very much wants to return to work, as she is aware that work helps center her and supports her self-esteem.

Interpersonally she would be described as warm, loyal, generous, and thoughtful. When she is not depressed, she has a dry but sharp sense of humor. She is cautious to a fault and never makes a move without first searching for every possible thing that could go wrong. She is not passive-aggressive, but any event or intervention that threatens change of any kind is met with fierce resistance. She is insecure, fearful, and obsessive. She is very bright and has a natural appreciation for art and music, but, with the exception of the foreshortened technical career, most of her talents remain relatively undeveloped and undifferentiated. She is forever planning to go to concerts or exhibits but usually cancels at the last minute, complaining of fatigue.

She lives several hours away from her mother and remains in a conflicted enmeshment with her that has resisted therapeutic attention. There is an obsessive quality about this enmeshment; it seems she perseverates in a desperate struggle to gain the emotional support and stability from her mother that she missed as a child. She complains of chronic exhaustion, which is exacerbated when she has engaged in yet another futile effort to extract nurturance from her mother. She has a few long-lasting and committed friendships, but most of the time she remains isolated, living alone with her cat.

She is not without the capacity to experience pleasure, but at the same time she has a remarkable capacity to cast a bleak, sad, hopeless complexion on whatever potential source of happiness or gratification may be available to her.

On Axis-I the working diagnosis is Major Depression, Dysthymia, and a Generalized Anxiety Disorder.

MCMI-III

She was tested periodically and her current MCMI-III results are presented in Table 9–2.

The Axis-I diagnoses are clearly revealed by MCMI-III elevations on the Major Depression, Dysthymia, and Anxiety scales. Further, the elevations on the Avoidant, Self-Defeating, and Dependent scales crisply and unambiguously describe her Axis-II personality disorder and confirm the direction

TABLE 9-2 MCMI-III of the Case Example

MCMI-III Inventory		Base Rate
	Validity	0
X	Disclosure	80*
Y	Desirability	20
Z	Debasement	72
1	Schizoid	62
2A	Avoidant	99***
2B	Depressive	0
3	Dependent	84*
4	Histrionic	46
5	Narcissistic	38
6A	Antisocial	36
6B	Aggressive (Sadistic)	48
7	Compulsive	63
8A	Negativistic	20
8B	Self-Defeating	93**
S	Schizotypal	61
C	Borderline	45
P	Paranoid	30
A	Anxiety	77*
H	Somatoform	66
N	Bipolar: Manic	62
D	Dysthymia	95***
B	Alcohol Dependence	60
T	Drug Dependence	25
PT	PTSD	65
SS	Thought Disorder	62
CC	Major Depression	88**
PP	Delusional Disorder	25

*BR 75–84
**BR 85–94
***BR 95 and above

the treatment took. The adjectives *fragile, inverted,* and *inchoate* exquisitely describe her personality and her struggles.

Psychoanalytic Psychotherapy

My therapeutic strategy with her employed some confrontation, particularly when she was especially avoidant or paralyzed with indecision or when the enmeshment (dependency) with her mother became especially destructive to both of them. The weak (fragile) self-image was routinely challenged. It was necessary to be especially reality-based and logical to provide a sort of psychological road map she could use as a guide in negotiating the precarious complex of tortuous emotions she experienced. Confrontation was also used extensively to deal with her avoidance of independence and her tendency to "enbleaken" (invert) every potential source of pleasure. However, the primary therapeutic effect was achieved by the "being with" aspects of the therapy. Cognitive clarity had to be balanced with a warm and accepting ambiance that soothed her anxiety while supporting and encouraging her growth toward competence and independence. In view of the wounds in her childhood and the ongoing pathological relationship with her mother, it was necessary to be modest in our expectations. This is a woman who had to be taken out of the hospital by the hand, literally, to live independently at the local YWCA. She also admits that the only reason she eventually left the Y to take an apartment was that the Y building was torn down. Yet, therapeutic progress measured in inches developed into miles. She had eventually managed a demanding technical job for 15 years; she mustered her courage to travel to New York City to hear her favorite opera singer; she took several long trips including one to eastern Europe, calling me only once for support when "she lost her insides" (her term for losing object constancy.) Great gains had been made in autonomy. Further, using money she earned on her job together with some inheritance money, she designed and contracted the construction of her own patio home, a gigantic achievement for her.

The MCMI-III clearly confirmed the types of deficits in morphologic structure that required intervention. Over time there were small but very important changes including greatly bolstered object constancy, increased capacity to experience pleasure, greater self-confidence, and a greater sense of personal responsibility. Unfortunately, her increasing physical problems have progressively exacerbated her emotional problems and she has become increasingly reclusive. It is hoped that her emotional condition will improve as she improves physically and gains greater mobility.

One particular incident in her psychotherapy captures the nature of progress with this type of patient. She was convinced that she was far too damaged to ever have a child of her own, yet she felt a natural longing for one. As an alternative she had discussed getting a pet for years, but she was reluctant to adopt one because she feared that she would be too unstable to be a "good enough mother" and she did not want to hurt or neglect any young thing as she had been. Finally, after much deliberation on her part and support on my part, she bought a kitten. It turned out that, in fact, she was a very good mother and she and the cat prospered emotionally. Reflecting on this outcome one day in my office, she said in a very soft voice, "You know, Dr. Dorr, I've come to realize that I'm a better mother to my cat than my mother was for me. Maybe I could have had a baby." She shared this moment with me calmly and without remorse. She was comforted to learn that she could take care of someone, maybe even herself. This event elegantly describes the morphological changes that occurred over the course of her therapy.

Summary

The morphological structure of the personality disorders is one of the richer domains. So too, psychoanalytic psychotherapy is one of the more complex and satisfying of the therapies. The structure of the character is an appropriate target for the traditional techniques of psychoanalytic theory. Through clarification and confrontation, many of the deficits of characterlogical morphology can be addressed. The MCMI-III is an excellent method by which to examine the underlying structures of our patients.

References

Blatt, S., & Shichman, S. (1981). Antisocial behavior and personality organization. In S. Tuttnam, C. Kaye, & M. Zimmerman (Eds.), *Object and self: A developmental approach: Essays in honor of Edith Jacobson.* New York: International Universities Press.

Chessick, R. D. (1977). *Intensive psychotherapy of the borderline patient.* Northvale, NJ: Aronson.

Mahler, M. S. (1968). *On human symbiosis and the vicissitudes of individuation.* New York: International Universities Press.

Millon, T. (1986). Personality prototypes and their diagnostic criteria. In T. Millon & G. L. Klerman (Eds.), *Contemporary directions in psychopathology: Toward the DSM-IV.* New York: Guilford Press.

Millon, T. (1990). *Toward a new personology: An evolutionary model.* New York: Guilford Press.

Stern, A. (1938). Psychoanalytic investigation of and therapy in the border line group of neuroses. *Psychoanalytic Quarterly, 7,* 467–489.

Winnicott, D. W. (1963). Psychiatric disorder in terms of infantile maturation processes. In D. W. Winnicott (Ed.), *The maturational processes and the facilitation environment: Studies in the theory of emotional development.* New York: International Universities Press.

Wolff, H. H. (1971). The therapeutic and developmental functions of psychotherapy. *British Journal of Medical Psychology, 44,* 117–130.

10

Experiential Mood Therapy with the MCMI-III

LEE HYER, JEFF BRANDSMA, *and* LUCINDA SHEALY

Against a backdrop of an often moribund theoretical ecosystem in personological psychology, Millon's model has remained alive and well. While there are many ways to parse this formulation, the primacy of people's redundant patterns (personality) is paramount. These styles of activity are captured in both a categorical and dimensional formulation (a class-quantitative approach) of distinctive domains, in which both components figure into the mosaic of the person. Millon (1984) has labeled these domains structural and functional attributes. Structural attributes represent deeply embedded and enduring templates that provide "important memories, attitudes, needs, fears, conflicts, etc., which guide and transform the nature of ongoing life events" (pp. 460–461). Functional attributes, on the other hand, are processes that transpire either within the person or between person and environment. They are less-enduring, only quasi-permanent features of the person that are visible and consistent. Use of both structural and functional components in the formulation of the person provides a way, then, to formulate problems for the human change process.

Affect is a functional attribute that is prepotent in the understanding of the person and in the change process. The purpose of this chapter is to highlight the affective domain of the Millon model (1969, 1981). In the context of this book it will involve a brief description of this paradigm and a more lengthy discussion of experiential therapies (ET). Our thesis is that the therapeutic algorithm specific to the complexity of a client's self-defeating styles involves two elements: a knowledge of these personality patterns (chiefly the ability to "unpack" styles from symptoms), and the ability to address "hot" issues (the affective domain). Since the first portion of this has already been articulated (Millon, 1969, 1981, 1983, 1987), our effort here is to discuss ET by highlighting one ET method, focused expressive psychotherapy (FEP). We intend to blend the importance of personality with the prepotency of the affective domain, to present the affective domain of each personality style, and to highlight several personality types. Next we examine the use of ET on the personalities from a domain perspective. Then we discuss modal issues and problems. Finally, we briefly describe a case study using the MCMI-III.

Experiential Therapies

ET represents a broad array of (sometimes strange) bedfellows whose posture toward psychotherapy has several common features. The most notable is a relentless dissection and focus on the client's current experiencing (sensations, feeling states, and emotions). Theories encompassing humanism (Rogers, 1961), existentialism (Jourard, 1971; Lang, 1975), gestalt (Perls, Hefferline, & Goodman, 1951), constructivism (Guidano, 1991), and, yes, experiential therapies themselves (Greenberg, Safran, & Rice, 1990; Safran & Greenberg, 1991b; Safran & Segal, 1990) have prospered. Additionally, updated versions of these positions have been perfected and retrofitted as central methods or techniques, including originally client-centered ones like focusing (Gendlin, 1991) and gestalt soft body techniques (Smith, 1985) (see Table 10-1). Many now exist independently, having a life of their own.

At its core, ET is elegant in its simplicity (see Table 10-2). The client determines the ongoing content and the therapist facilitates a moment-by-moment recounting of the client's experiencing with a special emphasis on affect. The heart of this matter involves the therapist's facilitation of experiential (emotional) processing, not (as is typically done) conceptual processing. Also, experiential knowing deploys attention to those "areas" of a person that are most relevant and optimal for change (Greenberg, Rice, & Elliott, 1993). Done well, this results in the awareness of the current state of the person; informed choices and improved psychological processing result.

Therapy then is the expansion of awareness, performed most efficiently via emotions: "The heart has its reasons, of which reason knows nothing" (Pascal). The datum and goal of therapy are one-fold—that is, expanded awareness. By means of this experiencing, self-referential core components of the person are addressed, differentiated, and liberated for meaning altering.

TABLE 10-1 Theories and Techniques of ET

Gestalt
Allow the natural flow of unfinished affective business—a completion of the awareness and expression cycles of human action in a "response-able" fashion.
Techniques: two-chair, soft-body.

Client-Centered
Active and empathic listening and reflection of feelings under safe conditions to allow natural growth and reprocessing.
Techniques: reflection of feelings, affect concentration in any of the time-limited psychotherapies (e.g., focusing).

Psychodynamic
Updated focus in the corrective emptional experience unfolding in an interpersonal dynamic, usually in a short-term psychotherapy.
Techniques: evocative unfolding, affect concentration in any of the time-limited psychotherapies.

Focused Expressive Psychotherapy
Process of unearthing in a structured content unfinished business (especially anger) for restructured emotional expressions.
Techniques: five-step procedure high-lighted by physiological and emotional involvement.

Schematic Restructuring
Complete unfinished business by accessing person and interpersonal schemas leading to a change in their core processes.
Techniques: decentering, disconformation.

TABLE 10-2 Tenets of ET*

1. Emotions are the primary biological and learned adaptations to living.
2. Emotions are motivational and organize all responses personally and interpersonally.
3. Emotions constitute the principal focus of human change but are coequal with and "known through" cognitions and actions.
4. Emotions are a form of meaning or appraisal accessed through experiential schemas.
5. Emotional awareness provides a tacit and direct understanding of human functioning.
6. Emotional restructuring requires schema activation or personologic pattern alteration.
7. Curative therapeutic components include the use of rationale, examination of current awareness, identification of problems or self-defeating patterns, and the presentation of options—all done experientially.

*Adapted from Greenburg and Safran (1991).

As the universal need for self-protective avoidance melts, a soft knowing evolves. From this expansion of "tacit" background come richer or different meanings and increased choices.

FEP is one experiential technique for loosening generally overcontrolled affect. This technique is especially helpful for clients who possess overcontrolled anger and who can identify significant others as adversaries or objects. If not anger, however, inhibited emotions (grief, sadness, joy, fear) are its targets. This technique assumes that a natural tendency exists for the human system to both remain dynamically homeostatic and to fulfill the self. This proclivity can be arrested when emotional expression is blocked and disorder results; compromise, placation, and conformity are the results.

The client is considered trapped in a state of incompleteness. In this formulation the client develops a "preattentive" formulation that is unfinished. Accordingly, therapy requires a stimulation of the unfinished emotional state, to be experienced at a level closer to its full intensity. In fact, the proponents of FEP posit that the patient transits through five phases, including disownment (denial of emotional experience), phobia (fear of the consequences of ownership of emotional reactions), implosion (an impasse characterized by lack of awareness, deadness, or numbness), explosion (acceptance of and expression of previously disowned emotion), and completion (a process characterized by decrease of emotional intensity, cognitive reprocessing, and a feeling of aliveness). This sequence is reprocessed at an attentive level into a "new experientially derived schemata" (Engle, Beutler, & Daldrup, 1991).

FEP does not attempt to alter information-processing deficits resulting from Axis I perturbations or Axis II patterns. Rather, this method addresses either the narrative part or experienced moments for purposes of recognition and reconstruction of new meaning: Experiential (emotional) processing at that moment in the on-going drama of the person is paramount. The roles assigned to the patient include acknowledging behavior, thought, and feelings; trusting one's own organism; and committing to work, monitoring that work, and performing homework assignments (Daldrup et al., 1988; see Table 10-3). Again, when a person's emotions are over- or undercontrolled, the person is cut off from self and a candidate for symptoms or self-alienation.

Procedurally FEP involves a five-step process (Table 10-3). Step 1 is the identification of a focus for work. As in any productive effort, the person who begins with a focused task, an end in mind, and a plan of action increases the chance of success. In this step the patient and therapist identify a piece of work or "unfinished business"—often a result of strange feelings, often related to a significant other, or often following logically and directly from undone emotional work with parents. One sure indicator is the presence of avoidant mechanisms preventing expression of unfinished business. Headaches, negative self-statements, and interpersonal fears are typical signposts indicative of needed change.

TABLE 10-3 Focused Expressive Psychotherapy*

Role of the Patient
1. To acknowledge behavior, thoughts, and feelings
2. To trust one's own organism
3. To make a definite commitment to work or not to work
4. To assess the work that has been done in the session
5. To carry out the homework assignments

Steps of FEP
1. Establishment of a focus for work
2. Elicitation of a commitment to work
3. Development of the work process itself to the point at which affective intensity peaks and then gradually begins to decline
4. Assessment or review of the work conducted, during which the patient reorganizes the experience
5. Development of plans and homework for the future

*Adapted from Daldrup, et al. (1988).

Step 2 is the commitment to work. As Daldrup et al. (1988) note, a query into the willingness or interest to change is sufficient: "Are you sure you want to work on this?" Hesitancy must be addressed and "therapeutically manipulated," if necessary—finessed, paradoxed ("you may not be ready to...."), or interpreted—exposing the ambivalence. This inquiry provides the gateway to accepting the work of ET, the understanding of the about-to-be systematic evocative unfolding (or the exploration of the resistance to enter the change facilitation process). At the worst, the split of the person to work is exposed; at best, the collaborative process unfolds.

Step 3 is the experiment itself—working through "unfinished business" via experiential learning. The target here is the what and how of avoidance; the client is avoiding either some expression or awareness of effect. The therapist is limited only by his or her creativity in the choice of FEP experiments, accessing motoric, sensory, verbal, and interpersonal patterns of expression. The guiding principle is to increase or magnify the client's current place in "real time" phenomenology. The now experience is exaggerated, polarized, cajoled, manipulated, or browbeaten until a change occurs or an impasse is reached. In the case of a change the affective schema is activated, experienced, and holistically integrated; in the case of an impasse a realization of the persistence of a stuck choice is highlighted. Often the increased use of affective expressiveness moves the client through the impasse. If an impass remains, a language tag places it in reachable storage, never too far from access.

The flagship exercise of FEP is the two-chair or empty-chair technique. Typically the client's conflict can be identified and this technique applied intrapsychically or interpersonally. Greenberg, Rice, and Elliott (1993) also identified two types of "splits," each a candidate for a different two-chair exercise. The first involves a conflict split, interruption of self-evaluation and self-coercion ("should do"); in the second, a self-interruptive split, involving an disruption of expression, one part of the self interrupts the other part. In both, ambivalence, battling selves, clouded affective processes, and natural "neurotic mechanisms" are classified, parsed, and emotionally completed. These are hygienically cleansed of confusion and allowed to remain as is. (An example is given in the case history). The empty-chair technique too is employed, but this method highlights unfinished business with others, often those who have been lost or who were abusers.

Steps 4 and 5 include an assessment of the impact of work and plan development and homework, respectively. After the emotional work of the experiment settles (impasse or completion), the assessment phase (Step 4) integrates this work at the cognitive level, a reformulation that impacts on the new current reality. Typical phases like "I feel loose," or "You know, this feels right to me" are uttered. The therapist has only to gently probe (or label) and recognize the new status. In Step 5, plans for the future are made and direction is provided for further experienced change. Experiences are emotionally or behaviorally based, always to move the new felt possibilities to a new integrated reality ("Stay with this feeling and say to your mother (in the empty chair). . .").

Primacy of Feelings

In this era of the "affective revolution" (Safran & Greenberg, 1991), one position regarding the many opinions of the "place" of emotion and cognition seems to be accepted, that is, that they are "fused" (Engle, Beutler, & Dalrup, 1991). While the form of this fusion varies with the specific theory (and clarity of operationalization is not evident), thoughts and emotions are seen to coexist and be co-determinant. The question of how to unpack these interdependent components most efficiently is, however, most relevant. When dealing with human data, the experiential therapist perforce addresses emotions in the creation of new cognitions and meaning structures. From a cognitive perspective, the experiential therapist examines unacknowledged experiences and facilitates discovery in the creation of new meanings. The access of uninformed, unknown, or inchoate feelings stimulates and helps integration in this process. Techniques include the stimulation of the inner experience, focusing attention, remaining with the target feeling, symbolizing the experience, and consolidating the new meanings. In the exploration of the inner world the client becomes aware of being an active agent in his or her symptom formation, of being the one who actively "meaning makes," and that through this awareness (content and process), past and present information commingle in new and fresh ways—change occurs. Relative to other domains, affect seems to facilitate the unfolding of this process; the current understanding of "feeling" now mixes with the "past" problem pattern or symptom to provide a reprocessing. Ultimately the client senses this process as his or her own and becomes an active information/emotion processor. This is a key part in experiential discovery.

Enter Schema/Personality

Just as any current diagnostic system necessitates some dependence on theory (e.g., mental disorders exist, symptoms result from stress, etc.), so too, a "little" assistance in person constructs on the part of the therapist is required and necessary. Borrowing from a host of theories including object relations and personologists (to wit, Millon and Benjamin), we can restate consensus by noting that each human possesses both genetic and environmental resilience and vulnerability factors, that the person adapts (even in psychopathological patterns), that this adaptation takes a logical and consistent form based on a replay of original object relations, and that people maintain this consistency across time. The product of this process is known as personality.

Several issues require attention here to consolidate the importance of personality with the endorsement of the primacy of emotions in the change process. The key tenet is that personality provides the needed framework that allows for therapeutic vision and direction. (This is not to underplay the importance of dissonance inherent in this construct, perhaps chiefly the problems of co-morbidity and definition.) Where affect is concerned, however, other problems unfold. First, personality styles vary in the importance of the domain unique to each. Antisocial personalities, for example, are defined predominantly by their behaviors, histrionic styles are noted for their emotive states, et cetera. The relative salience of affect, then, must be determined differentially in each personality. Second, several personalities are emotionally unstable by nature. The borderline, histrionic, antisocial, and narcissistic personalities are of special concern. It is not unusual for these styles to segue into Axis I symptoms and therapeutic plans. The particular influence of each of these styles (and others), then, is a necessary concern of the therapist. Third, it appears that the distinction between traits (the hallmark of personality) and symptoms (the hallmark of disorders) is often blurry at best (Bronisch & Klerman, 1991). The affective domain especially fluctuates, confuses, and deceives even the careful provider. The source (trait or symptom) and purpose of affect, then, are often unclear, requiring careful clinical deliberation. Knowledge of personality dynamics becomes important.

Personality

In recent years several models on the interaction of personality and symptom disorders have evolved. These include the paradigms that ascribe prepotency to personality (predisposition, common cause, and spectrum models); those that place importance on the influence of symptoms (scar and complication); and the pathoplasticy model, which argues for an interaction between these two constructs. A construct that assists in the understanding of how personality is important and can "lead" to various formations is schema. It also provides some understanding of how affect is central to personality and to the change process. Now popular (Freeman, 1992; Leventhal, 1984; Safran & Segal, 1990), schema is a constructionist concept of how the self is organized, regulated, and maintained. It is similar to the older idea of a complex. It refers to organizing the tacit knowledge that is self-referential. It monitors by an affective system that is always active. It modulates all person activities, including perceptual-motor and meaning making.

This process represents quite an undertaking, a whole-person learning. Early in life, core relational themes (Lazarus, 1991) develop, each encompassing components of interacting with the environment. As it becomes a complex knowing system, a schema becomes organizationally closed (relatively) and does not easily admit "other" meanings (Guidano, 1991). "Problem" stimuli (as in trauma) are not assimilated or accommodated, and inflexibility, maladaptation, and a pervasiveness of a new stuck position can be the result. In this framework, then, symptoms are the result of the rigid parameters of this normal schema processing.

What is central here is that schemas and personality dance together to define and direct the person. Millon (1984) considered schemas as structural attributes (noted in the Introduction, p. 451): "images and inclinations that provide a template of imprinted residues which guide and transform the nature of ongoing life events." These are the cognitive and affective substrates (invariant patterns) that contain residues of the past in the form of memories, intrapsychic constructs, and self-images. These are the core schemas that select and synthesize incoming data, direct actions, and organize the patterns of the person. In turn, schemas unfold, giving rise to personality styles or traits. Beck, Freeman, and associates (1990) wrote:

> Attributes such as dependency and autonomy, which are conceptualized in motivational theories of personality as basic drives, may be viewed as a function of a conglomerate of basic schema. In behavioral or functional terms, the attributes may be labeled as "basic strategies." These specific functions may be observed in an exaggerated way in some of the overt behavioral patterns attributed, for example, to the dependent or schizoid personality disorders. (p.7)

Personality "traits" identified by adjectives such as *dependent, withdrawn, arrogant,* or *extraverted* may be conceptualized as the overt expression of these underlying structures. By assigning meanings to events, the cognitive structures start a chain reaction culminating in the kinds of overt behavior (strategies) that are attributed to personality traits. Behavioral patterns that we commonly ascribe to personality traits or dispositions ("honest," "shy," "outgoing"), consequently represent interpersonal strategies developed from the interaction between innate dispositions and environmental influences.

Thus, the lines of demarcation between schema/personality and symptoms are not crystal clear. Schemas are "more core" and give rise to personality styles. Core schemas are "person" positions that provide the key elements of identity. In the thinking of the cognitive-behavioral therapists, they are "compelling" to the person, even when latent. Epstein (1991) even argues that such schemas are part of the self-theory, postulating that they are responsible for all coping or behavioral strategies of the person. Regarding personality, Sullivan (1953) noted that "security operations" are required during the normal development for protection from real or perceived threats. Adler (1964), too, labeled these (personality patterns) "safeguards" and "methods of operation," whose function it is to protect and foster the life style (schema). They consist of modal styles and self-perpetuated patterns of thoughts, feelings, and actions. The combination of schema and personality, then, incorporate the structural (hard-wired schema) and functional (personality-based, expressive modes of regulatory action) processes or attributes that transpire within the person and between him or her and others. The affective, cognitive, and behavioral complexes of the person together make up much of the person.

Symptoms

The last part of this model involves symptoms. Symptoms are descriptions or extensions of the client's coping style. They are anchored in the client's schemas and personality style(s) and take on significance and meaning in that context. Symptoms tend to be phasic and reactive to external as well as internal perturbations; they are also relatively transient. If a person does become symptomatic (depressed, anxious, or showing PTSD problems), he or she does so by undergoing a "shift," a stressor-influenced process whereby schema and personality styles become directed to and by the symptom or current disorder (Beck & Freeman, 1990). In the case of depression this would involve stressor-based rules of hopelessness and negativity; in the case of anxiety, danger and uncertainty.

As we transit into the therapy section, the interaction of these constructs in this human change process is relevant. How does the therapist alter such a stable formation? While the complexity of the person may be beyond personologic explanation (Wiggins & Schwartz, 1991), it is argued that the plasticity of the person is only increased by an emotional self-awareness that reaches "more" tacit self-references. In this sense the person is an epistemological animal whose self theories must be addressed, challenged, and expanded. When askew (as in the stress of psychopathology), ET is optimal when it "tickles" the core schema and personality. The former (schema) has laid the foundation for the self ("this is who I am") and has organized the personality to protect it. It is now "experienced" closer to its depths. The latter (personality) becomes a "go-for," the resultant behavior of the schema, following in lock step in the therapeutic metamorphosis.

Therapy: Affect-Change Process

A key task in therapy is to develop an understanding and a translation of the schema/personality patterns into an increased awareness of choice points, complete with a scorecard on problem options. This is to say that the client needs to know the full experience of self patterns, experience their operations and impact, and try on options. Experiential therapists do this by highlighting the "hot" experience, tracking it, and perhaps later presenting choices. The position here is that an unearthing of affective-based styles is most important in the human change process and that this is best directed by the clinician's understanding of the organization of the person's personality (schemas).

In addition to Millon, Benjamin (1993) believes that clinical plans depend on the clinician's knowledge and use of the client's personality. She holds that success in therapy should be considered from a perspective of discrete changes (stages of progress, not final goals) such as enhancing collaboration and awareness of interpersonal patterns, blocking maladaptive patterns, enhancing the will to change, and teaching new patterns. Progress would involve the attainment of any change beyond the starting point. Importantly, progress depends on knowledge of interpersonal patterns (personality). Without this, one travels in an unknown land with no map or compass. An understanding of the personality is necessary for change because interventions are dependent upon this knowledge, and change occurs according to the stage of change the client is in and the rules of his or her personality. Those familiar with Millon's theory are not befuddled by these statements.

Benjamin (1993) also holds that affect is the most available domain in therapy (at least initially). Experiencing an emotion (or "felt sense") is the current condition of the person. The change process, therefore, must attend to markers of this experiencing, the subjective and emotional measures of the problem area. Change is a process of many small steps that slightly shift the information processing, a process of re-experiencing here and now the there and then. The present process "meaning shifts" the past; a stuck story becomes a "never-ending" story, always influenced by dynamics of the new now. In addition, a new present opens new steps for future change. A total process unfolds, pushed along by affect.

Emotionality is present in every act of mental processing and is likely the principal domain in the person-change process. It is the domain of ET. Also, since a self-referent modulation (schema) is ongoing and a constant governor of the "right amount" of self-identity versus environmental awareness, the client necessarily experiences this. Through the living interactions of ET, the pathogenesis of the client is put on display. The change process is complete when the client's self-defeating (Axis II) patterns are exposed, experienced, and experimented with in the therapeutic relationship itself—a "corrective emotional experience." Always, ET presses toward experiencing.

Safran and Greenberg (1991a) highlight the elements in the affective change process: emotional restructuring, catharsis, experiential symbolization, facilitation of cognitive reorganization, motivation of adaptive behavior, corrective emotional experience, and affect atunement. In each element, techniques have developed from any of several ETs. Change involves emotional processing—the awareness, trying on, and integration of pathological elements in the person's schema and personality.

ET Techniques with Personalities

Recall that ET addresses the affective adaptation of handling problems that remain beyond their time. Under normal circumstances, one part of the person becomes organized to control the actions of another (the personality style is born). With a maladaptive personality, information is not used effectively; emotions especially are used as armor to prevent attempts at change. For any given person this domain can have varying parameters, resulting in a unique signature that is the personality. Components variously defined as affect intensity, affect variability, positive and negative affect, a penchant for one particular affect (e.g., guilt or anger), and affect regulation, among others, are present. The goal of treatment here is to understand affect in the context of personality and by so doing facilitate change.

Affect of the Personality Disorders

Table 10-4 is a representation of the affect domain as described by Millon (1984). These affective components represent a concatenation of "affective parts"—styles, defenses, and loose interpersonal patterns distinctive of the personality. For the clinician, information on the personality style is implied, especially the affective component, therapeutic entry points (and problems unique to each), and modal interventions. The therapist who is sensitive to these issues and, most particularly, to the "bridging acts" of the affect domain (as it displays its characteristic personality styles) can facilitate an integrated and apt ET care regimen. What follows is a brief description of each personality style, highlighting the distinctive affective domain of each.

TABLE 10-4 Mood/Temperament Domain

Schizoid Personality
Apathetic Mood (e.g., is emotionally unexcitable, exhibiting an intrinsic unfeeling, cold, and stark quality; reports weak affectionate or erotic needs, rarely displaying warm or intense feelings, and apparently unable to experience most affects of pleasure, sadness, or anger in any depth)

Avoidant Personality
Anguished Mood (e.g., describes constant and confusing undercurrent of tension, sadness, and anger; vacillates between desire for affection, fear of rebuff, embarrassment, and numbness of feeling)

Depressive Personality
Melancholic Mood (e.g., is typically woeful, gloomy, tearful, joyless, and morose; characteristically worrisome and brooding, the low-spirited and dysphoric state rarely remits)

Dependent Personality
Pacific Mood (e.g., is characteristically warm, tender, and noncompetitive; timidly avoids social tension and interpersonal conflicts)

Histrionic Personality
Fickle Mood (e.g., displays rapidly shifting and shallow emotions; is vivacious, animated, and impetuous and exhibits tendencies to be easily enthused and as easily angered or bored)

Narcissistic Personality
Insouciant Mood (e.g., manifests a general air of nonchalance, imperturbability, and feigned tranquillity; appears coolly unimpressionable or buoyantly optimistic, except when narcissistic confidence is shaken, at which time either rage, shame, or emptiness is briefly displayed)

Antisocial Personality
Callous Mood (e.g., is insensitive, irritable, and aggressive, as expressed in a wide-ranging deficit in social charitableness, human compassion, or personal remorse; exhibits a coarse incivility, as well as an offensive, if not reckless, disregard for the safety of or others)

Sadistic (Aggressive) Personality
Hostile Mood (e.g., has an excitable and irritable temper that flares readily into contentious argument and physical belligerence; is cruel, mean-spirited, and fractious, willing to do harm, even persecute others to get one's way)

Compulsive Personality
Solemn Mood (e.g., is unrelaxed, tense, joyless, and grim; restrains warm feelings and keeps most emotions under tight control)

Continued

TABLE 10-4 *Continued*

Negativistic Personality
Irritable Mood (e.g., frequently touchy, temperamental, and peevish, followed in turn by sullen and moody withdrawal; is often petulant and impatient, unreasonably scorns those in authority, and reports being annoyed easily or frustrated by many)

Self-Defeating Personality
Dysphoric Mood (e.g., experiences a complex mix of emotions, at times anxiously apprehensive, at others forlorn and mournful, to feeling anguished and tormented; intentionally displays a plaintive and wistful appearance, frequently to induce guilt and discomfort in others)

Schizotypal Personality
Distraught or Insentient Mood (e.g, excessively apprehensive and ill at ease, particularly in social encounters; agitated and anxiously watchful, evincing distrust of others and suspicion of their motives that persists despite growing familiarity; or manifests drab, apathetic, sluggish, joyless, and spiritless appearance; reveals marked deficiencies in face-to-face rapport and emotional expression)

Borderline Personality
Labile Mood (e.g., fails to accord unstable mood level with external reality; has either marked shifts from normality to depression to excitement, or has periods of dejection and apathy, interspersed with episodes of inappropriate and intense anger, as well as brief spells of anxiety or euphoria)

Paranoid Personality
Irascible Mood (e.g., displays a cold, sullen, churlish, and humorless demeanor; attempts to appear unemotional and objective, but is edgy, envious, jealous, and quick to take personal offense and react angrily)

Schizoid

The schizoid personality is affectively flat, a deficient, insensitive, and *apathetic* person who is intrinsically bland. Such individuals enjoy little, lead unemotional lives, and are not introspective or involved with self or others. Affect plays a small role with this personality. The therapist generally structures everything, encourages contact and feelings, and rewards the schizoid struggle to maintain contact and organize thinking. Psychotherapy problems related to affect occur due largely to the schizoid's style of passivity and blankness. Often the therapist may become impatient or feel helpless. Typical ET interventions, however, include skill building around basic life issues and attention to patient markers of trust/distrust.

Avoidant

The avoidant personality adopts an *anguished* mood as the affective response, the result of a chronic undercurrent of need/fear conflicts and a trust dilemma.

Unlike the schizoid, this personality style is affectively loaded, beset with a chronic evaluation anxiety, low thresholds for criticism or pain, as well as a general social ineptness. These individuals present many opportunities for affective therapeutic interventions due to an undercurrent of tension and a fearful desire to become involved. The therapist might respond to the feeling tone of the client; "I notice that you become edgy when we discuss work." ET techniques that isolate and expose these avoidant components provide the clinician with a opportunity for "tasting" and influencing avoidant styles as they occur. Also, the two-chair technique allows the therapist to highlight the undercontrol (fear) and overcontrol (need) components characteristic of this style. Often behavioral homework, such as testing one's fear of criticism, can be prescribed later in the process.

Depressive

The mood and temperament domain is perfect for illuminating the depressive personality style. The cardinal symptom of this disorder is indeed a *melancholic* mood. The feeling of gloom is pervasive, and the result is often worry and brooding. These feelings are core to the personality and, as such, make it not only an obvious target for ET but also an extremely difficult one. Therapy should, of course, focus on the melancholia through an exploration of the original affects that have resulted in this singular mood. As the depressive personality is in many ways a "burned out" avoidant, returning to the original anxieties and fears of the avoidant is not necessarily negative. The experiential aspects of therapy should encourage the patient to explore new and broader emotions as a means to minimize the impairment brought on by a single depressive affect.

Dependent

For the dependent personality the affect is *pacific,* due largely to self-doubt and a clinging need to be rescued. The dependent personality plays out the weak/strong dimension and contaminates relationships with "I am not okay." As with the avoidant personality, this person presents many opportunities for ET, due mostly to an inferior and whining stance along with suppressed resentment. Basically, a supported and increasing "collaborative" emphasis on emotions related to ineffectual decision making or ambivalence about change is recommended. The two-chair technique (topdog/underdog) often can be dramatically effective with these personality styles.

But there can be many problems with this style. Often the therapist is interpersonally induced into rescuing a person with a dependent personality, as a result of the person's fears of abandonment, intense transference, and ineffectual stances on issues. Additionally, therapeutic attention to referents of emotional reactivity is often parried by this personality style. And the therapist who adopts such an active and directive short-term strategy may later pay with burnout and other problems, as there is little change, and dependent styles of ineffectuality become even more entrenched.

Histrionic

The histrionic personality is affectively *fickle*, a studied superficiality intended to impress. At base, this style fears rigor of any sort, as well as aloneness; involvement is salving and emotional. The truly accomplished histrionic struggles to avoid connection between feelings and thoughts or actions. The therapist's goal is to tighten this expression and expose emotional games and styles. ET interventions are omnipresent as the dramatic personality features abound. A special therapeutic emphasis might involve attention to fears related to the loss of the exciting life, aloneness, exposure of their controlling or reactive ways, and highlighting empathy deficits in a sea of cute gestures.

Narcissistic

The narcissistic personality is *insouciant*, a persistent and self-aggrandizing distortion of reality. The steady state of emotionality is underplayed with a shallow, belittling, and arrogant emotionality. On occasion these personalities are given to anger, but only to disavow others (or self) if not up to overvalued standards. ET interventions require a quiet and steady discipline by the therapist—waiting for moments of depression, displays of empathy failure, or a "failed want." Empathy training through role playing and experienced strategies is also fruitful.

Antisocial

The antisocial personality is known for a *callous* mood, the predatory and remorseless exploitation of others that is manipulative and cool. This rationalized and learned style is often low-keyed ("just the way I am"), but no less seductive and cynical in action or style (than when more outgoing). One key therapeutic goal is to allow the antisocial personality to feel safe, not to treat others as threats and to tolerate anxiety. In this effort the therapist may have to manage care with anger training, self coping skills, choice reviews, and problem solving (all behavioral interventions). ET interventions then are possible. These include experiencing or teaching gradation of responsibility; highlighting power or trust struggles; and allowing the expression of any "hurting" emotion, not unusual for a troubled antisocial.

Sadistic

The sadistic personality is affectively *hostile,* a first cousin to the antisocial but more intentionally mean-spirited, resentful, and persistent. The therapist's goal is to titrate uncaring and violent feelings to safety and an acceptance of others. Often, however, the projected fear of the aggressive style is unwavering, and the "desensitizing process" of these interventions must be persistent. Again, as with the antisocial personality, management of fearless and dogmatic attitudes is required. An effortless "don't feel or be close" response can be pervasive. Nevertheless, given patience, trust, and control, ET openings exist in overresponses to neutral issues, obvious self-satisfaction in the coercion of others, or a glaring gap in affect awareness. Grading tenderness also can be fruitful—but with the necessary ingredients of empathy and trust.

Compulsive

For the compulsive personality, affect is *solemn.* This style is restrained, structured, and compartmentalized to keep worry and fears at bay. Painfully and steadfastly these people know they are not okay and become overcontrolled to prove otherwise. Feelings of losing control, of being overwhelmed, and of being discovered abound. Despite efforts, affect oozes through. It is here that the ET therapist can provide a safe structure for the compulsive to stay with the feelings until a new awareness is reached. The full experience of a single recent episode of a compulsive can be highly enlightening. This has special benefits if the emotion is anger; inevitably the primary referents of hurt are "discovered," and the knee-jerk response of annoyance or low-grade anger is unearthed. FEP was especially intended for compulsive personalities. Superficially, ET strategies may involve the awareness of uncomfortable feelings, two-chair representations of their inherent ambivalence, and simple acts of enjoyment (as these personalities are devoid of being truly happy).

Negativistic

The negativistic personality is *irritable,* a frustrating and consistent pusher of varied emotions, most showing some form of complaint. The affective ploys indigenous to this personality are open lability and soft rebellion. The therapeutic goal here is to even out the expression of feelings, especially anger. Initially role playing, avoidant strategies, and oppositional fears (being controlled by others) can be surfaced and used as educative exercises. Subsequent to these interventions, many openings will exist in the pursuit of the decontamination of the feelings. Most of the "heavy duty" information-processing defenses of reaction formulation, displacement, protective identification, and rationalization can be reframed and anchored to a feeling. In turn, these can be highlighted and exposed. It is important for the therapist to be sensitive to stimuli that contribute to negative affect and to "demands" on self.

Self-Defeating

The self-defeating personality is *dysphoric* affectively, a planned helplessness inviting rejection. This style is draining, overly busy, and perpetually incomplete. Such individuals are affectively chocked, expecting and usually gathering the worst in any situation. Guilt is often a result of their ploys. The therapeutic goal is for this personality to see all sides and to accept pleasure. Their low energy, somatic complaints, and incomplete feeling patterns are omnipresent. ET interventions involve the "affective irrationally" of undermining pleasure, the exposition of the not-so-subtle components of guilt, and the highlighting of all-too-frequent negative therapeutic reactions. The self-defeating commitment to suffer and pride in suffering can be emotionally unearthed in a myriad of patient markers.

Schizotypal

The schizotypal personality is seen as a breakdown of either the schizoid or the avoidant basic personality disorder. As such, there are two possible moods. The schizotypal disorder is affectively *insentient* (schizoid variant) or *distraught* (avoidant variant). In fact, this disorder is often viewed in the spectrum model of personality and is a severe variant of several inflexible traits. Excessive psychopathology aside, therapeutic goals essentially revolve around the management of this personality's idiosyncratic and bizarre features, as well as social-skills deficits. ET interventions should be the result of a deliberative process: a clinical sensitivity to decompensation or perturbation should remain on ready alert. Often excessive anxiety, moderate levels of suspiciousness, and cognitive slippage are paramount. ET interventions that soothe anxious tensions (demonstrate a reduction), role play on necessary social-skills training, reduce probable suspicious "selves," or teach internal cues to cognitive disruptive patterns are helpful. ET can subtly be involved in these interventions but is not the treatment modality of choice.

Borderline

The borderline personality is affectively *labile,* a one-size-fits-all, externalized, and fearful response to virtually all contacts. In recent years several compelling books (e.g., Layden et al., 1993; Linehan, 1992) have described the treatment of this disorder and highlighted the affective domain. At base, this disorder can be considered both a cognitive-behavioral problem (problem solving) and an emotional expression deficit. Borderlines have, however, central conflicts based on affect: fear of abandonment, inability to tolerate frustration, undifferentiated self, disparaging self attitudes, and their hallmarks—intolerable relationships and affective instability. This style has a disparaging attitude toward its own internal reality and shows disgust in emotional ways.

ET is an important modality in the treatment of this personality. Opportunities for interventions abound. The borderline is similar to the histrionic personality, where tightening is required, but with a twist. Here there is a less controlled responsivity, as well as a suicidal program at the ready. Issues of splitting, protective identification, and core schema abuse and sensitivity (e.g., abandonment, unlovability, safety) are prolific and ripe for ET strategists. This disorder also possesses one other feature of concern, a fear of change. ET techniques that expose this core pattern can be most helpful.

Paranoid

The last personality disorder is the paranoid. *Irascible* is the affective description—hypervigilant to avoid surprises and blaming to avoid insecurity. Therapists who confront, do not allow for control to flow from the client, or take trust for granted are in for a therapeutic failure. When nurtured, however, the paranoid client can be receptive for "milder" ET interventions. This personality must feel safe. The judicious employment of more cognitive strategies of self-efficacy and mastery can be mixed with milder levels of ET experiences (often related to feelings of vulnerability). ET therapists can titrate the paranoid's fears of vulnerability and structure emotional exercises in anxiety expression. If the paranoid personality disorder does not experience exploitation, the usual guarded defenses can become allies.

General Considerations

In summary, several personality styles are special candidates for ET, being overcontrolled or having a deficient range of emotional expression. These include the compulsive, dependent, avoidant, passive-aggressive, narcissistic, and self-defeating personalities. Histrionic styles also are good candidates for ET, but with this style the therapeutic effort involves "tightening." Personality styles that are less amenable to ET methods or require special consideration include antisocial, sadistic, and schizoid. Personality styles with which the therapist should use more therapeutic caution include the more severe disorders, that is, schizotypal, borderline, and paranoid, as well as any of the less applicable styles that present with affective intensity or high levels of denial.

Since the interventions (of ET) are particular, directed, and persistent (in a collaborative and human way), care should always be taken and permission sought. The importance of the emphasis on personality is that it affords the therapist a model of behavior, a heuristic blueprint to predict more likely responses. Affect is often the most "visible" component of this process. Of course, each personality disorder can present its own problems. Co-morbidity (Axis II) provides another set of difficulties, as most clients possess several disordered traits. Nonetheless, entry into the affective domain allows the most propitious access to the person.

CASE STUDY

Background

Ms. L. was a 27-year-old white-Hispanic female, the eldest of three children born to her caucasian, military officer father and her Hispanic-American mother, an alcoholic homemaker. The family traveled from place to place throughout Europe and the United States during her developmental years. Her father was a Vietnam veteran and a strict disciplinarian. Ms. L. remembers herself being a well-behaved child in order to avoid his wrath. He gave very little approval.

During Ms. L.'s adolescence she went from being acquiescent to being rebellious toward her parents, one method being sexual promiscuity in peer relationships. Due to her mother's drinking problem, Ms. L. assumed the role of caretaker for her younger siblings. She remembered feeling like the "little adult" of the family and that she had to be "tough." She was labeled a "whore" at school, and was glad when it was time for the next family move. Ms. L has a sister two years younger and a brother six years younger. Her brother has been successful in his academic and military pursuits, but her younger sister has been hospitalized repeatedly for substance abuse and emotional problems.

Ms. L. is an intelligent and highly verbal individual. Always succeeding academically, she graduated from college with honors. She married at 21 only to divorce about a year later due to chronic physical abuse. During the divorce she became involved in a women's advocacy group, and she remains active. She is presently involved in a romantic relationship of 3 years' standing.

Ms. L. initiated outpatient therapy twice before, first to examine issues related to her abusive relationship with her ex-husband and then to deal with her difficult relationship with her alcoholic mother. Ms. L.'s current presenting problem of explosive, irrational anger directed toward her boyfriend was quite different. As an example, she reported that when she found out that he would be late in returning from a business trip, she emptied all his clothes onto the floor. This along with other incidents left this rational person baffled and feeling foolish. Additionally, she felt overwhelmed by her emotions and unable to change or control her behavior.

MCMI-III

Ms. L's MCMI-III profile (see Table 10-5) shows a female with Axis II problems, chiefly patterns of an outgoing, confident, and competitive female who is rather dramatic in presentation (Choca, Shanley, & Denberg, 1992). This profile is noteworthy also for its lack of endorsement of Axis I symp-

TABLE 10-5 MCMI-III of the Case Example

MCMI-III Inventory		Base Rate
	Validity	0
X	Disclosure	50
Y	Desirability	70
Z	Debasement	49
1	Schizoid	0
2A	Avoidant	66
2B	Depressive	0
3	Dependent	20
4	Histrionic	88**
5	Narcissistic	92**
6A	Antisocial	76*
6B	Aggressive (Sadistic)	63
7	Compulsive	32
8A	Negativistic	47
8B	Self-Defeating	12
S	Schizotypal	0
C	Borderline	22
P	Paranoid	0
A	Anxiety	0
H	Somatoform	0
N	Bipolar: Manic	48
D	Dysthymia	27
B	Alcohol Dependence	64
T	Drug Dependence	63
PT	PTSD	30
SS	Thought Disorder	0
CC	Major Depression	0
PP	Delusional Disorder	25

*BR 75–84
**BR 85–94

toms. She likely has a great need for attention and affection. She seeks excitement and cannot easily contain her emotions. Also, she appears fickle and often not genuine, as she will experience short-term "highs," tending to overcommit. In effect, her emotional stance often results in problems as she needs either to feel special or to show off in sometimes ostentatious ways. Self-assurance and conceit, therefore, mix with flair and, on occasion, arrogance.

Ms. L. values self in content and form. She values personal images and expresses herself easily and willingly. She enjoys her ability to attract attention. Often her valued positions are defended with vigor, and she can become a worthy foe if pressed. In service of defense, she could appear mistrustful or suspicious. She feels tough to have survived her experiences and to have her talents. It is noted that she can be an impressive person, conspicuous in making an impact.

A particularly challenging character problem is her fear of her surroundings. Often she feels as if she must defend herself and become strong and assertive to obtain superiority. So, if she does not have her attentional needs met or if she is in a competitive environment, she will become confrontive.

Course of Experiential Therapy

Initially in this, her third trial of therapy, Ms. L. was fast-paced and talkative, focusing on her presenting problems with anger control. However, as she was encouraged to slow her verbalizations and directed to attend to her body language and feelings of the moment, therapy began to take a new direction, one anchored in the past. As noted from the MCMI-III, Ms. L. had been active, assertive, and competitive her entire adult life. In this way she kept her conscious self away from the traumatic aspects of her past. Therefore, the aim of therapy was to aid her in slowing these defensive behaviors in a safe environment so that she could begin to understand herself in relation to her past emotive experiences.

Throughout the year, Ms. L. retrieved numerous detailed memories of her father's physical and sexual abuse, which began at age 3. As a child she learned to dissociate during sexual incidents and did not integrate these experiences well into her consciousness. So as memories became available to her, they were raw events that were new, horrifying, and unprocessed. The first memory of her father's having intercourse with her unfolded as if she were reliving the experience. From that point, techniques were employed in therapy to help Ms. L. keep past and present separate. For instance, she was encouraged to describe memories as if she were watching them on a movie screen, and dialogue with the therapist was continual throughout to protect against her completely reliving traumatic experiences.

Once Ms. L. was slowed enough to touch on the memories that she had been defending against, the therapy became focused on coaching her (again in a safe environment) to follow feelings and connect them with trauma. Initially this was accomplished by simply directing her to focus on her breathing and to slow her talking. Focusing on affectively loaded words and concentrating on the feeling of the moment often helped bridge from the feeling in the present to that feeling in the past and the incident that produced it.

Several ET therapeutic interventions were employed before and during FEP. Ms. L. often covered her mouth as she was trying to be more specific about her feelings of discomfort. This use of the hand helped her to identify that her learned fear of "telling the secret" of her sexual abuse was still present. This was the starting point of Ms. L.'s affective work, and it resulted in her first verbalization that she had been abused by her father. This verbalization resulted in the first emotional (cathartic) experience for her in therapy, which was anxiety-laden sobbing. It ended abruptly, soon after it had begun. During this and subsequent recountings of abuse, Ms. L. held her breath; spoke choppily; and remained tense, fearful, and constricted.

Another therapeutic intervention that represented a significant development in the therapy process was simply the coaching that helped Ms. L. lengthen her verbalizations and reduce her fearfulness. She let her words be carried by first taking a long inhalation ("strong breath"), then following by sustaining exhalation and words. This aided not only in slowing and relaxing Ms. L., but also in helping her become less tentative concerning her affect and less fearful of the expression of her other negative emotions. On one occasion, when Ms. L. held her hand over her mouth, she quickly whispered, "I think my father molested me." She started sobbing and looked up as if watching for "the other shoe to drop." She gradually became able to slowly recount a memory and express her anger, fear, and disgust in lengthy detail.

The most important technique that was employed for Ms. L. was the empty-chair technique (FEP). Having Ms. L. talk to the therapist about her emotions was ineffectual, an intellectualized description of emotion. Use of the empty chair allowed not only for continued affective expression, but also set the stage for the cognitive work that followed, making the ineffable "real and felt." Due to previous therapy and the success of the other ET techniques, steps 1 (identification) and 2 (commitment) were easily accepted. It was obvious that Ms. L. was carrying many negative feelings affecting her relationships with both her father, boyfriend, and her mother. Keeping the awareness of a memory, she was guided to express her feelings concerning the memory and her parents' roles in her abuse (Step 3). It was through these "talks" with her parents that she gained the ability to protest and to finally fight back for herself. It was then that she began to feel some sense of closure concerning that traumatic period of her life.

For Ms. L., several affective problems existed: her fear of feeling and expressing what she is feeling as well as battling "parts" of self. Early on, "patient markers" were noted: "I became furious with my father at the mention of his name"; "I feel suffocated and then angry with sex"; "I must be the best, on top of everything." These markers were identified (Stage 4) during early therapy stages, stated and restated during two chair and soft-body techniques (breathing), and, as noted, were "let go."

Ms. L. was able to show many changes as a result of these experiences (Step 4). Early on she described the therapy process as a ride on an "emotional roller-coaster." The roller-coaster changed from one of peaks of hope and denial ("I remembered, I'm better now") and swift swoops downward to a less labile process in which memories and thoughts were given a "fair hearing." The therapy was focused and represented work; she did not feel "cured" when she completed a memory, but neither did she feel hopeless and out of control during the process of remembering and integrating.

Initially the experiencing of new emotional material tended to come in spurts of emotion with racking sobs and labored breathing. As with the other developments in therapy, however, this became more modulated as she worked along. In several months she was able to stay with her emotions, talking through them with even breathing and without fear of loss of control, to some point of closure or partial resolution. It was after these times that Ms. L. reported her greatest sense of relief.

Step 5 also followed smoothly. Where symptomatic relief of PTSD symptomatology and excessive, overdetermined emotional responses in her romantic relationship served as benchmarks for Ms. L., work to integrate her experience cognitively into her present understanding of herself was established. As Ms. L. began to experience and understand her memories as memories, she slowly began to make linkages between her past abuse and her overdetermined behavior in present relationships. Generally, her anxiety and dysphoric symptoms declined along with continued processing of a memory. Following this process, another memory or series of memories would come. There was a definite, progressive development in therapy of a pattern of affective work resulting in memory revelation that led to fear and emotional symptoms, followed by "finishing business," relationship work, and finally a cognitive sorting and processing of this newly salient information.

Summary

In any formulation of psychotherapy the ratio of speculation to facts is large. As a compromise, information on treatment is often the result of a "middle knowledge" based on theory and experience. This chapter is no different in this regard. Here three "persuasive" positions are advocated: (1) The client brings dysfunctions of personality/schema patterns into treatment, (2) affect is the "squeaky" wheel and the one that most quickly accesses the core issues of the person, and (3) the therapist who knows and isolates these patterns (especially affect) can assist the client in the "best" type of re-experiencing in the process of therapy.

To be effective, ET therapists help clients carefully attend to these (affective) signals, provide validation and empathy as these patterns are exposed, and allow the curative process of unfinished tasks to complete. The idea that the affective domain of the person by itself is an organized, meaningful structure of the person is a welcome learning. In a hierarchical way this position holds strongly to the view that each person (personality/schema) is a whole, a gestalt: One that is far from an enumeration of traits. How this self-referential process unfolds awaits decades of research; that it does is face-valid.

When all is said and done, psychotherapy is a simple human process in which two people share a myth about humankind and what it takes to change it. Through its inventively compelling approach to change, ET has added to the increasingly understood parametric constraints of personality consistency. It appears to be one of the better "myths" extant.

References

Adler, A. (1964). *Problems of neurosis: A book of case histories.* New York: Harper Torchbooks.

Beck, A. T., Freeman, A., & Associates (1990). *Cognitive therapy of personality disorders.* New York: Guilford Press.

Benjamin, L. S. (1993). Every psychopathology is a gift of love. *Psychotherapy Research, 3*, 1–24.

Bronisch, T., & Klerman, G. L. (1991). Personality functioning: Change and stability in relationship to symptoms and psychopathology. *Journal of Personality Disorders, 5*, 307–317.

Choca, J. P., Shanley, L. A., & Van Denburg, E. (1992). *Interpretative guide to the Millon Clinical Multiaxial Inventory.* Washington, DC: American Psychological Association.

Daldrup, R. J., Beutler, L. E., Engle, D., & Greenberg, L. S. (1988). *Focused expressive psychotherapy.* New York: Guilford Press.

Engle, D., Beutler, L. E., & Dalrup, R. J. (1991). Focused expressive psychotherapy: Treating blocked emotions. In J. Savran & L. Greenberg (Eds.), *Emotion, psychotherapy, and change* (pp. 169–196). New York: Guilford Press.

Epstein, S. (1991). The self-concept, the traumatic neurosis, and the structure of personality. In D. Ozer, J. M. Healy, Jr., & A. J. Stewart (Eds.), *Perspectives on personality* (vol. 3). London: Kingsley.

Freeman, A. (1992). The development of treatment conceptualizations in cognitive therapy. In A. Freeman & F. M. Dattilio (Eds.), *Comprehensive casebook of cognitive therapy* (pp. 13–27). New York: Plenum Press.

Gendlin, E. T. (1991). On emotion in therapy. In J. Safran & L. Greenberg (Eds.), *Emotion, psychotherapy, and change* (pp. 255–279). New York: Guilford Press.

Greenberg, L. S., Safran, J., & Rice, L. (1990). Experiential therapy: Its relation to cognitive therapy. In A. Freeman & F. M. Dattilio (Eds.), *Comprehensive casebook of cognitive therapy* (pp. 169–187). New York: Plenum.

Greenberg, L. S., Rice, L., & Elliott, R. (1993). *Facilitating emotional change: The moment-by-moment process.* New York: Guilford Press.

Guidano, V. F. (1991). Affective change events in a cognitive therapy system approach. In J. Safran & L. Greenberg (Eds.), *Emotion, psychotherapy, and change* (pp. 50–79). New York: Guilford Press.

Jourard, S. M. (1971). *The transparent self* (rev. ed.). New York: Van Nostrand Reinhold.

Lang, P. J. (1977). Imagery in therapy: An information processing analysis of fear. *Behavior Therapy, 8*, 862–886.

Layden, M. A., Newman, C. F., Freeman, A., & Morse, S. B. (1993).*Cognitive therapy of borderline personality disorder.* Needham Heights, MA: Allyn and Bacon.

Lazarus, R. S. (1991). Emotion theory and psychotherapy. In J. Safran & L. Greenberg (Eds.), *Emotion, psychotherapy, and change* (pp. 290–301). New York: Guilford Press.

Leventhal, H. (1984). A perceptual-motor theory of emotion. In L. Berkowitz (Ed.), *Advances in experimental social psychology.* New York: Academic Press.

Linehan, M. M. (1993). *Skills training manual for treating borderline personality disorder.* New York: Guilford Press.

Millon, T. (1969). *Modern psychopathology.* Philadelphia: Saunders.

Millon, T. (1981). *Disorders of personality.* DSM-III: *Axis II.* New York: Wiley.

Millon, T. (1983). *Millon Clinical Multiaxial Inventory manual* (3d ed.). Minneapolis, MN: National Computer Systems.

Millon, T. (1984). On the renaissance of personality assessment and personality theory. *Journal of Personality Assessment, 48,* 450–466.

Millon, T. (1987). *Manual for the MCMI-II* (2d ed.). Minneapolis, MN: National Computer Systems.

Perls, F., Hefferline, R. E., & Goodman, P. (1951). *Gestalt therapy.* New York: Julian Press.

Rogers, C. R. (1961). *On becoming a person.* Boston: Houghton Mifflin.

Safran, J. D., & Greenberg, L. S. (1991b). Emotion in human functioning: Theory and therapeutic implications. In *Emotion, psychotherapy, and change* (pp. 3–15). New York: Guilford Press.

Safran, J. D., & Greenberg, L. S. (1991a). Affective change processes: A synthesis and critical analysis. In *Emotion, psychotherapy, and change* (pp. 339–362). New York: Guilford Press.

Safran, J. D., & Segal, Z. S. (1990). *Interpersonal process in cognitive therapy.* New York: Basic Books.

Smith, E. W. (1985). *The body in psychotherapy.* Jefferson, NC: McFarland & Company.

Sullivan, H. S. (1953). *The interpersonal theory of psychiatry.* New York: Norton.

Wiggins, O. P., & Schwartz, M. A. (1991). Research into personality disorders: The alternatives of dimensions and ideal types. *Journal of Personality Disorders, 5,* 69–81.

Author Index

A

Acklin, M. W., 161–163, 183
Adler, A., 90, 109, 218, 233
Adler, G., 127, 133
American Psychiatric Association, 2, 6, 22, 24, 25, 39, 45, 46, 62
Arnow, D., 165, 184
Atwood, G. E., 159, 182, 185
Auerbach, J., 127, 134
Axelrod, S., 42, 62
Azim, H., 118, 133

B

Bacal, H., 111, 133
Bechtel, D. R., 42, 63
Beck, A. T., 75, 89–94, 96, 98, 99, 101, 103, 109, 110, 119, 134, 217, 218, 233
Becker, B., 118, 134
Becker, R. E., 41, 62
Beckham, E., 75, 89
Bellack, A. S., 41, 62
Bell, M., 118, 134
Benjamin, L. S., 216, 219, 233
Berg, J. L., 173, 184
Bergman, A., 115, 135
Beutler, L. E., 213–215, 233
Bickhard, M., 116, 134
Biglan, A., 45, 64
Billington, R., 118, 134
Bion, W. R., 113, 134
Blaine, J., 75, 89
Blanchard, E. B., 43, 44, 62
Blatt, S. J., 118, 127, 134, 161, 163, 164, 172, 174, 177, 183, 199, 209
Blom, G. F., 45, 63
Borkovec, T. D., 43, 44, 62
Bowen, M., 68, 88
Brandchaft, B., 159, 185
Brandenburg, N., 16, 22
Brandsma, J., 210
Brenneis, C., 118, 134
Bronisch, T., 216, 233
Burish, M., 183

C

Campbell, R., 111, 134
Camp, B. W., 45, 63
Cantor, N., 27, 39
Carroll, K. M., 75, 88
Cautela, J. R., 41, 43, 63

Chancer, L. S., 176, 184
Chaplin, J. P., 118, 134
Chessick, R., 127, 134
Chessick, R. D., 192, 209
Chevron, E. S., 68, 72, 88
Choca, J. P., 20, 22, 122, 134, 229, 233
Christopher, J., 116, 134
Collins, J. F., 74, 75, 88, 89
Cooper, S. H., 165, 184
Cornelison, A., 68, 88
Craig, R. J., 20, 22, 66, 72, 85, 88
Cramer, P., 164, 166, 184
Curran, J. P., 45, 63

D

Daldrup, R. J., 213–215, 233
Davis, M., 159, 185
Davis, R., 33, 39
Deffenbacher, J., 45, 64
DeWald, P., 126, 134
DiMascio, A., 74, 88, 89
Docherty, J. P., 74, 75, 88, 89
Donat, D. C., 40, 59, 61, 63, 64, 123, 134
Dorr, D., 186, 209
Dowd, E. T., 42–44, 63
Drake, R., 25, 39
D'Zurilla, T. J., 45, 63

E

Elkin, I., 74, 75, 88, 89
Elliott, R., 211, 214, 234
Ellis, A., 90
Emery, G., 91, 92, 110
Engle, D., 213–215, 233
Epictetus, 90
Epstein, L. H., 43, 44, 62
Epstein, S., 218, 233

Everly, G. S., Jr., 21, 24, 26, 33, 39, 170, 184

F

Fairbairn, W. R. D., 159, 167, 184
Fairbairn, W. T., 113, 114, 134
Fiel, A., 4, 23
Fischer, D. C., 158, 184
Fleck, S., 68, 88
Forehand, R., 42, 63
Foxx, R. M., 42, 63
Freeman, A., 96, 98, 99, 101, 110, 119, 134, 217, 218, 226, 233, 234
French, R., 27, 39
Freud, A., 113
Freud, S., 26, 39, 67, 90, 110–113, 115, 119, 134, 187, 209

G

Gacono, C. B., 173, 184
Gambril, E., 45, 63
Gawin, F. H., 75, 88
Geczy, B., 59, 61, 63, 64, 123, 134
Gendlin, E. T., 211, 234
Gergen, K. J., 158, 184
Gibertini, M., 9, 16, 22
Glass, D. R., 74, 88
Glazer, W., 74, 89
Glick, M., 118, 134
Goklaney, M., 74, 89
Goldfried, M., 33, 39
Goodman, P., 211, 234
Greenberg, D., 111–114, 134
Greenberg, L. S., 211–215, 220, 233, 234
Greenburg, R. L., 93, 109
Grinberg, L., 113, 134
Gross, A. E., 43, 63
Guidano, V. F., 211, 217, 234
Guntrip, H., 113, 122, 134

H

Haberman, J., 160, 184
Hall, C., 25, 39
Hamilton, N. G., 113, 134
Hare, R., 125, 134
Hefferline, R. E., 211, 234
Helmrich, J., 59, 63, 123, 134
Hepburn, A., 158, 184
Heraclitis, 25
Herbert, F., 45, 63
Herman, I., 75, 89
Hersen, M., 41–43, 62
Hibbard, S., 118, 134
Hinsie, L., 111, 134
Hole, A., 75, 89
Homer, A. L., 42, 64
Horner, A., 119, 121, 135
Horowitz, M., 115, 135
Hume, A., 59, 63
Hyer, L., 20–23, 210

I

Imber, S. D., 74, 88

J

Jaffe, L. S., 158, 184
James, W., 68
Jourard, S. M., 211, 234

K

Kazdin, A. E., 42, 44, 64
Kernberg, O., 115, 116, 135
Kernberg, O. F., 161, 163–166, 172, 184
Kilgore, R. B., 118, 136, 158, 185
Kleber, H. D., 74, 89
Klein, M., 113, 115, 127, 135

Klerman, G. L., 68, 72, 74, 88, 89, 216, 233
Kohut, H., 111, 117, 124, 135, 137–139, 141, 143, 144, 156, 159, 162, 172, 184
Kubacki, S. R., 158, 160, 184

L

Lachman, F. M., 164, 185
Lambeth, G., 116, 134
Lang, P. J., 211, 234
LaPlanche, J., 112, 135
Layden, M. A., 226, 234
Lazarus, R. S., 217, 234
Leber, W. R., 74, 88
LeMay, M., 59, 63, 123, 134
Lentz, R. J., 41, 64
Lerner, P. M., 161, 163, 165, 167, 184
Leventhal, H., 217, 234
Lewin, K., 26, 39
Lewinsohn, P. M., 45, 64
Lidz, T., 68, 88
Lindzey, G., 25, 39
Linehan, M. M., 226, 234
Lorr, M., 10, 23
Lovaas, I. O., 42, 64
Luborsky, L., 75, 89

M

McCann, J. T., 137, 159
MacIssac, D. S., 140, 157
McKeegan, G. F., 61, 64
McLellan, A. A., 75, 89
Mahler, M. S., 115, 135, 188, 209
Marchione, K., 45, 64
Marmar, C., 115, 135
Marshall, W. L., 41, 64
Materson, J., 115, 116, 127, 128, 135
Matheson, S., 20, 23

Meehl, P., 127, 135
Meehl, P. E., 158, 184
Meichenbaum, D., 45, 64
Meissner, W., 128, 135
Meloy, J. R., 125, 135, 173, 184
Merikangas, K. R., 24, 39
Meyer, A., 67, 68, 88
Mezzich, J., 27, 39
Michelson, L., 41, 64
Millon, T., 1–6, 9, 10, 19, 22, 25–28, 33, 35, 39, 40, 45, 46, 62, 64, 76, 88, 95, 110, 111, 118, 119, 122–124, 126,132, 135, 137–139, 141, 144, 145, 156–158, 162–164, 166, 167, 169–175, 178,179, 184, 193, 196, 199, 201, 203, 204, 209, 211, 216, 217, 219, 234
Mitchell, S., 111–114, 134
Monti, P. M., 45, 63
Morse, S. B., 226, 234

N

Neu, C., 74, 88, 89
Newman, C. F., 226, 234
Newman, K., 111, 133
Norcross, J., 33, 39
Novaco, R., 45, 64
Nunnally, J. C., 9, 11, 22

O

O'Brien, C. P., 75, 89
Ofman, P., 20, 23
Olson, D. H., 42, 63

P

Parloff, M. B., 74, 88
Pascal, 211
Paul, G. L., 41, 64
Pavlov, I., 41

Perls, F., 211, 234
Perry, J. C., 165, 184
Peterson, L., 42, 64
Pilkonis, P. A., 74, 75, 88, 89
Pine, F., 115, 135
Pontalis, J., 112, 135
Prusoff, B. A., 74, 88, 89
Pruyser, P., 115, 135

R

Racker, H., 115, 135
Rado, S., 127, 135
Rayner, R., 41
Rescorla, R. A., 42, 64
Retzlaff, P., 1, 4, 9–11, 16, 20, 22, 23
Rice, L., 211, 214, 234
Rinsley, D., 115, 116, 127, 128, 135
Rogers, C. R., 67, 68, 89, 211, 234
Rounsaville, B. J., 68, 72, 74, 75, 88, 89
Rowe, C. E., 140, 157
Rush, A. J., 91, 92, 110

S

Safran, J. D., 211, 212, 215, 217, 220, 234
Schafer, R., 161, 166, 184
Schichman, S., 161, 163, 164, 172, 174, 177,183
Schimek, J., 118, 134
Schreibman, L., 44, 64
Schwartz, M. A., 218, 234
Segal, Z. S., 211, 217, 234
Seinfeld, J., 167, 185
Shanley, L. A., 20, 22, 122, 134, 229, 233
Shapiro, D., 98, 110, 161, 185
Shaw, B. F., 91, 92, 110
Shealy, L., 210
Shea, M. T., 74, 75, 88, 89

Sheehan, E., 4, 10, 23
Shepard, R., 159, 185
Shichman, , S., 199, 209
Sides, J. K., 43, 44, 62
Singer, M., 68, 89
Skinner, B. F., 41
Smith, E. W., 27, 39, 211, 234
Smith, P. R., 158
Sor, D., 113, 134
Sotsky, S. M., 74, 75, 88, 89
Stern, A., 187, 209
Stern, D., 116, 136
Stolorow, R. D., 159, 164, 182, 185
Stone, M., 127, 136
Storr, A., 124, 136
Suen, H. K., 9, 23
Sugarman, A., 158, 162, 185
Suinn, R., 45, 64
Sullivan, H. S., 67, 68, 72, 89, 111, 114, 117, 136, 218, 234
Sundberg, N. D., 66, 89

T

Tabak de Bianchedi, E., 113, 134
Trimboli, F., 118, 136, 158, 185
Turner, S. M., 41, 64
Tyler, L. E., 66, 89

V

Vaillant, G. E., 25, 39, 125, 136, 161, 163, 164, 167, 170, 171, 175, 179, 185

Van Denburg, E. J., 20, 22, 111, 122, 134, 229, 233
van Doornick, W. J., 45, 63

W

Walters, J., 59, 63
Watkins, J. T., 74, 88
Watson, J. B., 41
Watson, R. I., 41, 64
Weissman, M. M., 24, 39, 68, 72, 74, 88, 89
Westen, D., 119, 136
Wiggins, O. P., 218, 234
Wilber, C. H., 74, 89
Willick, M. S., 164, 185
Will, T. E., 90
Winnicott, D., 112, 114, 115, 136, 159, 185, 192, 209
Wisocki, P., 43, 65
Wolf, E. S., 124, 135, 139, 140, 141, 157, 159, 172
Wolff, H. H., 192, 209
Wolpe, J., 40–42, 44, 45, 65
Woody, G. E., 75, 89
Wynne, L., 68, 89

Z

Zeiss, A. M., 45, 64
Zwilling, M., 74, 88

Subject Index

A

Acting out, 168, 172–173
Affect
 in experiential mood therapy, 211–212, 215–216, 219–220
 in personality disorders, 220–227
Aggressive personality (*see* Sadistic personality disorder)
Alcohol abuse scale, 7–8, 18
Antisocial personality disorder
 affect in, 221, 224
 behavioral treatment of, 53
 cognitive style of, 99, 107
 cognitive therapy of, 99–100
 experiential mood therapy of, 224
 expressive acts of, 47, 53
 impediments to therapy, 81
 interpersonal conduct in, 77, 80
 interpersonal treatment of, 81
 intersubjective treatment of, 173
 morphological organization of, 194, 199
 object relations psychotherapy of, 124–125
 object representation in, 120, 124
 psychoanalytic treatment of, 199–200
 regulatory mechanisms in, 168, 172–173
 self-image in, 142, 144, 148
 self-psychology psychotherapy of, 148
Antisocial personality disorder scale, 5
Anxiety disorder scale, 7, 18
Asceticism, 168, 169–170
Aversive counterconditioning, 41
Avoidant personality disorder
 affect in, 221, 222–223
 behavioral treatment of, 49
 cognitive style of, 95–96, 107
 cognitive therapy of, 96
 domains of, 33, 34
 domain-specific therapies for, 37
 experiential mood therapy of, 223
 expressive acts of, 47, 49
 interpersonal conduct of, 77, 78
 interpersonal treatment of, 79
 intersubjective treatment of, 167, 169
 morphological organization of, 194, 196

241

object relations psychotherapy of, 123
object representations of, 120, 122–123
psychoanalytic treatment of, 196–197
regulatory mechanisms in, 167, 168
self-image in, 141, 142, 146
self-psychology psychotherapy of, 146
Avoidant personality disorder scale, 5

B

Base rate scores, 11–15
Basic Clinical Syndromes scale, 7–8
  Alcohol abuse scale, 7–8
  Anxiety disorder scale, 7
  Bipolar disorder scale, 7
  Drug Dependence scale, 8
  Dysthymia scale, 7
  Post traumatic stress disorder scale, 8
  Somatoform disorder scale, 7
Basic personality disorders, 2
Basic personality disorders scale, 2, 3, 5–6
  Antisocial personality scale, 5
  Avoidant personality disorder scale, 5
  Compulsive personality disorder scale, 6
  Dependent personality disorder scale, 5
  Depressive personality disorder scale, 5
  Histrionic personality scale, 5
  interpretation of, 20
  Narcissism scale, 5
  Negativistic personality disorder scale, 6
Sadistic personality disorder scale, 6
Schizoid personality disorder scale, 5
Self-defeating personality disorder scale, 6
Behavioral domains of personality, 28–29
  cognitive style, 29
  expressive acts, 28
  interpersonal conduct, 28
  object representations, 29–30
  self-image, 30
Behavior therapy, 40–46
  case example, 58–61
  classical conditioning, 41
  and Million's personality theory, 45–46
  multicomponent treatment packages, 45
  operant conditioning, 41–42
  of personality disorders, 46–57
  recent trends related to, 42–43
  techniques of, 41, 42, 43–45
Biofeedback, 43
Biophysical domains of personality, 31–32
  mood/temperament, 31–32
Bipolar disorder scale, 7, 18
Borderline personality disorder
  affect in, 222, 226
  behavioral treatment of, 57
  cognitive style of, 103, 108
  cognitive therapy of, 103–104
  experiential mood therapy of, 227
  expressive acts of, 48, 56–57
  interpersonal conduct in, 78, 83
  interpersonal treatment of, 83
  intersubjective treatment of, 177
  morphological organization of, 195, 203–204
  object relations psychotherapy of, 127–128

Subject Index   **243**

object representation in, 121, 127
psychoanalytic treatment of, 204
regulatory mechanisms of, 169, 177
self-image in, 143, 144–145, 151
self-psychology psychotherapy of, 151
Borderline personality disorder scale, 6

C

Choice-review exercise, 99–100
Clarification, psychoanalytic technique, 190–191
Classical conditioning, 41
Client-centered theory, 68
Cognitions, meaning of, 92–93
Cognitive style
  of basic personality disorders, 95–104, 107–108
  evaluation of, 29, 30
Cognitive therapy, 90–106
  basic assumptions in, 91
  behavioral techniques used with, 94–95
  case example, 104–106
  dysfunctional cognitive functioning, nature of, 92
  compared to other therapies, 91–92
  of personality disorders, 95–104
  echniques in, 93–94
  thought and emotion linkage, 93
Compulsive personality disorder
  affect in, 221, 225
  behavioral treatment of, 54
  cognitive style of, 100, 107
  cognitive therapy of, 100–101
  experiential mood therapy of, 225
  expressive acts of, 47, 54
  interpersonal conduct in, 77, 81
  interpersonal treatment of, 81
  intersubjective treatment of, 174–175

morphological organization of, 195, 200
object relations psychotherapy of, 125–126
object representation in, 121, 125
psychoanalytic treatment of, 201
regulatory mechanisms of, 168, 174
self-image in, 142, 144, 149
self-psychology psychotherapy of, 149
Compulsive personality disorder scale, 6
Confrontation, psychoanalytic technique, 191
Contingency contracting, 42
Contingency management, 43
Counterconditioning, 43
Countertransference, nature of, 67
Covert positive reinforcement, 43
Covert sensitization, 41
Criterion referencing, 12, 13

D

Debasement scale, 2, 4
Defense mechanisms (see Regulatory techanisms)
Delusional disorder scale, 8, 18
Denial, 167
Dependent personality disorder
  affect in, 221, 223
  behavioral treatment of, 50–51
  cognitive style of, 97, 107
  cognitive therapy of, 97
  experiential mood therapy of, 223–224
  expressive acts of, 47, 50–51
  interpersonal conduct in, 77, 79
  interpersonal treatment of, 79
  intersubjective treatment of, 170–171
  morphological organization of, 194, 197

object relations psychotherapy of, 123–124
object representations of, 120, 123
psychoanalytic treatment of, 197–198
regulatory mechanisms in, 168, 170
self-image in, 142, 143, 147
self-psychology psychotherapy of, 147
Dependent personality disorder scale, 5
Depressive personality disorder
affect in, 221, 223
behavioral treatment of, 50
cognitive style of, 96, 107
cognitive therapy of, 96–97
experiential mood therapy of, 223
expressive acts of, 47, 49–50
interpersonal conduct in, 77, 79
interpersonal therapeutic of, 79
intersubjective treatment of, 170
morphological organization of, 194, 197
object relations psychotherapy of, 123
object representations of, 120, 123
psychoanalytic treatment of, 197
regulatory mechanisms in, 168, 169–170
self–image in, 142, 143, 146
self–psychology psychotherapy of, 146
Depressive personality disorder scale, 5
Desirability scale, 1, 4
Diagnostic and Statistical Manual of Mental Disorders (see DSM-IV)
Differential reinforcement, 42
Disclosure scale, 1, 4
interpretation of, 15

Displacement, 169, 175
Dissociation, 168, 171
Domain construction approach, 9
Dreams
interpersonal approach to, 70–71
intrapsychic approach to, 70
Drug Dependence scale, 8, 18
DSM-IV
compared to MCMI, 2, 5–7, 18
new format, 24
Dysthymia scale, 7, 18

E

Ego, in object relations theory, 113–114
Ego defenses (see Regulatory mechanisms)
Empty-chair technique, 214–215, 231
Exaggeration, 169, 176
Experiential mood therapy, 210–233
affect/emotionality in, 211–212, 215–216, 219–220
affect and personality disorders, 220–227
basic concepts in, 211–213
case example, 228–232
emotional processing in, 215–216
focused expressive psychotherapy, 213–215
goals of, 219
personality, concept in, 216–218
schemas in, 217–218
symptoms in, 218–219
techniques of, 212
theories of, 212
treatment of personality disorders, 220–233
Expressive acts
domain-targeted interventions, 35
evaluation of, 28, 29, 40
in personality disorders, 46–57

F

Fantasy, 167, 172, 196–197
Flooding, 41
Focused expressive psychotherapy, 213–215
  basic concepts in, 213
  steps in process, 213–215
Free association, 69
Freudian theory, 67, 112–113
Functional domains, of personality, 32, 210

G

Group therapy, 36

H

Histrionic personality disorder
  affect in, 221, 224
  behavioral treatment of, 51–52
  cognitive style of, 97–98, 107
  cognitive therapy of, 98
  experiential mood therapy of, 224
  expressive acts of, 47, 51–52
  interpersonal conduct in, 77, 79–80
  interpersonal treatment of, 80
  intersubjective treatment of, 171
  morphological organization of, 194, 198
  object relations psychotherapy of, 124
  object representation in, 120, 124
  psychoanalytic treatment of, 198
  regulatory mechanisms of, 168, 171
  self-image in, 142, 143, 147
  self-psychology psychotherapy of, 147–148
Histrionic personality disorder scale, 5

I

Intellectualization, 167, 168
Internal corrections, 15–16
Interpersonal conduct
  of basic personality disorders, 76–83
  domain-targeted interventions, 35
  evaluation of, 28, 29
Interpersonal psychotherapy, 66–87
  case examples, 71–72, 84–87
  dreams, use of, 69–71
  empirical findings related to, 74–75
  focus of, 69
  goals of, 72–73
  history of, 67–68
  and Millon's personality theory, 75–76
  of personality disorders, 76–83
  personality in, 71
  techniques of, 73–74
  time-frame for, 68
Interpersonal theory, 67, 68, 114
Intersubjective approach, 158–183
  basic concepts of, 159–161
  case example, 178–183
  psychoanalytic assessment approach, 161–164
  regulatory mechanisms in, 164–177
  treatment of personality disorders, 166–183
  view of therapy, 160–161
Intrapsychic domains of personality, 30–31
  morphological organization, 30–31
  regulatory mechanisms, 30
Introjection, 168, 170
In vivo desensitization, 41
Isolation, 168, 174

K

K correction, 15

M

Major depression scale, 8, 18
Masochism, 176
MCMI–III
   base rate scores, 11–15
   development of, 8–11
   internal corrections, 15–16
   interpretive approach to, 19–21
   item content, 3–4
   positive predictive powers of, 18–19
   reliability of, 11
   response bias scales, 4
   scale interpretation, 15
   scales of, 1–3
   validity of, 16–18
Mental representations, nature of, 67
Million Clinical Multiaxial Inventory (*see also* MCMI–III)
   MCMI–I, 9–10
   MCMI–II, 10
   MCMI–III, 10–11
Mixed personality disorder, characteristics of, 83
Mood/temperament
   domain-targeted interventions, 35
   evaluation of, 31, 32
Morphological organization
   domain-targeted interventions, 35
   evaluation of, 30, 31
   of personality disorders, 193–204
Morphology, meaning of, 186

N

Narcissistic personality disorder scale, 5
Narcissistic personality disorder
   affect in, 221, 224
   behavioral treatment of, 52–53
   cognitive style of, 98, 107
   cognitive therapy of, 98–99
   experiential mood therapy of, 224
   expressive acts of, 47, 52–53, 77
   interpersonal conduct in, 80
   interpersonal treatment of, 80
   intersubjective treatment of, 171–172
   morphological organization of, 194, 198
   object relations psychotherapy of, 124
   object representations of, 120, 124
   psychoanalytic treatment of, 199
   regulatory mechanisms of, 168, 171–172
   self-image in, 142, 144, 148
   self-psychology psychotherapy of, 148
Negative predictive power, 16, 17
Negativistic personality disorder
   affect in, 222, 225
   behavioral treatment of, 55
   cognitive style of, 101, 108
   cognitive therapy of, 101–102
   experiential mood therapy of, 225–226
   expressive acts of, 48, 54–55
   interpersonal conduct in, 78, 82
   interpersonal treatment of, 82
   intersubjective treatment of, 175
   morphological organization of, 195, 201
   object relations psychotherapy of, 126
   object representation in, 121, 126
   psychoanalytic treatment of, 201–202
   regulatory mechanisms in, 169, 175
   self-image in, 143, 144, 149–150
   self-psychology psychotherapy of, 150
Negativistic personality disorder scale, 6

Neurosis, psychoanalytic view of, 188
Norm referencing, 11–12

O

Object constancy, 112
Object permanence, 112
Object relations theory
  case examples, 116–117, 128–132
  contemporary focus, 115–117
  history of, 112–114
  and Million's personality theory, 118–119
  object, meaning of, 112
  object representations, meaning of, 112, 118–119
  therapeutic techniques of, 119–122
  treatment of personality disorders, 120–128
Object representations
  domain-targeted interventions, 35
  evaluation of, 29, 30
Operant conditioning, 41–42
Operating characteristics, 16–17

P

Paranoid personality disorder
  affect in, 222, 227
  behavioral treatment of, 57–58
  cognitive style of, 104, 108
  cognitive therapy of, 104
  experiential mood therapy of, 227
  expressive acts of, 48, 57–58
  interpersonal conduct in, 78, 83
  interpersonal treatment of, 83
  intersubjective treatment of, 178
  morphological organization of, 195, 204
  object relations psychotherapy of, 128
  object representations in, 121, 128
  psychoanalytic treatment of, 204–205
  regulatory mechanisms in, 169, 177–178
  self-image in, 143, 144–145, 151
  self-psychology psychotherapy of, 152
Paranoid personality disorder scale, 6–7
Passive aggression, 175
Personality
  behavioral domains, 28–29
  biophysical domains, 31, 32
  concept of, 25
  functional domains of, 32
  intrapsychic domains, 30–31
  phenomenological domains, 29–30
  structural domains, 31–32
Personality disorders *(see also specific disorders)*
  basic personality disorders, 2
  definition of, 25
  Million's conception of, 26–27
  prevalence of, 24–25
  prototypal model, 27–28
  severe personality disorders, 2
  systems view of, 25–26
Phenomenological domains, of personality, 29–30
Positive predictive power, 16, 17, 19
Post traumatic stress disorder scale, 8, 21
Predictive power, positive and negative, 16, 17, 19
Prevalence, operating characteristics, 16, 17
Projection, 169, 178
Psychoanalytic assessment, 161–164
  dimensions in, 161–164
  and MCMI-III, 162
Psychoanalytic psychotherapy, 187–209

case example, 205–209
confrontation in, 191
etiology of personality disorders, 188–189
goals of, 187, 189
and Million's theory, 193–196
morphological organization of personality disorders, 193–204
and personality disorders, 187–188, 190–193
transference in, 191–192
treatment of personality disorders, 196–209
Psychobiological theory, 67–68
Psychotherapy
integrative psychotherapy, 36–37
interpersonal psychotherapy, 66–83

R

Rationalization, 168, 171–172
Reaction formation, 168, 174
Reciprocal inhibition, 41
Referencing
criterion referencing, 13
norm referencing, 12
Regression, 169, 177
Regulatory mechanisms
acting out, 168, 172–173
asceticism, 168, 169–170
denial, 167
displacement, 169, 175
dissociation, 168, 171
domain–targeted interventions, 35
evaluation of, 30, 31
exaggeration, 169, 176
fantasy, 167, 168, 172
intellectualization, 167, 168
introjection, 168, 170
isolation, 168, 173
and MCMI-III, 164–165
projection, 169, 178
rationalization, 168, 171–172
reaction formation, 168, 174
regression, 169, 177
undoing, 169, 176
Relaxation training, 43
Reliability, of MCMI-III, 11
Response cost, 42

S

Sadistic personality disorder
affect in, 221, 225
behavioral treatment of, 54
cognitive style of, 100, 107
cognitive therapy of, 100
experiential mood therapy of, 225
expressive acts of, 47, 53–54
interpersonal conduct in, 77, 81
interpersonal treatment of, 81
intersubjective treatment of, 173–174
morphological organization of, 195, 200
object relations psychotherapy of, 125
object representation in, 120, 125
psychoanalytic treatment of, 200
regulatory mechanisms in, 168, 173
self-image in, 142, 144, 149
self-psychology psychotherapy of, 149
Sadistic personality disorder scale, 6, 18
Scales, 6–7
Basic clinical syndromes scale, 2, 3, 7–8
Basic personality disorders scale, 2, 3, 5–6
Severe clinical syndromes scale, 2–3, 8
Severe personality disorders scale, 2, 3
Validity scales, 1–2, 3, 4

Subject Index

Schizoid personality disorder
  affect in, 221, 222
  behavioral treatment of, 48–49
  cognitive style of, 95, 107, 108
  cognitive therapy of, 95
  experiential mood therapy of, 222
  expressive acts of, 46–48
  interpersonal conduct in, 76, 77
  interpersonal treatment of, 76, 78, 83
  intersubjective treatment of, 167
  morphological organization of, 194, 196
  object relations psychotherapy of, 122
  object representations of, 120, 122
  psychoanalytic treatment of, 196
  regulatory mechanisms of, 166–167, 168
  self-image in, 141, 142, 145
  self-psychology psychotherapy of, 145–146
Schizoid personality disorder scale, 5, 18
Schizotypal personality disorder
  affect in, 222, 226
  behavioral treatment of, 56
  cognitive style of, 102
  cognitive therapy of, 102–103
  experiential mood therapy of, 226
  expressive acts of, 48, 56
  interpersonal conduct in, 78, 82
  intersubjective treatment of, 176–177
  morphological organization of, 195, 203
  object relations psychotherapy of, 127
  object representations in, 121, 127
  psychoanalytic treatment of, 203
  regulatory mechanisms in, 169, 176
  self-image in, 143, 144–145, 151

  sel-psychology psychotherapy of, 151
Schizotypal personality disorder scale, 6
Scoring
  base rate scores, 11–15
  item weighting, 11
  scale interpretation, 15, 19–21
Self-defeating personality disorder
  affect in, 222, 226
  behavioral treatment of, 56
  cognitive style of, 102, 108
  cognitive therapy of, 102
  experiential mood therapy of, 226
  expressive acts of, 48, 55–56
  interpersonal conduct in, 78, 82
  interpersonal treatment of, 82
  intersubjective treatment of, 176
  morphological organization of, 195, 202
  object relations psychotherapy of, 126–127
  object representations in, 121, 126
  psychoanalytic treatment of, 202–203
  regulatory mechanisms of, 169, 175–176
  self-image in, 143, 144, 150
  self-psychology psychotherapy of, 150
Self-defeating personality disorder scale, 6, 18
Self-image
  domain-targeted interventions, 35
  evaluation of, 30
  in personality disorders, 142–143, 145–152
Self-management programs, 43–44
Self-monitoring, 44
Selfobjects, 159–160
Self-psychology, 137–152
  case example, 152–156
  Kohut's view, 139–140

250 *Subject Index*

Million's concept of self, 138–139
self in personality disorders, 141–151
therapeutic techniques of, 140–141
treatment of personality disorders, 145–152
Self-statement modification, 43, 44
Self-talk, 43
Sensitivity, operating characteristic, 16, 17
Severe clinical syndromes scale, 2–3, 8
  Delusional disorder scale, 8
  interpretation of, 20–21
  Major depression scale, 8
  Thought disorder scale, 8
Severe personality disorders, 2
Severe personality disorders scale, 6–7
  Borderline personality disorder scale, 6
  interpretation of, 20
  Paranoid personality disorder scale, 6–7
  Schizotypal personality disorder scale, 6
Shaping, 42
  Somatoform disorder scale, 7, 18
Specificity, operating characteristic, 16, 17
Splitting, 115, 116, 165
Structural domains, of personality, 31–32, 210

T

Temperament (see Mood/temperament)
Thought disorder scale, 8, 18
Thought stopping, 43
Time out, 42

Token economy, 42
Transference
  mirror and idealizing transference, 117
  nature of, 67
  in psychoanalytic psychotherapy, 191–192
Transitional object, 112
Treatment
  behavior therapy, 40–46
  cognitive therapy, 90–106
  and domain-related theory, 32–33
  domain-targeted interventions, 35, 37
  experiential mood therapy, 220–233
  integrative psychotherapy, 36–37
  interpersonal psychotherapy, 66–87
  intersubjective approach, 166–183
  object relations psychotherapy, 120–132
  psychoanalytic psychotherapy, 196–209
  self-psychology approach, 145–156
  treatment planning, 33–36

U

Undoing, 169, 176

V

Validity
  of MCMI-III, 16–18
  operating characteristics, 16–17
Validity scales, 1–2, 3, 4
  Debasement scale, 2, 4
  Desirability scale, 1, 4
  Disclosure scale, 1, 4
  interpretation of, 20